Implementing the Primary

Implementing the Primary Curriculum:
A Teacher's Guide

Edited by

Kate Ashcroft and David Palacio

 The Falmer Press

(A member of the Taylor & Francis Group)
London • Washington, D.C.

| UK | Falmer Press, 1 Gunpowder Square, London EC4A 3DE |
| USA | Falmer Press, Taylor & Francis Inc., 1900 Frost Road, Suite 101, Bristol, PA 19007 |

First published in 1997

A catalogue record for this book is available from the British Library

Library of Congress Cataloging-in-Publication Data are available on request

ISBN 0 7507 0592 2 Cased
ISBN 0 7507 0593 0 Paper

Jacket design by Caroline Archer

Typeset in 10/12pt Times by
Graphicraft Typesetters Ltd., Hong Kong.

Printed in Great Britain by Biddles Ltd., Guildford and King's Lynn on paper which has a specified pH value on final paper manufacture of not less than 7.5 and is therefore 'acid free'.

Contents

Contents

List of Figures

Section 1

Introduction

1   Introduction to the Primary School Curriculum

Kate Ashcroft and David Palacio

Introduction and Overview

To many people outside education, and perhaps yourself if you are just about to begin your course of initial teacher training, the terms *the primary school curriculum* and *the National Curriculum for primary schools* mean the same thing. However, to people more closely involved with schools the two terms are, for a number of reasons, quite distinct. In focusing on the primary school curriculum (sometimes called the whole curriculum), rather than the National Curriculum, one purpose for this chapter is to make explicit the differences that exist between the two. In doing so, this book should serve not only as a guide to the major features and key ideas underpinning the (whole) primary curriculum but also as a guide to how each subject comprising the National Curriculum may be implemented in a typical primary school classroom.

The nature of the primary school curriculum and the climate in which schools function changed quite dramatically following the passing of the Education Reform Act in 1988. Not only was the National Curriculum introduced by this Act but schools became much more publicly accountable for their actions and for the ways in which they have deployed the resources made available to them; for example, the governing body of a school and the parents of the pupils attending that school were given increased rights and responsibilities regarding the curriculum. You might like to compile a more comprehensive list of the changes that have occurred since the passing of the 1988 Act and the ways in which schools have changed to accommodate these new circumstances (the implications of these changes are considered more fully in a later enquiry task in this chapter, see p. 8). Because of all the changes that have occurred to the educational system and the impact these have had on schools, this book should prove to be essential reading not only for anyone who is new to teaching but also for anyone who is returning to teaching after a break away from a primary school classroom.

We suspect that most people are aware that schools are required by law to teach the National Curriculum. However, the National Curriculum is not the only component of the curriculum which all publicly funded (often referred to as *maintained*) primary schools have to include as part of the education they offer. Providing some form of religious education has been a legal requirement of all maintained schools

— secondary as well as primary — since the 1944 Education Act. Therefore, in this book you will find, in addition to a full consideration of the National Curriculum, a discussion of the recently introduced curriculum guidelines for religious education together with consideration of some of the major issues which emerge when schools attempt to implement these guidelines. At this point, pause for a moment and consider: if both the National Curriculum and religious education are required by law, why is not religious education part of the National Curriculum?

The total primary school curriculum is much wider than what is termed the Basic Curriculum — the teaching of the National Curriculum and religious education. In fact, one key objective which underpinned the recent review of the National Curriculum (Dearing, 1994) was to slim down the statutory curriculum so as to enable schools to devote more time to providing a curriculum which is broader than that which has to be taught by law and one which is more responsive to the needs and interests of individual schools and children. (As a consequence of the Dearing Review, the estimated time that primary schools can devote to non-National Curriculum work amounts to the equivalent of one day per week.)

You will wish to consider what you might include in this 'optional' part of the curriculum. One obvious suggestion might be to introduce new material or new experiences which enable you to teach aspects of the National Curriculum in greater depth and/or breadth than is required by law (practical suggestions of what this might be are provided in the chapters of this book). Another possibility, perhaps more imaginative than the previous one, is to introduce subjects/areas of experience which do not come within the present National Curriculum for primary schools; for example, a modern foreign language and aspects of dance and drama. Including additional subjects, or aspects of them, should not only enable you to broaden the subject base of the curriculum, but it should also enable you to offer new and more innovative ways to teach the existing curriculum: for example, you might consider teaching some science work through drama. Adopting approaches such as those outlined in this paragraph, and others mentioned throughout this book, should enable you to enhance and enrich the (National Curriculum) experience of the children in your class.

National Curriculum documents are, quite often, written in a style that can make them difficult to understand, particularly if you are new to teaching the National Curriculum (such as a student beginning a course of initial teacher education), or if you are an interested lay person, such as a parent or a school governor. Furthermore, the use of familiar words but with meanings which differ from their everyday usage, or unfamiliar technical words which have no meaning outside of the subject, makes these documents more difficult to understand. Because of these problems, the authors of this book, and especially the authors of chapters which deal with individual subjects of the National Curriculum, have tried to clarify meaning and suggest practical ways in which you can turn National Curriculum words into classroom action. In this sense, the book can be read in its entirety, thus giving you an immediate overview of the primary curriculum, perhaps re-reading chapters as and when necessary. Alternatively, you might like to use the book for reference purposes and perhaps gain a fairly detailed insight into just one chapter at a time.

Used in this latter way, the relatively short chapters should enable you to gain a detailed understanding of a subject in a single session.

Enquiry Task

If you are new to the primary curriculum and how it may be implemented, especially the National Curriculum, one of the first tasks you will have to undertake is to make yourself familiar with the terminology which surrounds it. Another early task will be to get to know the names of some of the new, and not so new, organizations that have responsibility for the curriculum and what their actual responsibilities are.

Find out what the following terms mean and how they relate to each other:

- Key Stage
- R and Year 5
- Programme of Study
- Profile Component
- Attainment Target and Level Description
- Assessment Weighting
- Ten Level Scale
- Basic Curriculum
- National Curriculum

Find out the full name of the bodies represented by the following abbreviations:

- SCAA
- TGAT
- OFSTED
- HMI and HMCI
- NCC and SEAC

What is the function of each body, and what are their responsibilities regarding the primary curriculum?

To find out answers to any of the above questions talk to an experienced teacher or consult a book (for example, Ashcroft and Palacio, 1995). Finding answers to each of these questions will not only aid your understanding of the primary curriculum but it will also enable you to come to a better, and quicker, understanding of the contents of this book.

We hope that this book will provide you with an accessible starting point in the process of developing further your *professional* knowledge and understanding of the contemporary primary curriculum. More than this, we hope that reading this book and undertaking the various enquiry tasks will lead directly to your increased effectiveness in the classroom.

Content and Structure of the Book

This book has been written with the intention of helping people who are having to implement the whole primary curriculum: the overall style is, therefore, practical in orientation. This notwithstanding, we nevertheless wanted the book to put forward a consistent and explicitly stated educational philosophy. This philosophy — the reflective practitioner approach to teaching and learning, which is explained more fully in a later section of this chapter — underpins the enquiry tasks you will find in every chapter. More importantly, perhaps, the reflective practitioner approach to teaching and learning can serve to guide you during all stages of your work with children.

Enquiry tasks serve an important function in that we hope they will take you beyond mere factual knowledge of the primary school curriculum. By focusing on your developing understanding of key ideas which underpin the curriculum and the ways that these ideas may be put into effect in the classroom, it is our intention that enquiry tasks will aid your overall awareness and understanding of the primary curriculum. More importantly, through a process of reflection and action we hope that these tasks will take further your own practical theory of teaching and learning, and thus increase even further your effectiveness in the classroom.

The sixteen chapters in this book are divided into three sections. Apart from this first chapter, which in addition to serving as an introduction to the whole book begins the process of taking further your understanding of the various elements of the primary curriculum, the other chapter in Section 1 introduces you to issues associated with the primary school curriculum when considered from a whole school perspective. Each chapter in Section 2 takes one subject of the National Curriculum and considers in some depth practical issues associated with the teaching and learning of the subject. Section 3 goes beyond the National Curriculum; the first chapter describes current thinking in religious education whilst two further chapters explore ways in which the curriculum may be enriched through work in dance, and in drama: the final chapter in this section returns to whole school issues by way of a discussion of curriculum implications for the teaching of children with special educational needs.

The chapters in all three sections:

- explore the values and assumptions which underpin the way that the 'subject' under discussion has been defined;
- include enquiry-based tasks as described earlier in this section;
- contain a bibliography together with a short, usually annotated, reading list designed to take further your understanding of the primary school curriculum;
- provide, where appropriate, suggestions as to how you might use the one-day-per-week equivalent that is free from National Curriculum work to broaden, deepen and enrich children's learning experiences.

The chapters in Sections 2 and 3 discuss practical matters concerned with the teaching and learning of the subject under consideration. Areas covered include:

- planning for progression;
- practical options for teaching;
- the provision of appropriate resources;
- assessment and the implications for teachers of assessment practice.

Practical suggestions as to how you might incorporate into the curriculum cross-curriculum issues, such as equal opportunities and information technology, are also provided. Current major concerns within each subject are discussed and explored, and, where it is considered appropriate, a glossary of terms used in the chapter is provided.

Nature and Structure of the Curriculum in Primary Schools

The idea of a centrally devised, externally developed, and politically tightly controlled school curriculum which is enforceable in law may not be contentious to you, especially if you have only recently left school and have, therefore, experienced the National Curriculum first hand as part of your own secondary education. However, for many other people, especially those with a relatively long experience of teaching and who have had to expend much time and effort implementing the National Curriculum and its many revisions, the notion is far from straightforward: many issues, personal and professional as well as simply practical, have had, and are still having, to be addressed. One significant issue for many teachers has been how to resolve the conflict arising out of the mismatch between their personal views about the aims and objectives of primary education and the rôle schools play in meeting these, and the requirements placed on teachers by a government that has very different views. Furthermore, the significance of many of these issues can only be appreciated fully after you have tried to implement a curriculum for which you have had little, if any, direct involvement with during its development, and for which you therefore feel no ownership.

If you are one of those people for whom a National Curriculum is not a contentious issue, then perhaps your initial visits to school as a beginning, or a returning, teacher may bring to your attention points of view which you have not considered previously.

Many informed and readable critiques of the concept of a National Curriculum for schools, practical as well as philosophical, were written soon after its introduction, (see, for instance, Kelly, 1990): since these critiques go beyond the scope of this book, which is essentially about implementing the curriculum and, through the enquiry tasks, enabling you to think more deeply about the curriculum and its relationship to your practice, why not consult one of them?

Following a review (Dearing, 1994) of the National Curriculum, (DES, 1989) the primary school curriculum for England may be described by reference to the components listed below. (In Wales, Welsh is an additional Core Foundation Subject in Welsh medium schools and an Other Foundation Subject in other schools.)

A National Curriculum comprising,

- Core Foundation Subjects (English, mathematics and science);
- Other Foundation Subjects (art, design and technology, geography, history, information technology, music, and physical education);
- Cross-curricular issues, e.g., health education, personal and social education, consideration of equal opportunities — gender and multi-cultural issues;

- Cross-curricular competences, e.g., language, literacy, numeracy, information technology skills, application of the 'scientific method', use of equipment;
- Cross-curricular themes, e.g., economic and industrial understanding, environmental education.

Religious education.

Other (non-statutorily required) curriculum material, e.g., content outside an existing subject Order, additional subjects such as dance, drama, a modern foreign language.

How these various components interrelate, one with another, and the terminology used to describe them, is shown by the diagram below.

Figure 1.1:   *Model of a primary school curriculum for England and Wales — as envisaged by the Department of Education and Science (DES, 1989) and subsequently modified as part of the Dearing Review of the National Curriculum (Dearing, 1994)*

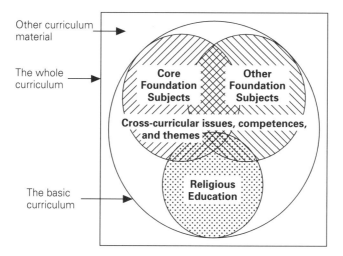

For more detail of the National Curriculum, and in particular a brief historical background to its introduction, see Ashcroft and Palacio (1995).

Enquiry Task

Consider the National Curriculum for Key Stages 1 and 2, and in particular the subject focus of its description.

Do you consider *subjects* to be the most appropriate way to define the framework around which *all* primary schools are required to build their curriculum? What alternatives are possible? How might these form the basis for an alternative National (common) Curriculum? How, for example, might a National Curriculum based around *aims and objectives* differ from the current *content* (subject) model? What would a National Curriculum organized around *principles and processes of learning* look like?

Do you consider there to be an educational case for a National Curriculum and, if so, how strong is this case?

(For a discussion and exploration of the issues raised in this enquiry task, see below and, for example, Kelly, 1990.)

As has been suggested already, the nature of the primary curriculum changed quite considerably following the passing of the Education Reform Act in 1988. The effects of some changes became apparent more or less immediately following the passing of this Act, but others took time for their impact to be felt. You may wish to explore what have been the main changes to the primary school curriculum since 1988.

Enquiry Task

Consider the curriculum of a primary school that you know well: this school could be the one you are working in at the moment. Observe this curriculum in action, but also take note of any description of the curriculum provided in, for example, the school brochure.

- In what ways is the model of the (official) primary school curriculum presented earlier in this chapter an accurate description of what actually happens in primary schools? For example, to what extent do you consider the overlap between the Core and Other Foundation Subjects, shown on the diagram above, to be a curriculum reality? Here you will need to draw distinctions between curriculum conception (how the curriculum is described by, for example, central government planners — individual subjects linked by overarching themes and skills), curriculum organization and curriculum 'delivery'; you will also need to refer to a copy of Key Stages 1 and 2 of the National Curriculum; for example DFE (1995).
- In what ways is the presented model deficient? For example, the model of the curriculum stresses subject content and, to a lesser extent, cognitive skills. How might children acquire personal qualities, such as values and attitudes?
- In what ways is the model in tune with common practice in primary schools? In what ways is the model at odds with this practice? What issues emerge for primary schools?

Now consider the primary school in which you were a pupil.

- Draw a model similar to the one given above but which describes that school's curriculum.
- Compare the two models. What similarities do you notice? What differences are there?
- What curriculum issues emerge now for today's primary schools?

Many issues are likely to have emerged following your analysis of the primary school curriculum which you undertook during the last enquiry task. Almost certainly, some issues will relate to the whole curriculum and will be similar to those discussed further in Chapter 2. For example, you might want to explore how a school, and in particular an infant or a first school, can accommodate within its curriculum, which is described mainly in terms of integrated themes or topics, a 'given' curriculum described mainly in terms of subjects. You could investigate how schools such as these adapt their curriculum philosophy, which in the past has laid emphasis on the 'basics', to one in which 'content from a diverse range of subjects' is the focus.

Other issues to emerge as a result of the last enquiry task are likely to be concerned more with individual subjects. For example, how teachers, especially those working with Years 5 and 6, acquire the skills and conceptual understanding necessary to teach 'new' subjects (such as design and technology), or subjects (such as mathematics and science) where the curriculum emphasis has changed. Issues such as these will be discussed further in Chapters 3 onwards, since it is these chapters that deal with individual subjects within the curriculum.

The Reflective Teacher Model

We have stated earlier that the underlying philosophy of this book is that of reflective teaching. This model is based on ideas first developed by Dewey (1916) and subsequently by, for example, Zeichner (1982), Pollard and Tann (1993), Ashcroft and Griffiths (1990), and Ashcroft and Foreman-Peck (1995). This model sees reflective practice as an essentially moral activity, which is designed to enable you to explore the congruity between your values and your practice and, where these are not compatible, to explore the issues that are raised.

We see teaching as requiring quick, informed decisions about complex issues in a fast-moving and dynamic set of situations. In this context, it is essential that your actions are moral, designed to meet the needs of all those within the situation, practical (and this includes the need for efficiency) and effective. The problem is that these objectives are not always compatible. For instance, it may be more efficient in terms of time to teach a class as a whole, but this may be ineffective since it leads to the individual needs of particular children being ignored. Teaching the class as a whole may be especially problematic for those children whose needs fall furthest from the 'norm' — the very able and those with learning difficulties. You might wish to consider what could happen to the move to integrate children with special educational needs into mainstream classrooms if whole class teaching becomes the new educational orthodoxy. On the other hand, it is clearly impracticable and ineffective to treat every child as an individual with their own special needs for the whole of the time. If you did so, each child might be taught only for a few moments each day and you would have to design (perhaps) thirty individual schemes of work. The children would in effect be following individual correspondence courses.

Reflective practice recognizes these dilemmas, and provides a language and set of actions for analysing them, so as to enable you to make decisions that are educationally and morally defensible. It does so by building on three qualities which we suggest are characteristic of reflective teaching. The first of these qualities is *openmindedness*. This quality implies that you look at the situation from the point of view of all the people within it and also from the point of view of others who are particularly well qualified to comment. Thus, if you have a problem (for instance, a child whose behaviour you find challenging), you might seek evidence as to what the situation looks like from the child's point of view. You would do this by collecting actual evidence yourself but you might also seek evidence from others involved in the situation and perhaps from other experts. You would seek and evaluate this evidence and maybe consider how you could work with others to reach a better way of managing the problem. In other words, not to blindly accept, or reject, those perspectives which do not agree with your own. In doing so you would be accepting some responsibility for it.

Responsibility is the second of the qualities that underpin reflective practice. It implies that, in the situation above, you do not see the problem as residing 'within the child' (and therefore insoluble) but rather as one that you have some duty to ameliorate by finding better ways of working. Responsibility requires that you look at the long-term consequences of your own, and other people's actions, rather than merely considering 'what works'. In doing so, you move away from a purely utilitarian standpoint, to one where questions of 'worthwhileness' are asked. In the case above, you might be able to 'solve' the problem of the child's behaviour from your point of view by moving him or her away from their peers, perhaps to work in an isolated part of the classroom. As a reflective teacher, you would ask yourself whether making a child with few social skills work in isolation was in his or her long-term interests. You might conclude that you needed to seek a better solution, even if this would be more difficult and demanding in the short term.

The final quality that underpins reflective practice is that of wholeheartedness or *commitment*. This implies that reflective practice permeates all of your work and is not assumed only for particular purposes or to gain advantages. It means that you are willing to stand up for what you consider to be 'right', even when this is not in your best interests (it can be dangerous to be a whistle blower). On the other hand, you would not stand out against your peers without very careful consideration of all the long-term effects of that action and of their point of view. Essentially, your decision would be an ethical one.

We have stated above that, in the course of a day, teaching requires you to make numerous decisions about quite complex matters. These decisions can only be truly moral and educational ones if you have done a lot of your thinking about educational priorities and dilemmas beforehand, and if you analyse your actions after each significant event, so that next time you can act with greater integrity and effectiveness. This preparatory thinking and evaluative analysis requires long-term commitment. It also implies that reflective teaching is not something you achieve once and for all, but rather is an aspiration that you will strive for throughout your career that will never be neither wholly nor permanently achieved.

Reflective practice is perhaps the only way that you can deal ethically and morally with circumstances where your room to manoeuvre is limited. It does not require perfect circumstances. We believe that it is an important tool for solving, or at least exploring, ethical and educational problems that may arise because of a prescribed curriculum. For instance, you might be working in an inner-city classroom, which contains children from a variety of cultures. An unreflective teacher might teach the History National Curriculum 'straight'. As a reflective teacher, you would wish to inform yourself about the perspectives of members of each of the cultures represented in your classroom on their own, as well as on British, history. Your 'treatment' of the history curriculum — the connections that you encourage the children to make, and the way that you approach it — might be very different from that you would have taken without the collection of evidence and your reflection upon it.

From the analysis above, it it clear that we believe that reflective practice depends on you developing a set of prerequisite skills. These include skills in the collection and analysis of evidence. That is why many of the enquiry tasks in this book ask you to collect and examine evidence related to the delivery of the curriculum in practice. In addition, it requires that you develop a variety of interpersonal skills. These skills enable you to collect the evidence (for instance, by building the children's trust sufficiently for them to be honest about their perspectives) that you will need for proper reflection. Interpersonal skills also enable solutions to be found to many of the problems in teaching and learning that stem from difficulties in relationships. You will also require these skills in order to seek the support you will need in your reflection. Solitary reflection can lead you into a self-serving analysis of problems and to solutions that fit your prejudices rather than the perspectives of others. Throughout this book, we suggest that reflection should be a social activity. You need to build the sort of relationships with others that will enable them to challenge your assumptions and solutions, such challenges being supportive, rather than destructive, of the relationship. This requires trust on both sides, but can lead to the best kind of professional relationships, with high levels of discourse and analysis, and useful, but unsentimental, support being available for you in dealing with the difficult issues that every teacher must face.

Evaluation and Reflective Practice

Evaluation is basic to reflective practice. It provides the raw material for reflection, the evidence to underpin changes in action and the means by which openmindedness and responsibility are exercised. In the model below, we describe reflective practice as an evaluation-led activity in which collection and evaluation of evidence leads to reflection on the significance of that evidence, which in turn informs subsequent planning, provision and action. On the completion of this cycle, evaluation again takes place, this time into the effectiveness of action, leading to another cycle of reflection, planning and action, as shown in Figure 1.2.

This model of reflection has much in common with the model of action research developed by Stenhouse (1987) and others (for instance, Carr and Kemmis, 1986, and Elliott, 1991). It also relates closely to Argyris and Schön's (1974) notion of the development of theory from practice. This suggests that part of what

Figure 1.2: *Model of reflective action*

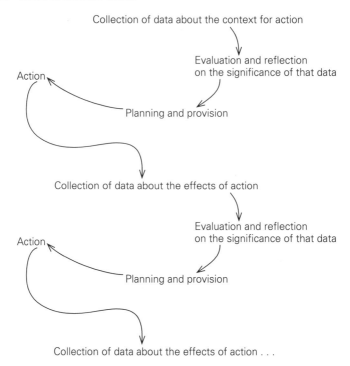

Collection of data about the context for action

Evaluation and reflection
on the significance of that data

Action

Planning and provision

Collection of data about the effects of action

Evaluation and reflection
on the significance of that data

Action

Planning and provision

Collection of data about the effects of action . . .

you are doing as a reflective teacher is developing and refining your own theories of teaching and learning.

The main difference between action research and reflective practice is that action research tends to be focused on a problem whereas reflective practice is not necessarily problem based. On the other hand, both require enquiry into practice and are centred on the improvement of practice. The close relationship between the notion of reflective practice and action research makes action research a particularly appropriate model for an evaluation-based enquiry into your practice.

Action research is a good method of improving practice, but the results may tend to be situation-specific and unverifiable; they may not generalize to other contexts. Action research can lead you astray, because you may be asking the wrong questions or failing to interpret your evidence critically enough. These disadvantages may be minimized if you use more than one method to collect data about the problem and evaluate your research at all stages with colleagues (these are both forms of *triangulation* — for more details of this concept, see, for example, Chapter 11 in Cohen and Manion, 1994). You will need to be openminded and willing to change your definition of the problem, your methods, and your interpretation of results in the light of your experience and discussion with others. On the other hand, action research does allow you to recognize that your values are part of the research context and, provided you are modest about what you claim for your results, it can lead to real insights into some of the troubling situations that teachers face.

Enquiry Task

Identify a child with the 'problem' outlined above: i.e., one whose behaviour you find challenging, perhaps because s/he lacks basic social skills and disrupts other children's work.

Use the action research model outlined below to enquire into the context of the problem, to decide on a possible solution and to evaluate the effectiveness of that solution.

At each stage:

- share your planning and reflection with one or more colleagues; **and**
- keep detailed notes about what you did as they occur (for example, your conversations with colleagues, what happened and your reflections on this).

The process of action research involves undertaking at least two cycles of enquiry as outlined below (adapted from Kemmis, 1988).

Identify the problem that will be the focus for your enquiry and find out as much as you can about the context in which it occurs.

- Whose problem is it?
- Why is it important? (Is it a problem for the child as well as for you? If so, in what ways?)
- What is happening now?
- What does the situation look like from the child's point of view? (For instance, the pattern of the school day, his or her interactions with you and with other children and the demands of the curriculum.)
- When does the problem occur, and how often?
- What form does it take?
- What triggers it?
- What are the alternative explanations for the problem? (You may need to talk to or observe the child; you may need to seek evidence from others involved in the situation, for example, parents, other teachers, other children. You might also seek the advice of experts: by talking to those in the advisory or educational psychology service, or through reading the research literature.)

Decide on an intervention that you hope will improve the situation.

- What might a better situation look like? (You might decide on one aspect of the child's behaviour that you particularly want to change.)
- Why would it be better?

Plan the intervention in some detail.

- What actions might improve the situation? (For instance, you might decide to spend a set period of time each day when you will actively look for aspects of the child's social interaction with others to praise; or you might set up enjoyable learning experiences that require the child to work on a task with one or two others, in order to experience more or less instant success.)
- How should your actions be sequenced?
- What criteria would indicate 'success' in dealing with the situation? (For instance, the ability to be able to regularly praise the child for working for a

ten-minute period, twice a day, on an enjoyable cooperative task, without being unpleasant to his or her partner.)

Discuss your plans with colleagues.

Implement the plan.

Collect data on the effect of the intervention on the problem.

- What techniques will you use to collect your data? (You might observe the child, or assess the quality of the outcomes of cooperative tasks.)
- What are the advantages and disadvantages of each?
- How might you triangulate findings? (Can you seek views from various participants in the process — perhaps the child her/himself or other children, or use more than one data collection technique?)

Evaluate the data.

- What patterns are emerging?
- What have you learned about the problem and your solution to it?

Discuss your evaluation with colleagues.

Revise your original plan.

- Are new ways of looking at the problem emerging from the evidence?
- Did you ask the right questions in the first place?
- Does your initial interpretation of the problem need to be revised?
- What values and assumptions about education were implied by your original approach?
- What ethical issues are raised by your research?

Discuss your revised plan with colleagues.

Implement the revised plan.

Repeat the data collection/evaluation cycle.

The Conceptual Structure of the Curriculum

In 1988, when Kenneth Baker, then Secretary of State for Education and Science, established the National Curriculum, there were various approaches he might have taken. Each of these are based on a different conception of the curriculum and each empowers a particular set of stakeholders (individuals or groups of people with a legitimate interest in the educational process).

The first approach that he might have taken was to decide what children should know, feel and be able to do at each stage of their schooling in order for them to develop as rounded, knowledgable and competent people. This approach suggests that the child is at the heart of the educational process, and that education is for his or her benefit. Because of the reaction by some politicians at the time against so-called 'child-centred' education, no such analysis was undertaken.

Another approach to the development of a National Curriculum might have been to decide who the stakeholders of school education are (parents, employers, educationalists — teachers, advisors, inspectors, academics — local and national government politicians, etc.) and to ask representatives of them to come to a consensus about what should comprise a rounded and complete education for children during their compulsory years of schooling. This consensus could then form the basis for the development of a common curriculum. Although representatives from some of these groups were included on the National Curriculum Council (NCC), the body set up to oversee the development and introduction of the National Curriculum, the curriculum was not designed on this basis, and anyway the NCC was only set up after the broad structure (the consensus) had been determined by the government.

A third model of curriculum planning that might have been considered was to base the National Curriculum around those subjects which comprise the existing (secondary) school curriculum. In fact, this was the approach taken. Having determined the subjects to be included in the National Curriculum, the Secretary of State then set up subject groups, each of which recommended the statutorily required material that should be taught in all schools, primary as well as secondary. This approach led to a subject-based curriculum and had the unintended (perhaps) consequence of giving power to members of subject disciplines at the expense of the other stakeholders in the educational process. In particular, the interests of children with special educational needs and members of ethnic minority groups were not well served by this process, a situation which you might find unexpected given that the National Curriculum was intended, with only a few exceptions, to be a curriculum for all.

The lack of holistic planning of the curriculum led to a situation where most subject Orders were well designed and could serve subject interests well in their own terms, but when seen together, led to an overcrowded, over-assessed and incoherent curriculum that did not encompass everything necessary to make rounded, knowledgable and competent citizens. It was also recognized that some powerful vested interests had not been represented in the curriculum.

The National Curriculum, right from its inception, was beset by major weaknesses. The crowded curriculum was overlaid with additional material in the form of cross-curriculum themes and dimensions that dealt with 'content' that could not be achieved through a study of individual subjects. Some of these, such as *Economic and Industrial Awareness*, were designed to meet the needs of powerful stakeholders in education such as employers. Some of the content of the curriculum, especially that within the humanities, was changed to make it more UK-centred, to reflect the views of a powerful right-wing establishment. Although there was some tinkering with the curriculum between 1988 and 1994 (in some subjects, such as science, those changes were by no means minor), the problem of an overcrowded and over-assessed curriculum was not solved until the Dearing Report (Dearing, 1994) was implemented. This report considered for the first time the curriculum and its assessment holistically, and recommended slimming down both the compulsory requirements of the curriculum and the means by which children were assessed.

Curriculum planning can focus on content and/or process. The National Curriculum was focused on content only. This was in part a reaction against the so-called 'process approach' that had been seen by some right-wing politicians as dominating 'trendy' educational thought. This led to a curriculum that focused on what children should *know*, *understand* and be able to *do*. The affective curriculum, for instance, the 'teaching' of particular attitudes, was largely ignored. Arts-based and Physical Education subject Orders were determined late in the process of putting the National Curriculum in place: these subjects had less prescribed content and assessment, and came to be seen as being of lesser importance than, for example, mathematics and science, perceived by some as more cognitively based subjects. Although many subject Orders implied the development of particular skills, teaching methods were not prescribed overtly. Recently, there has been an attempt by the last Conservative government to impose particular teaching methods on schools; for instance, by using inspection to reward particular approaches to teaching through the OFSTED (Office for Standards in Education) school assessment and reporting system.

Much of the debate about the form that the National Curriculum should take and of the educational reforms that would be necessary to bring this about was based on a spurious analysis of what was actually happening in schools. For instance, the notion that, before the reforms, most primary classrooms were wholly 'child-centred' needs to be challenged, as does the contention that most teachers fail to use as part of their overall teaching approaches whole class methods. As a reflective teacher, you should be able to analyse the prevailing education orthodoxy at any one time, look at the evidence upon which it is based and consider its value in your own teaching context.

In this book, we suggest that you should recognize the current National Curriculum for what it is, namely specified content and assessment arrangements; designed by 'experts'; that contain much of value; and which, despite our earlier comments, still gives you plenty of scope for interpretation in a way that meets your children's needs. Finally, we hope that you will come to a realization of how the National Curriculum can fit within your educationally — and ethically — grounded developing theory of practice.

References

ARGYRIS, C. and SCHÖN, D. (1974) *Theory into Practice: Increasing Professional Effectiveness*, London, Jossey-Bass.

ASHCROFT, K. and FOREMAN-PECK, L. (1995) *The Lecturer's Guide to Quality and Standards in Colleges and Universities*, London, Falmer Press.

ASHCROFT, K. and GRIFFITHS, M. (1990) 'Action research in initial teacher education,' in ZUBER-SKERRITT, O. *Action Research in Higher Education*, Brisbane, Griffith University Press.

ASHCROFT, K. and PALACIO, K. (eds) (1995) *The Primary Teacher's Guide to the New National Curriculum*, London, Falmer Press.

CARR, W. and KEMMIS, S. (1986) *Becoming Critical: Education, Knowledge and Action Research*, London, Falmer Press.

COHEN, L. and MANION, L. (1994) *Research Methods in Education* (4th Edition), London, Routledge.

DEARING, R. (1994) *The National Curriculum and its Assessment, final report*, London, School Curriculum and Assessment Authority.

DEPARTMENT OF EDUCATION AND SCIENCE (DES) (1989) *National Curriculum: From Policy to Practice*, Stanmore, DES.

DEPARTMENT FOR EDUCATION (DFE) (1995) *Key Stages 1 and 2 of the National Curriculum England*, London, HMSO.

DEWEY, J. (1916) *Democracy and Education*, New York, The Free Press.

ELLIOTT, J. (1991) *Action Research for Educational Change*, Milton Keynes, Open University Press.

KELLY, A.V. (1990) *The National Curriculum: A Critical Review*, London, Paul Chapman Publishing.

KEMMIS, S. (1988) 'Action research,' in KEEVES, J.P. (ed.) *Educational Research, Methodology and Measurement: An International Handbook*, Oxford, Pergamon.

POLLARD, A. and TANN, S. (1993) *Reflective Teaching in the Primary School: A Handbook for the Classroom* (2nd Edition), London, Cassell.

STENHOUSE, L. (1987) 'The conduct, analysis and reporting of case study in educational research and evaluation,' in MURPHY, R. and TORRANCE, H. (eds) *Evaluating Education: Issues and Methods*, London, Harper and Row.

ZEICHNER, K. (1982) 'Reflective teaching and field-based experience in teacher education,' *Interchange*, **12**, 4, pp. 1–22.

Annotated List of Suggested Reading

DEAKIN (1988) *The Action Research Reader*, Waun Ponds, Victoria, Deakin University Press.
(A set of very useful papers giving a range of theoretical perspectives on the process of action research and describing some projects in action.)

KEMMIS, S. (1982) *The Action Research Planner* (2nd Edition), Waun Ponds, Victoria, Deakin University Press.
(A short book that serves as a useful and practical guide to the process of action research.)

2   Planning Across the Curriculum

Mike Threlfall

In this chapter I aim to provide an introduction to, and an overview of, the issues, features, processes and implications of planning across the curriculum, which you are encouraged to consider by way of enquiry tasks. These will focus on wide ranging aspects of planning. As in all fields of educational enquiry, there are many sources of ideas and opinions, theories and models concerning planning. I make reference to some of these. An annotated reading list is provided at the end of the chapter.

A useful working definition of 'curriculum' can be found in Stenhouse (1975; see especially Chapters 5, 6 and 14):

> A curriculum is an attempt to communicate the essential principles and features of an educational proposal in such a form that it is open to critical scrutiny and capable of effective translation into practice. (p. 4)

The proposal, formulated into a plan will contain certain principles:

- selection of content: what is to be learned and what is to be taught;
- development of a teaching strategy: how it is to be learned and taught;
- decision-making about sequence;
- strengths and needs of individual children: differentiation;
- studying and evaluating the progress of children and teachers;
- recognition of varying contexts; school, pupils, environment, culture and climate. (p. 5)

Therefore, there is the need to formulate intentions and aims into policies and practice which are subject to critical scrutiny from interested and involved parties.

Issues, Aspects and Implications of Planning

Planning is usually a feature of all aspects of our lives. A quick trawl through a newspaper on one day (the *Guardian*, 24 September 1996) verifies the fact that planning is regarded as a high profile and necessary activity:

| *Planning your next step?* | 'Make more of your future. Now is the time to plan the next success of your |

	life. A few places still left for 1996 entry. Ring today.'
Planning to learn a new language?	'Tick the language you want to speak in twelve weeks' time. This method enables you to learn easily, enjoyably, naturally and the freedom to learn at your own pace.'
Planning a qualification for aspiring headteachers	'The qualification will cover five key areas, each dealt with in a discrete module; strategic direction and development, learning and teaching, people and relationships, human and material resources and their development and accountability for both the school's efficiency and effectiveness.'
Planning development for IT	'Our aim is to create easy-to-use and easy-to-manage integrated solutions to school's everyday IT needs. In short, solutions both child-compatible and teacher-friendly.'
Job advertisement	'We are currently planning changes for a new county structure to improve every aspect of our service. We need a special individual to join our management team.'
Planning a carbon tax	'This must be introduced gradually and in a way that does not prejudice those on low incomes.'
Planning to buy a new car?	'With a Personal Contract Plan you can drive a family sized car for as little as £116 per month ... at the end of your agreement you will have three choices ...'

Enquiry Task

Design and detail a plan for a day's educational visit as a starting point for a half-term project on the theme of 'Movement'.

From the information above and your experience of planning, list specific issues, aspects and implications that concern, 'planning'. For instance, you might include 'planning of resources, time ... ; planning with children, colleagues ... , planning in the short-term, the medium term, planning in order to promote values, promote conceptual development ...' (See Preedy 1993, Chapter 5)

Morrison and Ridley (1988) point out that curriculum planning occurs at many stages, levels of abstraction and application. It may be concerned with different foci, be top-down or bottom-up and it may be a response to your own ideas, the demands of the school or to outside influences. Any curriculum planning model should answer the following questions:

- What sort of learning experiences do we plan for children?
- Who will be involved in the planning?
- How do we go about making plans?
- What are our own views of curriculum policy?
- Decisions in relation to content . . . topic, themes, subjects?
- How will children and classrooms be organized and managed?
- What resources are needed and available?
- How will we monitor and evaluate our plans?

As you work through the enquiry tasks and your reading, you may find that planning is a process where many issues have to be addressed in terms of prior questions, clarifying purposes, gathering information, ways of working and formulating action that takes into account what is happening, what is going well and what could be better. The Coverdale Organization suggest a systematic approach to planning. Below, are a list of key words that you might use as a starting point as you attempt to structure the task of planning across the curriculum:

choice and values	framework	process	content
selection of methods	justification	context	analysis
learning styles	teaching strategies	sequence	continuity and
match	differentiation	records	progression
evaluation	and access	communication	entitlement
accountability	assessment	cycles	involvement
systems	inspection		culture
monitoring	models		time
	approaches		

If your planning is to be as systematic as possible, each of the concepts represented by the words above needs to be considered and decisions made about them. For example, you may need to think about what values you wish to underpin your planning, how the culture of the school, the community and the UK as a multicultural society should affect your planning, and so on.

Enquiry Task

Think about the way that you might approach planning for differentiation over the next term. Consider the following steps and concepts in planning:

Background: What are the circumstances, difficulties, opportunities and reasons which stimulate the need for thought and action?

Task: What emerges or is given, for instance, in the activities that may be or must be covered?

Aims:	Purposes: why do you plan, what for, who for? Who benefits? What might be desired end results? What might be your success criteria?
Information:	What resources, data, skills and experiences are available? What resources do you need? What ideas, options, risks, and consequences might result?
What has to be done:	What curriculum and policies are prescribed? What freedoms do you have?
Plan:	Who does what, when, where and how?
Action:	What *will* you do?
Review:	How will you record progress or achievement against aims, successes and difficulties in order to improve?

Choices, Values and Framework of the Curriculum

It is assumed that every *educational choice* is based upon a *value commitment* to some *interpretative framework* by those involved in the *curriculum process*. (van Manen, 1977)

The assumption underpinning this chapter is that you believe that schools exist for children. The school may express itself as a lively and purposeful community through the ways in which children are treated. The framework and expression of education and the context of a positive, caring and controlled atmosphere of a school will in part rely upon your commitment to the question; will what I do benefit children? The excitement, possibility and adventure implied by this vision depends on a commitment to this belief. The organized and planned curriculum of school generally flow from this. As an educator, on whatever level, you have an exciting and problematical task: how can you best prepare your children for life within a constantly changing society and how can you effectively organize and plan the curriculum to that end?

Thus, choices have to be made. You become a 'chooser', basing decision upon what is considered to be worthwhile, essential, relevant and acceptable. The basis for that choice is in some sense double-edged: it includes examining and reflecting upon your own views and the values that you bring to the educational context and the views and values of the society in which you find yourselves. Choice, through thinking and analysis, involves you in decisions about the interpretative framework for the curriculum; who should be involved in the curriculum process; how to plan appropriate and significant activity; how to translate this process into practice? (See Morrison and Ridley, 1988, Chapters 1 and 2.)

In the context of Western, and specifically British, institutions of education, planning models for the curriculum involve clarifying and outlining specific aims and objectives. These aims and objectives should be formulated in such a way that they are capable of implementation in the classroom.

The education of children is both orientation and induction into a particular society taking into account their individual need. The aim is a clarification of, 'ways of knowing' with 'ways of being practical' (van Manen, 1977). The implication of this is that you may wish to pay critical attention to the philosophies of knowledge in which our planned curriculum is grounded. You may decide to involve yourselves in raising questions as to what is the case (ways of knowing) and to raise questions as to what should be done in real classrooms (ways of being practical). Values and commitments may need to be located within an interpretative framework (that asks what do we bring to the task?): a stated and articulated philosophy of education:

> A philosophy of education, like any theory has to be stated in words, in symbols. But so far as it is more than verbal it is a plan for conducting education. Like any plan it must be framed with reference to what is to be done and how it is to be done. (Dewey, 1963, p. 28)

Thus planning becomes a means by which we attempt to bring together theory and practice.

Enquiry Task

- What do you consider to be the essential features of a curriculum?
- In planning across the curriculum what views, values and interpretative framework (your philosophy of education) do you bring to this task?
- Analyse the SCAA document: *Planning the Curriculum at Key Stages 1 and 2* and its 'assumptions' regarding choices, values, frameworks and curriculum process. (See Hooper, 1971, Chapters 3, 4, and 5.)

The National Curriculum and Planning

The National Curriculum is an example of an educational choice based upon a value commitment to a particular and stated interpretative framework. This is made explicit in the Education Reform Act (1988) when it states that the essential principles and features of the curriculum should:

a) provide the spiritual, moral, cultural, physical development of pupils at the school and of society, and

b) prepare such people for the opportunities, responsibility and experience of adult life.

This becomes the basis for the 'curriculum process' and has important implications for planning across the curriculum. The principles that underpin this curriculum process include:

- each child should have a broad and balanced curriculum which is relevant to his or her particular needs;

- this must be reflected in the curriculum of every pupil. It is not enough for such a curriculum to be offered by the school, it must be fully taken up by each individual pupil;
- the curriculum must promote development in all the main areas of learning and experiences which are widely accepted as important;
- the curriculum must also serve to develop the pupil as an individual, as a member of society and as a future adult member of the community with a range of personal and social opportunities and responsibilities;
- schools should develop a shared vision of a preferred and desired future for its children in an atmosphere and ethos of learning, support and cooperation.

Enquiry Task

Obtain a copy of a school prospectus (and if possible a school development plan) which will contain a statement of aims in relation to the overall curriculum (including National Curriculum)

Analyse how it is planning to fulfil those stated aims through its organization, budgeting, systems and procedures (focused in the school development plan).

The National Curriculum is a 'given' (in terms of content and arrangement) within the interpretative framework (which may include the views of children and society). Decisions in relation to the curriculum process are translated by schools into planning. In the planning process, schools and teachers attempt to organize and manage the curriculum in such a way that what is considered to be worthwhile is arranged in continuous and progressive stages. In relation to the continuity and progression of the curriculum Spencer (1928) maintained that the steps in the curriculum should be matched to children's development so that learning is perceived as easy and satisfying by the child.

The vocabulary may have changed, but, essentially, the SCAA (1995) document *Planning the Curriculum at Key Stages 1 and 2* is also focused on progression, balance, coherence and continuity (see pp. 8 and 9). Thus, planning across the curriculum should be:

- set within a broader set of principles outlined in the Education Reform Act (1988);
- related to the range of curricular provision implicit in the schools' aims and policies;
- translated by schools into specific, well-defined elements of the curriculum which will in turn need to be included in the overall planning process;
- carried out by individuals and groups of teachers at different levels of detail — long-term, medium-term and short-term plans.

In the SCAA document (1995, p. 10) these three levels of planning (long-, medium- and short-term) are represented:

Figure 2.1:   Three levels of curriculum planning (source: SCAA, 1995)

Planning level	Participants	Purposes	Outcomes for each year group
Long-term: key stage or year group plans.	Headteacher, all staff and governors.	To ensure: • coverage of all aspects of the school curriculum (including the National Curriculum and religious education) across key stages; • balance within and across all aspects of the curriculum in each year of each key stage; • coherence within and between all aspects of the curriculum; • continuity between key stages.	A broad framework of curricular provision for each year of each key stage, which reflects the school's overall aims, objectives and policies. For each year group it should: • specify the content to be taught; • organize content into manageable and coherent units of work, each with a clear focus for learning; • identify links between different aspects of the curricular provision; • allocate a notional time to teach and assess work; • sequence work into three terms.
Medium-term: termly or half-termly plans.	Class teachers supported by subject coordinators and/or year group coordinators.	To develop each year group plan into a detailed sequence of continuing, blocked and linked units of work.	A detailed specification for each unit of work which sets out: • the learning objectives; • emphases and depth of treatment: • resource requirements; • links and references to other units of work; • suggested teaching strategies and pupil groupings; • strategies for differentiating work; • assessment opportunities.
Short-term: weekly or daily plans.	Class teachers.	To ensure: • differentiation; • a balance of different types of activity throughout a week; • appropriate pace; • time for teacher assessment; • time for constructive feedback for pupils; • monitoring evaluation and (if required) modifications to the medium-term plan.	Detailed daily or weekly lesson plans and appropriate records to ensure day-to-day teaching and assessment. They will include suitably differentiated pupil activities based on clear learning objectives.

Section 2 of the SCAA document gives a systematic step-by-step process for whole school planning and is illustrated with examples from schools which have used this approach with the revised Orders. *Key Stages 1 and 2 of the National Curriculum* (DFE, 1995) brings together in a single volume the revised National Curriculum for 5–11-year-olds (Key Stages 1 and 2) in England. It covers all the required subjects and has been produced to aid teachers' planning of the curriculum for Key Stages 1 and 2.

Approaches to Planning Across the Curriculum

Planning should be structured and systematic. These structures and systems may be formulated into a whole school approach to planning across the curriculum. In order to answer the question: 'Will what we do benefit our children?', this approach may then be expressed as a policy which attempts to address the complex issues in planning (ways of knowing) and translate these into systems of organizing and managing the curriculum (ways of being practical) as in the following model:

Issue	*Focus*	*Expression*
Choices, values and framework for decisions in relation to the curriculum.	The planning process; approaches and systems centred upon children.	The scope, content and arrangement of the curriculum.

In looking at issues and deciding on foci and means of expression, you may need to bear in mind that school contexts are different and schools will vary in the way that they approach issues and priorities when designing systems for planning across the curriculum. However, whatever the context:

> Planning cannot mean unthinking implementation. The National Curriculum is defined through brief Attainment Targets and Programmes of Study. It provides a framework only. The breadth and balance of the curriculum and the progression of children through it still have to be *secured by teachers*. Much of the planning has to be across the school. (Preedy, 1993, p. 65)

Planning, 'secured by teachers':

> does not dictate precisely the form of action, but it ensures that one thinks through *possibilities and contingencies* and provides a resource upon which one can draw if necessary. (Alexander, Willcocks, Kinder and Nelson, 1995, p. 30)

You may need to think about how best you can consider the many 'possibilities and contingencies' that affect our decision making in planning and how best you might work together with others in a collaborative, positive and supportive way that ensures a balance between systems of planning and the needs of children. Schools may need to use a particular planning process so that:

> they can address key planning issues in an objective and systematic way and arrive at a framework for the curriculum which reflects their own individual aims, circumstances and priorities, thus preparing the ground for subsequent more detailed planning of specific classroom activities. (SCAA, 1995, p. 5)

Figure 2.2: *Establishing connections and planning processes*

Issues →	Children →	Teachers →	Classrooms →	Schools →	Curriculum →	Planning
	• Developing confidence and self-esteem.	• Values, beliefs and attitudes.	• Management and organization. . . . messages	• Legal framework	• Approaches, scope, content, arrangement. . . .	
	• Involvement and responsibility for planning and assessing learning.	• Own concept of and sharing good practice.	layout resources	• School Development Plan	topic themes	
	• Needs, interests, skills and circumstances of individual children.	• Managing oneself: coping with pressures and demands.	labelling display routines	• Staff Development	subjects	
	• Children's rights to be safe, valued and supported.	• Organizational and management skills. Time management.	good behaviour equal opportunities	• Parents, governors and the wider community	• Schemes of work	
	• Acknowledging and planning for children learning in different ways.	• Commitment to professional development.	decision making plan-do-review	• Philosophy: vision, aims, atmosphere and ethos	• The National Curriculum	
	• Children's understanding of and involvement in school and classroom routines and procedures.	• Developing and evaluating teaching and learning styles.	use of time negotiation planning	• Procedures/Politics/ Systems	• RE	
	• How are children presented with opportunities for thinking and creativity?	• Whole class teaching, group and individual work.	cooperation centres of interest storage	• School context	• Time allocation to units of work	
	• How do we secure for all children access and entitlement to a broad and balanced curriculum?	• Grouping of children.		• Planning processes and cycles	• Cross-curricular themes, dimensions and skills	
	• Expectations in relation to good behaviour.	• Systems of record-keeping and assessment.		• Classroom and curriculum organization	• Access and entitlement	
	• Ways of working and relationships with others.	• Planning for match, differentiation and pace.		• Accountability	• Continuity and progression	
		• Positive language, approaches to children, good behaviour.		• Planning for improvement and effectiveness	• Coverage and coherence	
		• Commitment to collaborative and supportive ways of working: whole school approach and context.		• Ensuring quality of outcomes	• Balance	
		• Own planning systems in the context of continuity of approach through the school.		• Achieving high standards	• Extra-curricular	
		• Planning cooperation.		• Celebrating success	• Spiritual, moral, social and cultural	
		• Balance needs of individual with needs of the class.		• Staff, roles, rights and responsibilities . . . ways of working	• Knowledge, skills, concepts and attitudes	
				• Budgeting . . . resources and their allocation	• Special Needs	
				• Communication systems	• Subject knowledge	
				• Use of school environment	• Role of coordinators	
				• Health and Safety		
				• Monitoring and evaluation		

See also HMI (1991), especially the summary of the characteristics of well-managed classes that includes: planning for teaching and learning; classroom context; assessment, diagnosis and task setting; organizational strategies and teaching techniques.

Enquiry Task

Take an issue from the text under the heading of 'Children' above and use a systematic approach (discussed at the beginning of the chapter) and the rest of the chart to devise and design a plan for developing and implementing this issue in your classroom.

In the demanding task of planning across the curriculum, schools have to take into account many issues. There are many contexts for this planning process, including planning for: school improvement; assessment; special needs; inspection; the National Curriculum; health and safety; cooperative and collaborative ways of working; staff development; and so on. Whatever the issue, focus or demand, the process is likely to be translated into a policy — a system that works. The planning policy may contain certain elements, each one of which will need to be addressed in a structured and systematic way. Further to this, a school or individual teacher's planning policy should contain the necessity to review: to assess progress or achievement against aims, successes and difficulties, in order to improve each of the elements listed in the enquiry task below:

Enquiry Task

Look at planning within an individual school. How does the school assess:

- what happens now?
- what is going well?
- what could be better in relation to the elements or features of a planning policy?

Can you identify ways that the school has considered some of the following:

Context and culture	Documentation
Communication	Staff development and training
Role of senior management	Role of curriculum coordinators
Cycles of planning	Monitoring and evaluation
Children's involvement	Equal opportunities
Planning meetings and systems	Relationship to other policies
Content and approach	Classroom management and organization
Resources	

Discuss with a colleague what other factors you would wish to take into account (for example, a good behaviour policy or the school environment).

You may wish to use these headings as a focus and framework for the review of your own planning.

Conclusion

Throughout this brief introduction to and overview of planning across the curriculum, I have stated that the aim of planning across the curriculum is to balance the needs of children and those of staff with the necessary systems, procedures and policies in relation to planning. I have indicated a need to plan thoroughly and carefully but you will also need to find a place for flexibility, spontaneity and imagination. A colleague of mine asked their 4-year-old son the usual teatime question: 'and what have you done at school today?' The 4-year-old replied, 'I did some technology without any planning.'

References

ALEXANDER, R., WILLCOCKS, J., KINDER, K., and NELSON, N. (1995) *Versions of Primary Education*, London, Routledge.

COVERDALE ORGANISATION (1986) *A Systematic Approach to Getting Things Done*, London, Coverdale.

DEWEY, J. (1963) *Experience and Education*, London, Macmillan.

DFE (1995) *Key Stages 1 and 2 of the National Curriculum*, London, HMSO.

GUARDIAN (1996) Extracts from various advertisements, September, 24.

HMI (1991) *Well Managed Classrooms: Case Studies*, London, HMI.

HOOPER, R. (ed.) (1971) *The Curriculum: Context, Design and Development*, London, Oliver and Boyd and OU Press.

MORRISON, K. and RIDLEY, K. (1988) *Curriculum Planning and the Primary School*, London, Paul Chapman.

PLAYFOOT, D., SKELTON, M. and SOUTHWORTH, G. (1989) *The Primary School Management Book*, London, Mary Glasgow Publications.

PREEDY, M. (1993) *Managing the Effective School*, London, Paul Chapman and OU Press.

SCAA (1995) *Planning the Curriculum at Key Stages 1 and 2*, London, HMSO.

SPENCER, H. (1928) *Essays on Education* (first written 1861), London, M. Dent & Sons Ltd.

STENHOUSE, L. (1975) *An Introduction to Curriculum Research and Development*, Oxford, Heinemann.

VAN MANEN, M. (1977) 'Linking ways of knowing with ways of being practical', *Curriculum Inquiry*, **6**; 3.

Annotated List of Suggested Reading

ASHCROFT, K. and PALACIO, P. (eds) (1995) *The Primary Teacher's Guide to the New National Curriculum*, London, Falmer Press.

(This book provides a quick and accessible overview of the curriculum arrangements that came into force in August 1995. It outlines the main changes, provides examples of creative ways of delivering the new curriculum and provides enquiry tasks to take the reflective teacher forward, locating issues and subjects within a context of whole curriculum planning.)

AVON LEA (1995) *Planning for Effective Schools*, Bristol, County of Avon.

(This material takes into account the findings relating to effective schools in the context of planning for school development. The central message is that the needs of children should be at the heart of planning.)

BLYTH, W.A.L. (1984) *Development, Experience and Curriculum in Primary Education*, Beckenham, Croom Helm.

(The author presents a convincing case for a primary curriculum carefully constructed to enhance the relationship between the various aspects of the child's development and total experience.)

CRAFT, A. (ed.) (1996) *Primary Education: Assessing and Planning Learning*, London, Routledge and OU Press.

(This wide-ranging source book draws together some of the issues at the heart of planning and assessing learning in primary schools.)

DEWEY, J. (1956) *The Child and the Curriculum* and *The School and Society*, London, University of Chicago Press.

(These two small but influential essays were first published in 1902 and 1899. They represent the earliest of Dewey's work on education as an experimental, child-centred process.)

FISHER, R. (1990) *Teaching Children to Think*, London, Simon and Schuster.

(This book discusses the nature of thinking and thinking skills. It explores current developments in the teaching of thinking skills and evaluates research in this field; see especially Chapter 8 'Teaching for thinking across the curriculum'.)

MERRTENS, R. and VASS, J. (1990) *How to Plan and Assess the National Curriculum in the Primary Classroom*, London, Heinemann (Chapters 4 and 5).

(This is a very practical book suggesting ideas and ways forward in planning for the National Curriculum and the implications for classroom management and organization.)

MORRISON, K. (1993) *Planning and Accomplishing School-Centred Evaluation*, Dereham, Peter Francis.

(This book provides a step-by-step practical guide to the key elements of planning, implementing and reporting both formal and informal evaluation, whether as part of a large-scale or small-scale evaluation scheme.)

NATIONAL PRIMARY CENTRE (1992) *Primary Schools in Action*, Oxford, Westminster College.

(This helpful pack focuses on a whole school approach to:

a)   planning the curriculum;

b)   developing a whole school approach;

c)   continuity.)

TRIGGS, P. (1994) *Understanding the Primary Curriculum*, Bristol, UWE.

(A valuable package aimed at school governors, but still a good resource for teachers in addressing aspects, issues and features of planning across the curriculum.)

Section 2

The Subjects in the National Curriculum

3   English

Helena Mitchell and Jenny Monk

Introduction

In this chapter we focus upon language-based topics in which the work is primarily concerned with reading and writing. Our intention is to provide you with suggestions from which you can plan individual lessons as part of a coherent programme. Clearly, speaking and listening will be an integral part of many of these activities and will underpin them. You will also need to consider what assessment opportunities the activities provide as assessment is an integral part of planning and teaching. Enquiry tasks are designed to provide suggestions for the ways you can plan and teach the English curriculum in your classroom. To begin with, we focus on planning.

Planning

Planning takes place on three levels: long, medium and short term. Long-term planning will, hopefully, already be in place and will be linked to your school's language policy *and* to the requirements of the National Curriculum for English (DFE, 1995). Long-term planning should ensure that children cover the National Curriculum in ways that let them experience progressively more challenging activities as they move through year groups. It should also establish curricular balance, coherence and continuity within and between Key Stages. Long-term planning is the key to effective medium- and short-term plans.

A successful and effective way of approaching medium-term planning is through a scheme of work. This is usually drawn up to cover approximately half a term's work in English. This approach contrasts with some earlier approaches where it was usual for English to be subsumed within a topic with a resulting loss of clarity and focus related to the teaching of English. For the purposes of this chapter, we will adopt an English-based scheme of work in which the focus is predominantly reading and writing. This is not to undermine speaking and listening. Indeed, we see these as integral to all curriculum planning.

Below, you will see a model plan, and our intention is to look at the issues raised by this approach. Although this scheme of work is directed towards a particular year group, it is nevertheless flexible. In devising any scheme of work, you will need to consider the previous experiences of the children you teach and their

Figure 3.1: Medium-term plan stage 2: Scheme of work planning sheet

Curriculum Area/Theme: LANGUAGE — ENGLISH				'PIRATES'
Programmes of Study/Learning Objectives	**Key Activities/Experiences/Questions**	**Resource Organization**	**Cross-curricular Aspects**	**Assessment Opportunities**
• developing ability to listen & respond to a novel over a period of time (R1a, 1c, 1d, 2b)	CLASS NOVEL: The Pirate Mixed-up Voyage, M. Mahy. Read at story time and used as a basis for language work.	Novel		Focus on 2–3 children: ability to discuss texts in depth; present and justify opinions; ability to make selections and give reasons; reading aloud; asking questions of texts/poems.
• developing ability to reflect on and respond to texts; express & support opinions; make informed choices (R2b)	DESERT ISLAND POEMS: Create a class book of favourite poems suitable to take on a desert island.	• I Like This Poem — K. Webb MUSIC. Access to writing materials. • Cassette and Tape Recorder • Computer — Flexiwrite	Technology	
• developing understanding of non-chronological writing — purpose and organization; improve knowledge of adjectives and use of metaphors and similes (W1a, 1b, 1c)	INTRODUCING THE PIRATES: A piece of non-chronological writing using imagination and prior knowledge. • Assessment piece to gauge where children are. Encourage use of adjectives. THE MAN WHOSE MOTHER WAS A PIRATE: Read and discuss.	• Descriptions of Pirates • 'Quiz aid' for some children • Whiteboard — brainstorm • Writing equipment		Assess writing in relation to level descriptors (choose 2 or 3 children). Include writing and commentaries in pupil profiles.
	ME THE PIRATE!: A different type of descriptive writing; drawing on language as used in the two Mahy books — point out alliteration, etc.	• Computer — Concept Keyboard		
• develop awareness of audience for writing; • developing letter writing skills (W1a, 1c, 2a)	MESSAGE IN A BOTTLE } To use different LETTERS HOME } types of communication as well as to learn the features of these two types.	• 'Aged' paper • Bottles • Models of letters		As above. Perhaps focus on same children in order to make comparisons and build portfolios.
• extending understanding of form — experimenting with elements of poetry — rhyme, rhythm, imagery; developing ability to write poetry (W1c, 2b)	SEA POEMS: Using two pirate stories as starting points, look at sea descriptions. Create own sea poems, focusing on aspects of sea. (Differentiation. Phrase cards — children in a group)	• Books with sea description • Sea music • Phrase cards		Discuss poems with children . . . ?
Comments/future action.				

current development. Within the scheme, there should be an opportunity to differentiate between the less and more experienced learners. If you look closely at this scheme of work, you will see that its emphasis is on writing rather than reading. Speaking and listening are part of the activities. It is your role to ensure that the curriculum is balanced, and that there is equal emphasis over time to each aspect of the English curriculum.

Although the selection of desert island poems for the class book does involve a focus on reading, nevertheless it also offers opportunities for developing speaking and listening. The following enquiry task illustrates how this can be done.

Enquiry Task — Speaking and Listening

Focus on the section of the planning sheet related to the choice of Desert Island Poems. In conjunction with the National Curriculum Programmes of Study for Speaking and Listening, consider how you would plan to provide Speaking and Listening opportunities for a range of children. This could be achieved in the context of:

- selecting the poems;
- justifying their inclusion;
- the layout of the book;
- its publication and presentation.

Assessment opportunities provided by this activity include:

- justifying opinions;
- developing response;
- skills of planning and organization;
- collaborative group work skills.

This activity should have provided you with an interesting starting point for further work, and illustrated the pattern of curriculum planning in English. However, in a chapter dedicated to English, the topic of reading must have a central place, because of its fundamental importance in education.

Reading

The debate continues to rage about reading. Teachers who are unable to articulate the reasons for their practice are likely to become the victims of every changing fashion. Results of research conducted over the last twenty-five years have demonstrated that reading is a complex and multi-faceted behaviour. As an adult, you will have become so accustomed to the ease with which you can read most texts that you probably haven't considered how you learnt to read.

The work of Goodman in 1968, and the introduction of miscue analysis and its development by researchers such as Marie Clay (1985), can help you to diagnose the strategies being used by a reader. More recent research than that of Goodman's, for example, Rumelhart and McClelland (1981), and Mitchell and

Dombey (1996), demonstrates how reading involves simultaneous processing of textual information on a range of different levels. The debate focuses on how children learn to become readers, and whether you should focus on specific aspects of reading behaviour at the expense of the full range.

The National Curriculum states, 'within a balanced and coherent programme, pupils should be taught to use the following knowledge, understanding and skills' (DFE, 1995, p. 7). The skills outlined in the National Curriculum are:

- phonic knowledge;
- graphic knowledge;
- word recognition;
- grammatical knowledge;
- contextual understanding.

In order to ensure a balanced and coherent scheme of work which encompasses the full range of knowledge and skills demanded, it is essential to plan an effective teaching programme which utilizes lively, stimulating and meaningful texts.

It is important to consider the features of an effective reading curriculum at Key Stage 1. For many early years teachers, the teaching and learning of reading is one of the most important aspects of the curriculum. It is impossible to discuss the full range of the reading curriculum at Key Stage 1 in the limited space of one chapter, but we will attempt to suggest some guidelines, illustrated by a range of activities which can be used in the classroom.

Reading at Key Stage 1

The range of reading specified in the National Curriculum for Key Stage 1 is very broad, and should include information texts as well as children's literature. Children's own writing should feature as part of the textual sources, and should be read to a range of audiences. The range of literature currently available is considerable, and there should be plenty of opportunities for you to ensure that a stimulating and inviting range of texts is presented to the class, and discussed by them. Such texts can also be used by you for a spectrum of literacy-based activities which will enable children to learn not only how such texts work and are structured, but also to encourage a closer focus on the components of the text. In order to fulfil the requirements of the National Curriculum, it will be necessary for you to regularly review the range of texts in your classroom, and to plan for the inclusion of different text types throughout the year.

The use of enlarged books, commonly called Big Books, is an excellent teaching aid for developing children's knowledge about literacy, both in terms of how the text is organized and as to how the smaller textual aspects operate. If you do not have any of these large-scale books in your school, you should be able to obtain some through local public libraries. Big books are now available in different text types, and include both popular story texts, such as *The Lighthouse Keeper's Lunch*

(Armitage and Armitage, 1989) and *Oscar Got the Blame* (Ross, 1989), as well as information texts such as the Magic Bean series published by Heinemann (1992).

Enquiry Task — Development of Range

Over the course of one week, note down the texts which you use with your class and consider the *range* with which you are presenting them. Consider also the texts which the children choose to read from the selection in your classroom:

- Does the selection include stories, plays, poetry and picture books?
- What opportunities are there for children to experience information texts, including those produced on disk/CD-ROM? How are such opportunities structured?
- In what ways do children present their writing to other children in the class?
- What other opportunities are there for children to present to other audiences; for example, parents?

Of course, it is not possible to ensure that children are exposed to the full range of texts every week, but this activity should help you to consider the balance of your provision for reading.

Key Skills

The key skills element of the National Curriculum is intended to focus you onto the particular strategies which children must acquire, demonstrate, and be able to orchestrate if they are to be competent readers. The term 'skills' implies a set of discrete items to be learnt, which can then be bolted together. It is probably easier for you to view them as part of the same conceptual framework. Although all of the key skills in Key Stage 1 of the document need specific teaching, the most effective way of doing this in order to ensure that you both focus on the concepts and also enable children to orchestrate them is to tackle the key skills within the context of a text. The use of Big Books forms an ideal resource for this type of teaching.

Enquiry Task

If you have not used a Big Book before, gather your class around you and share one with them, noting their response to the content of the text and any specific features of its construction.

- Read the text to them, pointing out the title and the name of the author and illustrator.
- As you read, run your finger along the bottom of the text in order to indicate directionality. You may also wish to focus on particular words and phrases if appropriate.
- To encourage prediction, pause at two or three points in the text to ask the children what they think will happen next.

- When you have read the text with them, get the children to retell the main events in sequence.
- You may wish to use the format of the text to create your own class Big Book with the children.

Big Books offer great versatility to the early years teacher, enabling much loved texts to be used effectively to teach textual structure, organization and context, as well as phonic and graphic knowledge, and knowledge about punctuation. The large-scale format makes the text clearly accessible to small or large groups of children.

Reading at Key Stage 2

In this section, we intend to focus on the effective planning of a reading curriculum at Key Stage 2. While it is true that there is a broadening of the curriculum at this stage, it is equally true that English is a curriculum subject requiring discrete planning. It should not be seen as simply integral to other curriculum areas. Indeed, we would argue that the view of English as a service subject has led to some of the present problems and to difficulties faced by the profession when asked to justify practice.

Reading at Key Stage 2 highlights the importance of a range of reading experience, enthusiasm for reading, and the development of independence, understanding and response. These were key features of the Cox Report (DES, 1985), and are fundamental to the development of reading from the initial stages through to GCSE and beyond. Recently, we expressed the view that:

> In order for the full range of texts to be available to, and read by pupils, the [book] collection in every classroom at Key Stage 2 should reflect diversity, sophistication and complexity and, in addition, cater for the differentiated needs of all children. (Mitchell and Monk, 1995, p. 41)

It is also clear that unguided choice does not develop critical reflective readers. The ability to make sense and to respond to any new text is dependent upon the following:

- past experience of stories and a range of genre;
- the opportunity to respond with peers and adults to texts in a variety of contexts;
- the recommendation of books at planned times on a regular basis;
- well documented reading records that include self-assessment, the recording of strategies used and recognition of the child's home literacy experiences as being supportive of, not in conflict with, school literacy;
- the opportunity to discuss texts, in both groups and pairs, for particular purposes and with specific outcomes in mind.

Figure 3.2: Planning the reading curriculum

	Hearing stories, poems etc.	Silent reading/Group reading (including reading for research)	Reading to a partner	Reading to an adult	Booktalk	Reading aloud: a performance

A starting point towards achieving the above is to consider the range of books available to your class or year group.

Enquiry Task

Carry out an audit to ascertain whether your collection of reading material in your classroom contains:

- books for inexperienced readers who still need support;
- books for newly independent and independent readers who are developing confidence and reading stamina;
- books for the experienced and fluent readers;
- a wide selection of poetry;
- media texts in a range of forms;
- books that cover the range of genre outlined in Key Stage 2 Reading (DFE, 1995), including traditional tales, stories from other cultures, translations, and both recent and long-established children's fiction.

Given that most classrooms are not well resourced, the aim is to maximize existing materials and to devise an appropriate curriculum. We would therefore challenge the underlying assumptions of the provision of a period of unstructured silent reading each day: instead, we would put in its place a well-planned curriculum that is both flexible and rigorous, and includes sessions such as group reading, booktalk, and shared reading. Figure 3.2 can be used by individuals, by the teacher as a class record or by a reading group to plan and record their reading experiences. Names of children or dates can be written into the boxes on the left hand side.

In providing this range of reading, you will be able to focus on the important ideas of *understanding* and *response*. We have explored these notions already (Mitchell and Monk, 1995). It is, however, worth considering the implications of such knowledge.

Understanding embodies notions of:

- confidence in choosing, discussing, and summarizing texts;
- appreciation of both the major points in a text, and its subtleties and ambiguities;
- familiarity with reference material and retrieval strategies.

Response involves the reader in:

- expressing opinions with reference to the text;
- being aware of themes and images, and considering the structure of texts and the use of language. (Mitchell and Monk, 1995, p. 41)

In developing group discussions of texts, you may wish to consider some or all of the following issues:

- your rôle in modelling and demonstrating the process of critical reflection;
- the involvement of learning support staff and parents in the reading process;
- the way in which discussions about texts can be structured and assessed.

Detailed accounts of the implementation of discussions related to texts can be found in three articles in Language and Learning (Davies, Karavis and Monk, 1993).

Planning text-related activities at Key Stage 2 has shown that even with a single book it is possible to develop activities that meet the needs of individuals, and at the same time involve all children in discussion of worthwhile texts. It should be emphasized that children who take longer than others in learning to read deserve the best reading material, not the cast offs that other children would never choose to read and that are an insult to intelligence and integrity. It is with this in mind that we present the example below. Having selected a text, you may decide to focus on one small part of the story or poem, but you will need to consider how you might introduce the whole text, and then look closely at the possibilities it holds. All the activities should add to the children's understanding of the text and, therefore, the choice of text and related activities need careful consideration. This approach is an effective way of teaching the key skills of reading at Key Stage Two, especially developing an understanding of the structure of texts. The following example is based upon the poem *The Nose* (Crichton-Smith, 1993), and outlines possible text-based activities for Year 6 children.

Example of Text-related Activity

Introduction

Before beginning focused work on this text, arouse the pupils' curiosity by displaying pictures by artists and illustrators, such as Magritte and Anthony Browne, showing surreal impressions of parts of the body. Make the display interactive by posing questions and providing answer spaces underneath where the children can write their ideas and responses.

Objectives: To develop children's knowledge and understanding of the ways in which a writer chooses to organize ideas, and focuses on use of language and cohesive features.

Differentiation: Consider how you group the children so that they are able to work with each other effectively.

Activity: Groups of children working in home or base groups. Each group is provided with an envelope containing the cut-up lines of one stanza of the poem. In their groups, the children are set the task of discussing the most appropriate order for the cut-up lines. Each reconstructed stanza is then combined with the others to produce the class version of the poem. The original poem is then read aloud. An overhead projector can be used effectively here to demonstrate the overall result and as a class the children can discuss similarities and differences between the original poem and their versions. You can use this discussion to draw out the structural implications of the use of grammar or syntax. The children choose and vote on a suitable title for the class poem. You re-read the original poem, returning to the subtleties of meaning in it; highlighting the differences in meaning between the versions, and impressing upon the children the need to respect the author's original structure and intention.

You may find the following headings useful as a planning grid to help you structure the activities:

Title of book;
Author;
Suggested age range for activities;
Organizational considerations;
Stage of reading development;
Learning objectives;
Activities;
Assessment opportunities.

Standard English and Language Study

By linking an understanding of text structure with knowledge about language, it is possible to develop schemes of work that include work on the following important areas of language study:

- explicit discussion of the comparative features of certain texts types, for example, narrative, information, argument;
- comparisons of texts to show how authors exploit creatively the features of a genre; for example, a modern version of a fairytale;
- awareness of how language changes over time; for example, compare dialogue between characters in the works of Enid Blyton and Jacqueline Wilson;
- discussion of word derivation, *root* words; for example, sign as in signature, signing, design, signal: *loan* words from other languages to aid understanding; for example, quiche, karate, discotheque;
- discussion of the differences between fact and opinion.

An ideal way of developing this knowledge is to focus on different tellings or versions of one fairytale. For example, you could ask your children to compare an Anthony Browne version of *Hansel and Gretel* with that by Tony Ross, and then they could compare these versions with the range found in story books at home, at school, and in the library. The work is recorded in *Becoming a Reader 2*, (Davies et al., 1993).

To help you plan effectively for work in this area, the annotated selection of books at the end of this chapter is focused on reading for information.

Writing at Key Stage 1

Planning

As with reading, the range of writing outlined by the National Curriculum for English at Key Stage 1 is broad. The underlying themes of *audience* and *purpose* are identified and highlighted by the inclusion of different forms of writing. The dilemma for the early years teacher is how to provide opportunities for children to learn to write fluently and competently when many of them do not yet have the knowledge to do so, and also find the physical demands of writing very difficult. There are many interwoven threads here. Clearly, as the National Curriculum states: 'Pupils' early experiments and independent attempts at communicating in writing, using letters and known words, should be encouraged' (DFE, 1995, p. 9, para. 2a).

In order to enable children to utilize their learning about how writing works, it is necessary to provide them with opportunities for using their knowledge. Planning for writing needs to take into account all the different threads of the National Curriculum for English, and to consider the overlap between reading too. With long-term planning, it is possible to see that the full range demanded by the Programme of Study is in place, but this needs to be carefully balanced by the planning undertaken at the medium-term stage. Opportunities for different types of writing need to be catered for throughout the year, and these need to be viewed in conjunction with the types of reading undertaken as part of the reading curriculum. Thus, work on a science-based topic, such as Living Things and their Environment, would also include class reading and writing of texts which fall into the report category. For further suggestions on work using such texts, see Derewianka (1990).

Teaching

Role play situations, as discussed in a previous publication (Mitchell and Monk, 1995), can offer opportunities for children to demonstrate and develop their independent spelling and writing. Private writing books, in which children experiment with writing, can also help to provide an opportunity for writing in which children feel able to experiment because they are not having to produce work for a specific audience unless, that is, they wish to share it. However, bearing in mind the themes of *audience* and *purpose*, it is important to ensure that children are aware of who the writing is intended to be for (see Figure 3.3).

Translation of Laura's writing:

> Once there was a giant who was selfish and he wouldn't let people into his garden so winter came and it stayed and one day he heard a lovely noise and he thought it was spring but it was birds singing and he saw children playing in his garden and then he saw a child in the corner in his garden crying because he couldn't get in the tree he was too small to get in the tree so the giant went over and put him [in] the tree.

Figure 3.3: Laura's writing

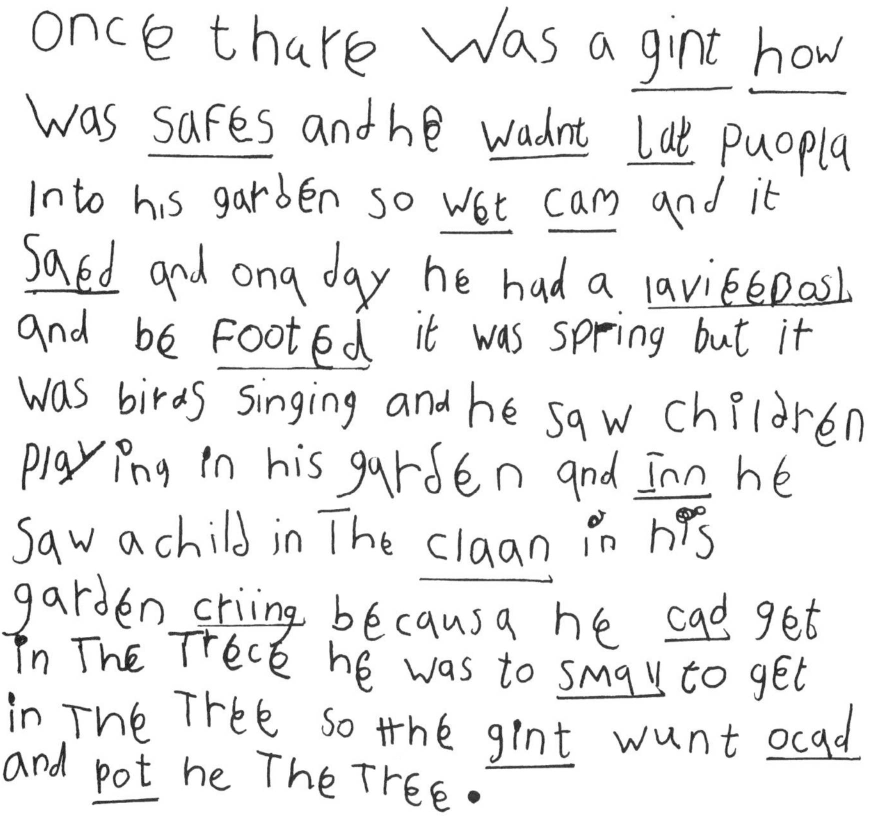

once thare Was a gint how
Was safes and he wadnt lat puopla
Into his garben so wet cam and it
Saed and ona day he had a lavieepasl
and be footed it was spring but it
Was birds singing and he saw children
playing in his garden and inn he
Saw a child in The claan in his
garden criing becausa he cad get
in The Treck he was to smay to get
in The Tree so the gint wunt ocad
and pot he The Tree.

In the piece of writing in Figure 3.3, a 6-year-old is retelling the story of *The Selfish Giant* by Oscar Wilde. If one of the children in your class produced a piece of writing such as this you would need to assess it on several levels, and use these assessments to plan further teaching. Firstly, you would wish to consider *content* and *structure* of the writing: Laura has used story language confidently, and has retold a particular incident in the story with detail beyond the simple. Her grasp of story structure and story language are developing well. Evidence for this can be found in phrases such as, *a giant who was selfish*, and *so winter came and it stayed*. This young writer is using both main clauses and subordinate clauses competently. For example, *he saw a child in the corner* is the main clause. Further information on the child is then provided by the phrase *in his garden crying*, and *because he couldn't get into the tree* is a subordinate clause of reason. However, it is also true that this young writer is using connectives such as 'and' as we do in spoken language to link the sequence of events. She needs to be introduced to the use of punctuation through reading her own writing aloud to hear the rhythm of the structure, and discussing where the punctuation should go. If children have writing partners, such discussions can be held on a regular basis as children progress through school.

Transcriptional skills (spelling and handwriting) also need to be considered. Laura has already begun to identify words which she recognizes as not being spelt correctly (they are underlined). This is an important stage in spelling development in that it gives the child responsibility for focusing on their own spelling. It is your rôle to provide an appropriate framework for spelling development.

The stages of spelling development (as defined by Gentry, 1981) provide clear guidance on the stages which children go through in order to become competent spellers. This spelling development needs to be promoted through specific teaching in the classroom, and also linked into the content and form of writing. Laura uses phonetic strategies when faced with a word she does not know; for example, *criing* (sic). In order to plan for the effective teaching of spelling, you need to ascertain children's stage of development. The best way of doing this is to collect and monitor examples of each child's developmental spelling, to diagnose their stage of development, and to plan for further teaching. Laura has identified the examples above as possible errors, and she should be introduced to the letter strings that underpin them.

Devices such as alphabets made with the children will be a useful teaching aid for developing knowledge of the structure and names of letters. Similarly, displays of functional writing in the classroom will create a writing environment to which children can be encouraged to contribute, perhaps with their own messages on a message board. Direct teaching can be achieved through class sessions in which you, as the scribe, write for the children, drawing their attention to particular features of writing, such as spelling patterns. The links between spelling and handwriting can also be explored, so that children are taught how to write certain letter patterns in cursive writing. These letter patterns, once learnt, can be utilized in other pieces of writing. Laura's writing also exhibits a need for work on handwriting development, particularly the formation of the vowels as a possible starting point. However, she would also have benefited from being introduced to cursive writing at an earlier stage. The rôle of information technology in promoting writing development must not be forgotten. Word processing programs enable children, working together, to construct and reconstruct complex texts which might otherwise be beyond their physical coordination to achieve.

Writing at Key Stage 2

Planning

Research by White (1986) for the Assessment of Performance Unit (APU), the work of Czerniewska (1992) and Medwell (1994), highlight the need for children to be more aware of the processes involved in the writing of different texts. It is also clear that children need explicit teaching and discussion about what it is that writers actually do. Firstly, you need to be clear in you own mind as to what is meant by *purpose* and *audience* in relation to the range of texts that Key Stage 2 children should be writing. We refer you to the grid (Mitchell and Monk, 1995,

p. 48) outlining the way in which both purpose and form need to be addressed in your planning. The purpose of a piece of writing may be to inform, entertain or instruct; for example, its form may be a letter, a poem, a poster or a novel. The success of any text is dependent upon its reception by the reader. When children receive a response, either written or oral, from an intended audience, the effect on their writing can be immediate. A classroom where writing is discussed and crafted is offering support to the apprentice writer. Fisher (1990) suggests that there are specific questions a child can ask before a piece of writing is started. These include: *Who will receive the message? Why are we writing? How should the message be presented?* and *What ideas have we got?* (p. 199). Children are generally quite happy for you to answer the last question in particular. It is important to set written work in a meaningful context and within a sound knowledge base. In this way, children will develop the confidence to express their ideas, to take risks, and to experiment with different text types. Take one or two of the following questions and then begin to address their underlying implications for classroom practice.

Enquiry Task

- Does your classroom provide at least some of the following range of materials? pens of all types, pencils, paper in a variety of sizes, book-making/ binding equipment, desktop publishing programs
- Do your children experiment with different forms of writing and types of texts?
- Do your children work together on collaborative tasks and as response partners for each others' work?
- Do your classroom displays reflect a range of writing, and do they show the process of writing; that is, from plans through drafts and revisions to a published text?

If children and teachers can define *purpose*, then it is far easier for feedback to be relevant and meaningful. The APU summary report (Gorman and White, 1989) indicates clearly the need for regular and systematic feedback about the quality of written work set in the context in which the writing was undertaken and *linked to a well-informed view of what constitutes development in children's writing abilities* (p. 33). Subsequent work by SCAA (1995) on the exemplification of standards and National Foundation for the Educational Research in their SAT support material (SCAA, 1995) have provided a framework for analysis and discussion. There is still much work to be done on teachers' understanding of language structures and grammatical terminology. Language in the National Curriculum project materials, so supportive of that knowledge, were not published but are used selectively by those leading INSET to build confidence and competence. It is our view that there has to be less hysteria and more critical analysis and reflection. When asked to share their concerns and to discuss gaps in their own knowledge, teachers, as with most professionals, respond and learn quickly. When criticized and attacked, they become defensive and do not make progress.

What Role Does Information Technology Play in the Writing Process?

In Chapter 12 of this book, you will see how the writing process described in the National Curriculum can be supported through the use of word processing. In spite of the few references to it in the Programmes of Study for English, it is important to consider the significant opportunities offered by IT. Consider, for example, the following in relation to the writing curriculum:

- photocopying drafts of a text allows them to be worked on without changing the original;
- a range of formats can be used in desktop publishing; for example, posters, newspaper layouts;
- CD-ROMs provide information in a range of forms that provide exemplars for children;
- communication through e-mail can provide instant and written feedback;
- skills of editing and proof-reading can be developed through word-processing.

There are many opportunities to use IT in the teaching of writing. To use IT purely as a tool for copying writing once complete is a waste of a valuable and scarce learning tool.

Planning and teaching an effective English curriculum is a most rewarding process which should not result in a series of unconnected lessons and activities. For both your children and yourself, English lessons should be meaningful and stimulating. Work in English should have a coherent and distinctive place in the curriculum: more than this, work in English should inform teaching and learning across the *whole* curriculum.

References

ARMITAGE, R. and ARMITAGE, D. (1989) *The Lighthouse Keeper's Lunch*, Oliver and Boyd Storytime Giant, Harlow, Longman.

BARRS, M., ELLIS, S., HESTER, H. and THOMAS, A. (1988) *The Primary Language Record*, London, CLPE.

BROWNE, A. [illus.] (1986) *The Brothers Grimm: Hansel and Gretel*, London, Methuen.

BRYANT, P. and BRADLEY, L. (1985) *Children's Reading Problems*, Oxford, Blackwell.

CARRE, C. (ed.) (1990) *Leverhulme Primary Project: Classroom Skills Series*, London, Routledge.

CHAMBERS, A. (1985) *Booktalk*, London, The Bodley Head.

CHAMBERS, A. (1993) *Tell Me*, Stroud, Thimble Press.

CLAY, M. (1985) *The Early Detection of Reading Difficulties*, Oxford, Heinemann.

CRIPPS, C. and EDE, J. (1991) *A Hand for Spelling*, Wisbech, LDA.

CRICHTON-SMITH, I. (1993) 'The nose', in HARRISON, M. and STUART-CLARK, C. (eds) *The Oxford Book of Story Poems*, Oxford, Oxford University Press.

Czerniewska, P. (1992) *How Children Learn to Write*, Oxford, Blackwell.

Davies, P., Karavis, S. and Monk, J. (1993) 'Becoming a reader', in *Language and Learning*, Birmingham, Questions Publishing Company.

Derewianka, B. (1990) *Exploring How Texts Work*, Sydney, Primary English Teaching Association, Australia.

DES (1975) *A Language for Life*, London, HMSO (also known as The Bullock Report).

DES (1985) *English from 5 to 16*, London, HMSO (also known as the Cox Report).

DFE (1995) *Key Stages 1 and 2 of the National Curriculum England*, London, HMSO.

Fisher, R. (1990) *Teaching Children to Think*, Oxford, Blackwell.

Gentry, R. (1981) 'Learning to spell developmentally', *The Reading Teacher*, **34**, 2, Newark, Delaware, International Reading Association.

Goodman, K. (1968) 'Reading: A psycholinguistic guessing game', in Singer, H. and Ruddell, R. (eds) (1994) *Theoretical Models and Processes of Reading*, Newark, Delaware, International Reading Association.

Gorman, T. and White, J. (1989) *Assessment Matters Number 4: Language and Learning*, London, HMSO.

Goswami, U. and Bryant, P. (1990) *Phonological Skills and Learning to Read*, Hove, Lawrence Erlbaum Associates Ltd.

Lewis, M. and Wray, D. (1996) *Writing Frames*, Reading RALIC.

Littlefair, A. (1991) *Reading All Types of Writing*, Milton Keynes, Open University Press.

Mallett, M. (1992) *Making Facts Matter: Reading Non-Fiction*, London, Paul Chapman.

Medwell, J. (1994) *Contexts for Writing: The Social Construction of Written Composition*, in Wray, D. and Medwell, J. (eds) *Teaching Primary English*, London, Routledge.

Mitchell, H. and Dombey, H. (1996) 'Analysing the strategies used by teachers of reception aged children in one to one reading sessions using non-scheme texts', unpublished paper presented at United Kingdom Reading Association conference, University of Northumbria.

Mitchell, H. and Monk, J. (1995) 'English', in Ashcroft, K. and Palacio, D. (eds) *The Primary Teacher's Guide to the New National Curriculum*, London, Falmer Press.

McNaughton, C. (1994) *Suddenly*, London, Andersen Press.

National Oracy Project/National Curriculum Council (1990) *Teaching, Talking and Learning in Key Stages One and Two*, NCC, York.

Neate, B. (1992) *Finding Out about Finding Out*, Sevenoaks, Hodder and Stoughton.

Noyes, A. (1981) *The Highwayman*, Oxford, Oxford University Press.

Oxfordshire County Council (1993) *OCM 8 Papers on the Teaching of Reading*, Oxford, OCC.

Perera, K. (1984) *Children's Writing and Reading: Analysing Classroom Language*, Oxford, Blackwell.

Reid, D. and Bentley, D. (eds) (1996) *Reading On!* Leamington Spa, Scholastic.

Ross, T. (1989) *Oscar Got the Blame*, Oliver and Boyd Storytime Giant, Harlow, Longman.

Ross, T. (1992) *Hansel and Gretel*, London, Red Fox.

Rumelhart, D. and McClelland, J. (1981) 'Interactive processes through spreading activation', in Lesgold, A. and Perfetti, C. (eds) *Interactive Processing in Reading*, New Jersey, Lawrence Erlbaum Associates.

School Curriculum and Assessment Authority (SCAA) (1994) *Key Stage 2 National Pilot: English Teachers' Guide*, London, SCAA.

School Curriculum and Assessment Authority (SCAA) (1995) *Exemplification of Standards in English: Key Stages 1 & 2, Levels 1 to 5 Reading and Writing*, London, HMSO.

Seuss, dr (1980) *The Cat in the Hat Series*, London, Collins.
Stubbs, M. (1976) *Language, Schools and Classrooms*, London, Methuen.
Warlow, A. (1987) *Reasons for Writing*, Aylesbury, Ginn.
Wells, G. (1986) *The Meaning Makers*, Sevenoaks, Hodder and Stoughton.
White, J. (1986) *The Assessment of Writing*, Windsor, NFER-Nelson.

Annotated List of Suggested Reading

Derewanika, B. (1990) *Exploring How Texts Work*, Sydney, Primary English Teaching Association.

(This Australian publication provides a clear structure to support teachers developing work with non-fiction texts. The book is divided into chapters which focus on different text types and age groups across the primary school. The author highlights particular features of each text type, and emphasizes what children need to learn in order to use the genre successfully and effectively.)

Lewis, M. and Wray, D. (1996) *Writing Frames*, RALIC Reading.

(These frames, developed and trialled by teachers and researchers on the EXEL project at Exeter University, have potential for children of all ages. Although it does not have to be, non-fiction writing is often difficult for children. The photocopiable writing frames offer children a structure within which to work. They are not a panacea, nor are they for use with all children, but they do offer a valuable starting point for the organization of the writing of non-fiction genre, such as reports, arguments and recounts.)

Littlefair, A. (1991) *Reading All Types of Writing*, Milton Keynes, Open University Press.

(Alison Littlefair was one of the first people in this country to study and write about the issues of teaching about genre and register. The significance of children developing a range of flexible reading strategies cannot be over-emphasized. Littlefair explains the thinking underpinning genre and register: implications for both primary and secondary schools are discussed.)

Mallett, M. (1992) *Making Facts Matter: Reading Non-Fiction*, London, Paul Chapman.

(Margaret Mallet's book is partly an account of her own work with primary-aged children, focusing on developing children's reading of non-fiction texts. As a result of her work, she makes a number of suggestions about how reading information texts with children should be structured in order to enable them to read such texts effectively. Her work builds upon previous work undertaken by the Schools' Council in the late 1970s, reinforcing teaching points made then and developing them further. The need for primary-aged children to be taught a range of effective reading strategies is emphasized.)

4   Mathematics

Margaret Jones

Introduction

In this chapter my intention, by considering mathematical activities, is to arrive at some conclusions about the teaching and learning of mathematics and related issues. The chapter contains five sections in addition to this introduction. Each section covers a specific aspect of mathematics education and, although each section could be read independently, there are on occasions references between sections which may need to be considered. There are suggestions for enquiry tasks: these are classroom based, and involve the collection and analysis of data in order to make changes in, or highlight, aspects of your classroom practice.

Practical Examples for Tackling the Content of National Curriculum Mathematics

This section will focus mainly on ideas for teaching mathematics. Number is an area of the curriculum which can either be taught in a lively and interesting manner, or it can be reduced to a series of exercises which are ineffective in allowing objectives to be achieved. The activities suggested in this section will all address the requirements of Using and Applying of the Mathematics National Curriculum (DFE, 1995), as well as specific areas of content. They are activities that encourage children not only to *communicate* the mathematics they have been doing but also to make *decisions* about how they tackle those activities.

Communication is a fundamental aspect in the learning of mathematics. The Open University in *Using Mathematical Thinking* identifies the sequence, 'Do, *Talk* and Record'. Pam Liebeck (1984) puts forward the acronym ELPS (Experience, *Language*, Pictures and Symbols), as a means of identifying the process of learning mathematics. George Ball (1990) regards *Talking* and Learning as being synonymous. 'Using and Applying' of the National Curriculum (DFE, 1995) clearly sets out the place of communication in children's learning of mathematics when at Key Stage 1 it states that:

> Pupils should be given opportunities to:
> . . .
> (b) explain their thinking to support the development of their reasoning.

and at Key Stage 2:

> Pupils should be given opportunities to:
> . . .
> (d) ask questions and follow alternative suggestions to support the development of reasoning.

At both Key Stage 1 and 2 the progression through the development of skills and concepts is well documented (see Hopkins, Gifford and Pepperell, 1996; Atkinson, 1996). I will consider activities from which I know surprising results sometimes emerge. For example, in the early years classroom, it is usual to use Plasticine and paper, cutting them up to demonstrate fractions. Instead, you might use biscuits. Group the children into sixes, for example, and give each group a packet or plate of biscuits, where the number of biscuits is not a multiple of six. Some suitable numbers might be 17, 23 or 29. Ask the children to share the biscuits so that they each get exactly the same. They can then record their findings and, if you wish, eat the biscuits afterwards. In deciding to do this activity, aspects of Health and Safety must be considered. The children should wash their hands before starting and handle the biscuits as little as possible.

Figures 4.1 and 4.2 show the recording carried out by two groups in one class of infant pupils working on sharing 29 biscuits between six people.

The children in these examples are quite comfortable using fractions; later in the assessment section I will return to an analysis of their work.

At the end of Key Stage 2, it is possible to use another idea based around the theme of food and to work on developing understanding of fractions with the following activity (see *Working Investigationally*, ATM, 1987, for further information). You need six large bars of chocolate which are laid out on three tables; three bars on the first, two bars on the second and one bar on the third. The children line up at the front of the classroom and have to choose where to sit one at a time. They have to choose the table where they will get the biggest share and justify their choice to the rest of the class. The first six who sit down will find it easy to share but as the rest of the class begin to sit down the fractions become increasingly difficult. It is useful to record the fractions as the children sit and to discuss the strategies for making decisions.

Enquiry Task — Practical Examples for Tackling the Content

The Teaching of Fractions

Working with other members of staff, or fellow students, try out the idea outlined in the paragraph above. In order to get enough results to make the activity viable, you will need to follow this through as though you had a whole class of children.

- What mathematics have you used during the activity?
- Did any patterns emerge? If so, what are they?
- Where do you have choices to make? In what ways do these choices change the outcomes?

Figure 4.1:   *Sharing 29 biscuits between 6 people*

Try out the activity with a class of children. (Try not to let your experience influence the work that the children do.)

In what respects were the children's actions the same as those of yourself and your colleagues? In what ways were they different?

What implications are there for your teaching of fractions?

Measures is an aspect of the curriculum that needs some consideration before teaching begins. Fundamental to its development is the notion of comparison; for example, longer than, heavier than. These concepts can be explored through direct comparison of the objects under consideration. Before progress can be made, the

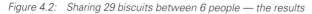

Figure 4.2: Sharing 29 biscuits between 6 people — the results

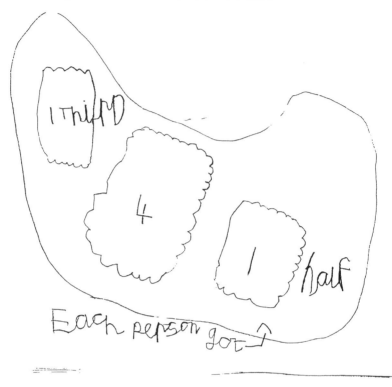

notion of a comparator, a tool which can measure many objects, needs to be introduced. Initially this will be something which is a non-standard measure, such as a footprint. Later, standard measures such as metre or centimetre can be introduced.

In teaching measures, Booth and Jones (1995) outline an activity called Giant's Hand, which works well with children of all ages. Another activity for measuring, which also works well with children of all ages, is one which involves different lengths of string. For the latter activity you will need an even number of envelopes with about five different lengths of different types of string in each. You will need thick string, thin string, twine, different coloured string, with lengths varying between 5 cm and 1 m. The lengths should not be the same in each envelope. The children should be grouped about four or five to each envelope. They look at what is in their envelope and then have to order, according to length, their own pieces of string. Whilst they are doing this the children have to consider how they will describe to another group the contents of the evelope so that their own set of string and the other group's set of string can be ordered whilst the string of both groups remains hidden from the other group. This must be done by using descriptive language and/or comparators. In this case, a comparator might be a book or the edge of the desk, but the children must decide for themselves that a comparator is needed. In this way the children can say that a piece of string is about half the width of the book or five times longer than the book. Rulers and standard measuring instruments are forbidden! This task helps the children realize the importance of standard comparators, such as scales and rulers.

For early years children, this activity can be adapted so that there are fewer lengths of string; for example, they might just decide which is the longer of pairs of string, and then a third and fourth length could be introduced.

The above activities allow for mathematical concepts to be explored whilst, at the same time, encouraging discussion as a key element of learning. In making decisions about the activities to use in your classroom, a number of factors need to be considered. Most important is the knowledge and understanding of the mathematics that you have. Also important is your ability to tailor the activity to the class using the unique knowledge that stems from the continuous assessment that any teacher makes of the children in the classroom. Alongside this, the children themselves must be considered: their previous experiences which prepare them for the activity that is offered, as well as their preferred learning styles. Just as you might have a preferred teaching style the children have preferred learning styles. Some children are extremely happy working on an abstract level and others require equipment to clarify their thinking. Some are happy with a 'page of sums' others are much happier working investigatively. In order to ensure maximum involvement it is, therefore, important that a range of approaches is used and the response of the children is carefully noted. Any activity offered by an external source, such as a book (including this one), a journal, or advisory staff, can only be a suggestion, and needs to be considered in the light of your unique knowledge about the children and the appropriateness of the activity at this particular stage of their learning.

It is possible to choose what appear to be interesting and stimulating ideas, but how will these translate into activities in the classroom? For example, you might want to consider a topic such as reflection and rotation which is found in the Programme of Study for Shape and Space (DFE, 1995). At Key Stage 1, Shape and Space is considered by many to be mainly about the development of language; it is possible to become so engrossed in the language issue that you fail to see that alongside this what also needs to be considered is the development of an understanding of the properties of shape (see Hopkins et al., 1996). There are many well-documented activities (see Edwards, 1992; Murray, 1994) as well as physical resources, such as Polydron, Clixi and Activity Tiles (see bibliography for further details) that can be used to stimulate interest. Care should be taken to ensure that the children see the mathematical links in work, which can become to them just a series of interesting art activities, such as mirror paintings or Celtic knotwork patterns. Even tessellations can be seen by a child as a series of elaborate jigsaws with no obvious mathematical content. You must point out the obvious mathematical features of the chosen activity, and take care that shape experience is a progressive one, giving new understanding and insights as the work unfolds. Children need to know that mathematics is a powerful tool for explaining the world around us.

You may need to consider what experiences the child needs to have, and what resources are available to aid a full understanding of reflection and rotation. Resources may include pinboards and/or dotty paper, mirrors, looking together at books such as *The Magic Mirror Book* (Walter, 1984), making kaleidoscopes, paper folding and cutting, ink blot paintings which fold, making faces of animals and considering the reflective symmetry, coordinate point diagrams to complete, making windmills, and kites. The teacher has to decide not only which of these practical experiences are appropriate but also how to make the mathematics of each situation overt so that the child sees not just the wonder and beauty of these situations but also the power of the mathematics which can be used and expressed in such a variety of practical situations.

Whilst we wish children to enjoy mathematics, we mustn't lose sight of the fact that, usually, we learn most from the things we struggle with. Activities should therefore also contain an element of challenge so as to push knowledge and understanding forward. You might collect ideas continually from a whole range of sources. The magazines *Junior Education* and *Child Education* often have interesting sections for the teaching of mathematics. The more specialized journals, *Maths Teaching* and *Maths in Schools* provide not only ideas but accounts of teachers working with those ideas in the classroom (more details at the end of this chapter). Having collected a range of ideas for teaching, you may need to consider which ideas will consolidate the existing knowledge that the children have, and which will push their thinking forward and provide a challenge for them.

In deciding on activities we should not lose sight of the need to provide a balance of experiences for the child. Paragraph 243 of the Cockcroft Report, *Mathematics Counts* (HMSO, 1982), exhorts teachers to develop a variety of styles for teaching and learning, stating:

Mathematics teaching at all levels should include opportunities for:

- exposition by the teacher;
- discussion between teacher and pupils and between pupils themselves;
- appropriate practical work;
- consolidation and practice of fundamental skills and routines;
- problem solving, including the application of mathematics to everyday situations;
- investigational work.

You may need to consider what constitutes the full range of teaching and learning styles so that you do not close down on the opportunities for variety, which, in turn, may disadvantage some children who have one of these methods as a preferred learning style.

Enquiry Task — Practical Examples for Tackling the Content

Collect together a number of practical activities around a mathematical theme, for example. These activities should vary in nature, such as those described for rotation and reflection above, and should cover the full range of teaching and learning styles as suggested by Cockcroft. In carrying out the activities in the classroom there are a number of things you might wish to consider and keep notes of in a field diary — a

---

note book in which you write down your observations of both the children and your-self as the activities are carried out.

- How is the mathematics for each situation being made explicit to the children?
- How, if at all, are the children's perceptions of mathematics changing? What is the evidence for your conclusions?
- What can you deduce about individual children's preferred learning styles? What evidence do you have for the claims you are making about their pre-ferred individual styles of learning?
- How will your knowledge of preferred learning styles affect your approaches to the teaching of mathematics?

Options for Teaching

The *Panorama* Programme, *Hard Lessons — Whole Class Teaching* (BBC, 1996), suggested that more whole class teaching needs to take place. The figure suggested for whole class teaching was about 50 per cent of the total teaching time allocated to mathematics. Many other teachers already carry out at least 50 per cent of their mathematics teaching with a whole class. Many do not feel that such a proportion of whole class teaching is appropriate for them because of either the wide spread of ability within the class or other organizational factors, such as insufficient re-sources. In this section, I wish to consider how this notion of whole class teaching might have different interpretations.

Whole class teaching may mean different things. It could be all children looking at the blackboard whilst a technique is demonstrated; for example, long multiplication. However, this may assume that all the children have the necessary previous knowledge to cope with the demonstration that is being offered. At best, those children who do not have the skills leading up to this step may rote learn a technique, at worst the children may become confused. If you decide to use this technique, you may need to have assessed what skills a child needs to have acquired before beginning long multiplication. For example, a facility with both addition and subtraction; knowledge of both number patterns and the multiplication tables themselves; a feel for number generally and what multiplying large numbers might mean. The Non-Statutory Guidance (DES, 1989a) gives exemplars of a feel for number in the section on 'Pupils Doing Calculations'. To have all the class at that stage at the same time with all the prerequisite skills seems an unlikely situation!

There are options for whole class teaching. The biscuit, chocolate, and string activities mentioned in a previous section are activities which can take place with the whole class working on the same activity and discussing that activity after it has happened. The discussion will provide opportunities for some input from you on skills and concepts within the context of the activity and a shared understanding of the activity. This should facilitate the development of the skills and concepts as they are clarified through discussion and exposition. In fact, if whole class teaching of a specific skill is to take place, it is probably best attempted under conditions where there is a common practical experience on which the children can build. HMI (1989) wrote:

> . . . . no class was expected to work in an exploratory way all the time. Children embarked on problem solving or investigative work using their existing skills and knowledge. The need to adapt and add to these quickly became apparent. It was here that more formal direct methods of teaching often proved effective.

One of my favourite activities that can be carried out with a whole class is Function Game. This is well documented in a number of places (for example, *Developing Algebra*, RLDU, 1990). The key aspect of this activity is the silence which allows the children to think without interruption and without there being pressure to respond. The nature of the task allows all to participate as they feel comfortable. At all times you, as the teacher, are in control of the situation and best able to make judgments about appropriateness and challenge. You decide on a rule for changing numbers that only you are aware of: at a simple level this may be, 'add 2'. You begin by writing on the board something that conveys this to the children in the form of a mapping, along with an invitation for one of them to write something, for example:

$$1 \rightarrow 3$$
$$2 \rightarrow$$

All of this is carried out in silence, although in practice the children will be anxious to come out to the board and write their answers and thus will be making noises to attract your attention. Whatever is written is then signified as correct or otherwise by the use of either a smiley face ☺ or a sad face ☹.

$$1 \rightarrow 3 \; ☺$$
$$2 \rightarrow 4 \; ☺$$

At this point, you decide either to write a $3 \rightarrow$ next or to write some other number such as $12 \rightarrow$. Continuing to write $3 \rightarrow$ followed by $4 \rightarrow$ will sometimes lead the children to focus on the patterns that are produced rather than the rule which generates them. Dotting about will not only lead to a greater focus on the rule but also provide you with the opportunity to move to and fro between larger and smaller numbers, thus controlling what you might choose as being appropriate for particular individuals. If a sad face is given, the number can be returned to until a happy face is achieved.

At some stage the word RULE? can be written up and the children invited to write what they think is happening. Always ask for alternatives by writing OR! repeatedly until all possibilities that the children might have thought of are exhausted. Children may not always be thinking of the rule in the same way as you are. For instance, you might be thinking of a rule which multiplies by two and then subtracts one. A child may see this as add one less than the number to itself, or double the number one less and then add on one, or add the number to itself and then take away one. All of these answers are correct, they are just different ways of expressing the same thing. This is part of the richness of mat' ematics and is, in part, what the Non-Statutory Guidance (DES, 1989) means when it states:

> Tasks should be both of the kind which have an exact result or answer and those which have many possible outcomes.

In this case there are a number of answers which are different but all are correct and mathematically have the same meaning.

Inverses can also be introduced using the Function Game. Here, having worked with the rule for a while, you then write down the number that is the answer and invite the children to write down what they think the input number might be.

$$\rightarrow 12$$

I think the silence required in this activity is a powerful device, allowing you to decide which child to select according to the feedback you receive by looking at their faces. There are some wonderful moments when you realize that the child who has been struggling for some time to come to terms with what is happening suddenly understands: her/his face lights up with a smile and you invite her/him to come and write down their answer. The silence allows for quality thinking time and the children don't feel pressured into making wild guesses. In fact, a talking point after the silence might be about the almost impossible task of knowing what the teacher is thinking if the only information they have is $1 \rightarrow 3$. Whilst $1 \rightarrow 3$ fits with the add 2 rule, it also fits with multiply by two and add one, or multiply by itself and add two, or multiply by five and take away two, and many, many, other rules. The list of possibilities is, in fact, endless: a good follow up is to say, 'This is my starting point so what might my rule be? How many different rules can you find?'

Whole class teaching, therefore, is not just exposition followed by an exercise, but can also be defined as an activity, practical or otherwise, worked on by the whole class and followed up by discussion and/or exposition.

Let us return to the topic of reflections mentioned in the previous section. A whole class introductory activity might be completing half pictures, drawn on dotty paper about a mirror line, with mirrors available. Your objective might be to achieve understanding that each line and point on the diagram for the right- and left-hand sides are equidistant from the mirror line. Completing the pictures and then having a discussion about what the children notice will enable the objective mentioned above to be pulled out of the whole range of other things noticed, such as the fact that the two halves are the same but opposite. This focusing happens by getting the children to explain in detail what they have noticed. You will need to make sure that the correct language is being used, such as line of symmetry, reflection, mirror image and equidistant. You can continue by asking the children to complete some more pictures and then to consider how this understanding of reflection, which has been made explicit in the discussion, contributes to the way in which the task was completed.

Enquiry Task — Practical Options for Teaching

Consider your teaching plan for next term or your next school experience. Look at what the options are for teaching the mathematics topics. Which activities will lend themselves to whole class teaching and which will need teaching in smaller groups?

Focus on the opportunities for whole class teaching. Divide the class into two large groups, as evenly matched as possible. One group to be taught traditionally using exposition; the other group to be taught with whole group introductory activities followed up by close attention to the explanation and teaching of the skills and concepts. (See the example of reflections outlined before this task.)

Set yourself some tight objectives for the outcomes and consider how the teaching style supports the achievement of the learning objectives.

- What do the children do, say or record that leads you to think that exposition and/or activities with follow-ups have been effective in achieving your objectives?
- Is there any difference between the two groups within any one topic?
- Do the children perform differently according to the topic or does one group consistently outperform the other?
- What evidence supports the statements you are making about the children's learning and the style of teaching?

In carrying out this enquiry you will be considering what are the advantages/disadvantages of whole class teaching in a didactic manner (using exposition) as opposed to using activities for the whole class which then lead into discussion and some exposition. It will be difficult to arrive at firm conclusions because even though the groups are supposed to be evenly matched there will still be differences. You will also have preferences for your teaching style which will to some extent interfere with the ability to arrive at firm and unbiased conclusions: the children will have their own preferred learning styles. Nevertheless, you will have experienced two distinct styles of teaching the same topic.

Assessment

Assessing Using and Applying mathematics appears to be the area that causes most problems, perhaps because traditionally we have assessed children using written tests. Using and Applying cannot be assessed within the context of a written test and therefore needs rather more open-ended tasks to allow the child to demonstrate her/his ability to think and work in a mathematical manner. These open tasks also allow the assessment of skills and concepts in other aspects of mathematics. Buckinghamshire County Council (1993) has produced an A4 booklet, *Teaching and Assessing Ma1 at Key Stage 1* (see references section at the end of this chapter for further details). What makes this book useful is its innovative approach through the use of story. Various story books and a wealth of activities arising from these have been considered. The outcomes of using these activities within the classroom are documented, with examples of children's work. Each activity illustrates aspects of the assessment of Using and Applying, as well as the skills, concepts and knowledge of the other Attainment Targets.

The key problem in assessing Using and Applying seems to be an attitude of mind. There is a need with Using and Applying to get the child to show that they can think mathematically. This means that a worksheet cannot be provided which will demonstrate the child's facility as a mathematician: only an activity that the child has to work through, demonstrating the ability to be logical, to communicate mathematically and to select appropriate materials to carry out the task will suffice. It is difficult to sit back and judge when, if at all, intervention may be appropriate. There is the danger of interfering in the logic before the child has had time to think things through and has, therefore, been unable to demonstrate the necessary skills. If the task is one in which assessment is the primary focus then intervention should be limited and possibly confined to enabling questions or statements such as: 'Tell me what you've done so far'; 'Can you explain why you think this?', or 'What could you try next?' These questions will stimulate the child's thinking but without interfering with the processes of thought in which the child is engaged.

However, there is a danger in expecting the child to play games with you. You should not be in the business of promoting the child's facility to 'guess what is in your mind' but rather the ability to think and act mathematically. However, some input should be given which moves the child forward, if you consider this to be appropriate. There are at least two reasons why input might be needed. Both are based on the same premise, that the child is not yet ready for the assessment of skills to be made because not enough work on inculcating those skills has been undertaken. The first is that the child has not been encouraged to think autonomously before, and is, therefore, unsure of how to proceed. If this is the case some suggestions about how to proceed might be needed but remember these will interfere with the objective of assessing the child's ability to think mathematically. Secondly, the task may not be suitable. Any task which will assess Using and Applying requires the child to know some mathematics: if the task is to assess the child's ability to think mathematically, it is usual to give them a task based on some familiar or already known mathematical concepts. Using and Applying cannot be assessed in isolation from mathematical content, and it is usual to set the assessment task around some mathematical content with which the child is already familiar.

In a previous section, the problem of sharing out 29 biscuits between 6 children was considered. This task should not be undertaken with children who have not been taught any of the language, or developed some understanding, of fractions. This task would be set after some experience and understanding of fractions has been gained, thus providing an ideal opportunity to assess the mathematics the child *chooses* to use, the way in which thoughts and ideas are *communicated*, and the *logic* of the approach in carrying out the activity. In fact, it is clear from both Figure 4.1 and Figure 4.2 (see earlier in the chapter) that the children have a clear understanding of simple fractions using *words* such as half, quarter and third.

In setting this task, the objectives could have been: to encourage the use of correct mathematical language and to encourage the children to record, and hence communicate, their mathematics. In Figure 4.1, the children communicate clearly in words the problem they have been asked to do but use only half and a quarter, resorting to the word 'bit' to describe smaller parts. In Figure 4.2, the children communicate using diagrams but the more sophisticated word 'third' appears; the method of dividing 29 biscuits allows them to arrive at a correct answer. There is also a more sophisticated representation of their findings using 1 biscuit with a 4 written on it to symbolize 4 biscuits. The children are beginning to use abstractions to represent their thinking. The presentation, with less words, might lead you to think that there was less sophisticated mathematics going on when in fact there is a greater degree of sophistication in mathematical terms.

In order to develop and consolidate the skills and concepts, the children need more activities where they share and cut up items into fraction parts. They also need to be introduced to the notation associated with fractions. In addition, those in the group associated with Figure 4.2 need to have more activities where they are required to explain their thinking not only in pictures but also in words. For both groups, you would need to consider not only what the children have done but also what needs to be done to develop their understanding. Assessment needs to be both summative and formative. More examples of assessment can be found in *Children's Work Assessed — English, Mathematics and Science* (SEAC, 1993). This publication was written prior to the current Orders (DFE, 1995) but the three portfolios of children's work that it contains are invaluable for considering not only how to assess children's work summatively but also how to consider it formatively.

Summative assessments, for the legal requirements of the National Curriculum, are generally carried out at the end of a Key Stage: here the progress of each child is reviewed and assessed by considering his/her performance against the Level Descriptions and finding that Level which best describes what she/he knows and can do. This is not a complicated process and is based on the knowledge that will have accumulated during the course of at least a year's teaching.

In general, most teachers carry out formative assessments, which aid them in their forward planning, based on their learning objectives for an activity. The Level Descriptions themselves are too coarse a measure to use for termly or even end of year assessments because children are unlikely to progress at the rate of one Level each year: in other words a given child might appear to be standing still when in fact much progress had been made. Forward plans, and the objectives they contain, drawn from the Programme of Study should be used to monitor each child's progress. In effect, the objectives for a term or year become the school's own descriptions against which a child's progress might be judged. This does not require evidence to be collected especially because the day-to-day work books of the child and/or your records of their progress should provide the evidence against which judgments can be made.

At Key Stage 1, when much of the work is oral and the children are unable to keep their own written records, teacher records may be kept of a child's progress based on the things that they say and make. These records provide what is known as ephemeral evidence and are an extremely valuable source for formative assessments. Ephemeral evidence continues to be important throughout a child's life at school: however, as the children become more adept at recording their thoughts and work, there is less need for extensive records of ephemeral evidence to be kept. Only ephemeral evidence which adds significantly to your assessment of the child needs to be kept.

Since assessment is usually carried out within the context of the teacher's objectives, it could be said that the National Curriculum Programme of Study is of little use other than in setting a broad framework for the teaching of the subject. It is certainly true that work needs to be done in breaking down broad statements into smaller developmental skills. As an illustration, consider 'Time'. This word implies many dimensions of teaching which happen over a number of years. There needs to be consideration of not only developing the skill of reading a clock face, but also of a whole host of associated language and mathematical complexities. First, there is the notion of time passing and the difficulties of understanding this complex concept. Then there is the variety of language and knowledge associated with *time* that needs to be developed. Below, in no particular order, are some of the words, skills and concepts which contribute towards the build up of an understanding of the passage of time:

> week; fortnight; day; month; year; time passing; next; before; after; next week; tomorrow; yesterday; soon; Autumn; Spring; Summer; Winter; Monday; Tuesday; Wednesday; Thursday; Friday; Saturday; Sunday; January; February; March; April; May; June; July; August; September; October; November; December; half past; quarter to; quarter past; five past; ten minutes past; twenty minutes past; o'clock; hour; minute; second; stop watch; timer; seasons; birthdays; festivals; Easter; Christmas; Divali; millennium; century; prehistoric; analogue and digital representations

Before a child can begin to tell the time, some of the language needs to be known, and the concepts of sequencing and time passing need to be taught. Having taught the child how to tell the time, next comes an understanding of the various types of clock and the way in which they represent time — analogue, digital, twenty-four hour clocks of both of these types, stop watches, and so on. Finally, there is the manipulation of these figures and the way in which time is used in society in timetables and lists, and the use made by other disciplines, such as science, history, and so on. All of this teaching is encompassed when we state that a child knows about and understands 'time'. Not all of this knowledge and understanding will be accomplished during the primary school, and understandings and perceptions of time will increase as the child develops into adulthood. Clearly, the need to identify those aspects upon which early objectives are focused will be the key to measuring the progress of a child's understanding.

In planning, you will have to consider which aspects of language and concept acquisition to focus on with your children: as mentioned earlier, this will come from the on-going informal assessments that you carry out as you work with the children. Inevitably, assessment is linked into future planning and one follows on from the other. We assess what we have planned to teach, and we use those assessments to inform future planning.

Enquiry Task — Assessment

Consider your teaching topic for mathematics. Look at your objectives and specify them clearly so that each small gain by a pupil can be identified. This will mean that you need to break down the statements in the Programme of Study into well defined skills and concepts; for a break down of concepts see Deboys and Pitt (1980).

Consider four or five specific pupils and follow their work closely for about a month. Set up pupil profiles for each child into which you put annotated samples of their work for each lesson as the topic progresses.

- How well are the children performing against your stated objectives?
- What evidence do you have in their profiles to support your judgments?
- How does your teaching plan get modified in the light of the children's progress?
- Consider your medium-term plans. How have the judgments you are making fed into these plans?

Cross-curricular Dimensions

As teachers, we can all point to examples of work which we do in the classroom that are cross-curricular in nature. What is more, we can all highlight the mathematical skills that are being used in this work but all too often these links across the curriculum are not made explicit to the children. It is my experience that children have a limited view of mathematics, and, in the main, believe mathematics to be a page of sums from a textbook. They don't see that they are using skills concerned with measuring when they are making a pop-up card in design and technology. For them, a pop-up card is a task for design and technology. Unless we make explicit the connections between the design and technology task *and* the measures work they have been doing in mathematics, the powerful way in which mathematics is all pervasive passes them by.

Enquiry Task — Cross-curricular Dimensions

Begin by asking the children to give you examples of when they are doing mathematics — this is to ascertain what they think mathematics is and when they think they are doing it. The children could be asked to write down their thoughts, if this is appropriate.

Next, set up a series of lessons which feature mathematics in a cross-curricular context. For instance, if you consider a topic about the local church, the children might be collecting: data for history, such as the dates on the grave stones in the cemetery; science data on the types of mini-beasts in the cemetery; constructing the arched windows in the church, using compasses, rulers and pencils; making pop-up cards for a religious festival; or making Easter biscuits.

All of the above activities have a mathematical element, and each of the skills and concepts being used should be made explicit to the children as each of the activities is happening. What mathematics skills, knowledge and understanding are being used in the activities you have chosen?

At the end of the sequence of work, ask the children to write down when they think mathematics is being done, giving examples. Compare and contrast their original thoughts with those they have just written. Is there any noticeable development in their thinking? How does it compare with your thinking?

Many adults when questioned believe that they do little or no mathematics in their everyday life, whilst in fact quite a lot of what they do is highly mathematical. If we can make clear to the children the cross-curricular links that we see so as to enable them to appreciate what a powerful tool mathematics is, in terms of both 'doing' and 'explaining' the world around them, their understanding of concepts will be improved by being able to relate them to the everyday activities.

Work in art and Shape and Space are a powerful combination; a book which gives lots of interesting ideas for working in this cross-curricular dimension is *Teaching Maths and Art* (Jones, 1991). Measures are used practically in cooking, in science and in design and technology. Data handling is the province of the geographer, historian and scientist: each one of these subjects can provide rich and stimulating ideas for cross-curricular work, as suggested in the enquiry task above.

It is useful to begin a collection of ideas that bring the cross-curricular dimensions of mathematics to the fore. I have a collection of books about: kites, boomerangs, paper aeroplanes, Victorian needlepoint, William Laurence fabrics and wallpaper, and braiding. I also have a collection of boxes and flats. (Flats are the cardboard model kits, that you can buy to cut out and assemble into a scale model of the building.)

There are two aspects to mathematics; the first is the power and wonder of mathematics as a discipline in its own right; the second is its applicability across, not only the curriculum, but also the world at large. As a teacher you should be continually looking for ways of presenting mathematics in interesting and varied contexts, both purely mathematical and applied, and which both stimulate and challenge the child's thinking. It is often felt that the second aspect, the applicability, is all that is needed to ensure understanding in mathematics. However, in order to ensure balance some of the wonder of mathematics as a discipline in its own right must also be conveyed.

References

ATKINSON, S. (1996) *Developing a Scheme of Work for Primary Mathematics*, London, Hodder & Stoughton.

ATM (1987) *Working Investigationally*, Derby, ATM.

BALL, G. (1990) *Talking and Learning*, Oxford, Blackwell.

BBC (1996) *Panorama: Hard Lessons — Whole Class Teaching*, London, BBC.

BOOTH, P. and JONES, M. (1995) 'Mathematics', in ASHCROFT, K. and PALACIO, D. (eds) *The Primary Teacher's Guide to the New National Curriculum*, London, Falmer Press.

Margaret Jones

BUCKINGHAMSHIRE COUNTY COUNCIL (1993) *Teaching and Assessing Ma1 at Key Stage 1*, Aylesbury, Buckinghamshire County Council.

DEBOYS, M. and PITT, E. (1980) *Lines of Development in Primary Mathematics*, Belfast, Blackstaff Press.

DES (1989a) *Mathematics in the National Curriculum — Non-Statutory Guidance*, London, HMSO.

DES (1989b) *Aspects of Primary Education: The Teaching and Learning of Mathematics*, London, HMSO.

DFE (1995) *Mathematics in the National Curriculum*, London, HMSO.

EDWARDS, C. (1992) *Tiles and Tiling*, Derby, Association of Teachers of Mathematics.

HMI (1989) *Aspects of Primary Education: The Teaching and Learning of Mathematics*, London, HMSO.

HMSO (1982) *Mathematics Counts*, London, HMSO.

HOPKINS, C., GIFFORD, S. and PEPPERELL, S. (1996) *Mathematics in the Primary School*, London, David Fulton.

JONES, L. (1991) *Teaching Maths and Art*, Cheltenham, Stanley Thornes.

LIEBECK, P. (1984) *How Children Learn Mathematics*, London, Penguin.

MURRAY, J. (1994) *Squares, Patterns and Quilts*, Derby, Association of Teachers of Mathematics.

OPEN UNIVERSITY *(Course ME234) Using Mathematical Thinking*, Buckingham, Open University Press.

RLDU (1990) *Developing Algebra*, Bristol, Avon RLDU.

WALTER, M. (1984) *The Magic Mirror Book*, London, Hippo Books.

SEAC (1993) *Children's Work Assessed; English, Mathematics and Science*, London, SEAC.

Annotated List of Suggested Reading

ASSOCIATION OF TEACHERS OF MATHEMATICS (undated) *Using and Applying Mathematics*, Derby, Association of Teachers of Mathematics.
(Good explanation of this aspect of the National Curriculum for Mathematics. Although published and linked to the original National Curriculum Order for Mathematics, it is still relevant to the present Order.)

ASSOCIATION OF TEACHERS OF MATHEMATICS (1994) *Teaching, Learning and Mathematics*, Derby, Association of Teachers of Mathematics.
(A collection of readings from the Association journal, *Mathematics Teaching*. This book has three sections of readings which consider Teaching and Learning Mathematics, Mathematics in the Classroom, and Debates and Issues.)

BLINKO, J. (1996) *Teaching and Learning Number*, Aylesbury, Buckinghamshire County Council.
(This book considers the critical issues and ideas associated with the teaching of number. A useful revision text because it considers both the theoretical and the practical.)

HUGHES, M. (1986) *Children and Number*, Oxford, Basil Blackwell.
(A useful text which outlines the writer's research into children's difficulties in learning mathematics.)

HUME, B. and BARRS, K. (1988) *Maths on Display*, Twickenham, Belair Publications.
(A simple attractive book which gives ideas for teaching and displaying mathematics. Useful for teachers of infants and lower juniors.)

Equipment

Polydron and *Clixi* are available through the major school suppliers.

Activity Tiles are available from the Association of Teachers of Mathematics, 7 Shaftesbury Street, Derby DE3 8YB.

Journals

Mathematics Teaching is the journal of the Association of Teachers of Mathematics, address above.

Maths in Schools is the journal of the Mathematics Association, 259 London Road, Leicester LE2 3BE.

Useful Addresses

Association of Teachers of Mathematics resources available from 7, Shaftesbury Street, Derby DE3 8YB.

Avon RLDU resources available from Laurinda Brown, University of Bristol Learning Resources, School of Education, University of Bristol, Berkeley Square, Bristol.

Buckinghamshire County Council resources available from Education Department, County Hall, Aylesbury, Bucks.

5   Science

Cliff Marshall and David Palacio

Introduction: What is *Science*?

In this section we will consider answers to this question from three differing perspectives; firstly, your own and other people like you; secondly, children of primary school age; and finally, the government perspective as embodied in the form of the *Science in the National Curriculum for England and Wales* (DFE/WO, 1995).

Enquiry Task

Look back on your own science experience at both primary and secondary schools. Consider what you did during science lessons, what you learnt, and how science was taught to you.

- Make a list of the main ideas or key points which come back to you. What images does school science conjure up in your mind?

Now look back over your out-of-school experiences. Consider how science has impacted upon your life.

- What ideas about science, and of scientists and their work come through now? In particular, what ideas are portrayed by the popular media?

In what ways are the ideas about science which you got through work in school in line with those acquired through out-of-school experiences? In what ways are they different?

How are your views about science similar to those of other people like yourself? If you are a student teacher, how similar are your views to those of students reported by Coates and Russell (1995) and by Wright (1990)?

How might your science experiences impact upon your work as a teacher?

Now, let us consider children's views.

Enquiry Task

Ask children individually to:

- draw a scientist so that anyone who looks at the drawing can see that they are a scientist, or

---

- draw a scientist at work.

Did the children draw a scientist who was male with horn-rimmed glasses, old, balding and wearing a white lab. coat? Was the scientist using large, expensive equipment or was he/she doing an experiment that was either dirty/smelly or dangerous? Have individual children produced a drawing which depicts what he/she really believes or has he/she simply reproduced a stereotypical scientist of the type seen in children's cartoons and, to a lesser extent now, in material produced ostensibly for adults; for example, some television advertisements?

To find out each child's real beliefs, you might need to ask a follow-up question:

- are scientists really like this?

Even though they will often acknowledge quite readily that their first drawings were not representative of what scientists really do, for many children — and despite the fact that they may make use of books with the word science written on them or hear their teacher use the word — real science doesn't take place in primary schools, since in the children's minds science is associated with a specialized room (laboratory) requiring specialist equipment, the study of science begins in the secondary school (see, for example, Hobden, 1993). Much work has been devoted to researching children's views about science; you might like to compare your findings with those of others (for example, Newton and Newton, 1991; Preston, 1995; Janniker, 1995). In what ways are your views similar to/different from those of children? What implications are there for the way in which you approach science-based work with children?

So, what *is* science? To answer this question we suggest that you have a go at the autogyro (sometimes called the helicopter) activity — this is seen by many people involved with science in primary schools as being 'good' science. Why is this? First, you need to make your autogyro. Mark out a 9 cm by 12 cm piece of paper as shown. Cut along the two thick vertical lines, folding the wings along the thin short horizontal line. Fold wing A towards you and wing B away from you. Hold the autogyro by its top and, from a height of about two metres, let go. Describe how your

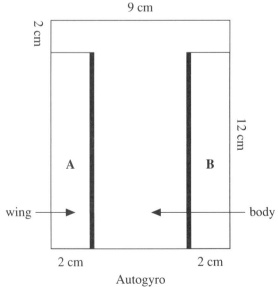

Autogyro
(for more information see
Richards and Kincaid, 1983)

autogyro falls to the ground. How might you change your autogyro so that it falls to the ground in a different way? For example, what happens when you fold the wings in the opposite direction and then let go? What happens when you change the height of drop from 2 metres to 3 metres/1 metre? What happens when you add a paper clip to the base of the body?

So far what you have done has been descriptive and based solely on changes which have occurred to a single autogyro: for example when wing A was folded towards you and wing B away from you did you notice that the autogyro spun clockwise? When the wing directions were reversed, did the autogyro spin in the same or the opposite, i.e., anti-clockwise, direction? Did you start to make predictions as to what you expected might happen on the basis of your previous experience (with the autogyro)? For example, when you dropped the autogyro for the first time did you simply predict *that* it would fall to the ground? When you dropped it a second time, did you mention *how* you expect the autogyro to fall to the floor? In other words was your second prediction more sophisticated (detailed) than the first?

In the activity so far, what have you been doing? Have you:

- been making observations, trying to make sense of them so as to determine possible future actions?
- been making observations and measurements, and using these to make predictions about the likely outcomes of that future action?
- been working systematically so as to only vary one factor (variable) at a time?

What other *skills* and *procedures* have you been involved with?

Have you exhausted all possible ways of changing how the autogyro drops to the ground? What would you need to do in order to find what effect (if any) changing the wing width had on how the autogyro fell? Based on the autogyro you have made already, you will not be able to make the wing width larger than 2 cm; therefore, you will need to make new autogyros. Since you probably found that changing the number of paper clips affected how the autogyro fell, how will you make sure that you do not change the weight of the autogyro at the same time as you change the wing width?

Now make a list of the skills and procedures that you have been deploying during this second example. Have you:

- been making careful observations and measurements involving direct comparison?
- planning out your work in a systematic way so as to be able to make fair comparisons — what is often called fair testing?
- been recording your results and looking for trends or patterns in them?
- have you been checking on the reliability of your measurements by repeating them?

What else has happened during this activity? For example, did you:

- persevere when things did not go the way you had planned them the first time?
- have 'respect' for your results even when they were not what you expected or what you had hoped for?
- been curious and wanted to find out more?

What other personal characteristics or qualities (sometimes called *attitudes*) have you shown during this activity?

Finally, did you try to *explain* why changing the number of paper clips on the body of the autogyro had the observed effect or why the wide-winged autogyro spun in a different way to the narrow-winged one? In other words, did you apply your pre-existing scientific knowledge and understanding to a new situation, and in doing so enlarge your scientific knowledge and understanding?

If, during the autogyro activity, you were involved in all three of the following:

- deploying cognitive and manipulative skills and procedures
- applying appropriate personal qualities and characteristics
- applying existing science knowledge and understanding

then the chances are you were involved in some *good* science. (For more detail as to how the autogyro activity can be good science see Ward, 1989.)

Science then is:

> the development of rational thinking, of ways of finding out about the world, of willingness and ability to seek and use evidence; it involves the gradual building of a framework of scientific ideas (concepts, knowledge and understanding) through experiment and testing, and the use of these ideas to make sense of further (new) experience; it includes the growth of readiness to be independent of thinking but open to new evidence and to be critical of one's own ideas and those of others. (adapted from Harlen, 1983)

Finally, we turn to a consideration of the meaning of science as seen from the requirements outlined in the National Curriculum: here you will need a copy of the Science National Curriculum, for example, DFE/WO (1995).

Enquiry Task

Familiarize yourself with the Programmes of Study, and the Attainment Targets and Level Descriptions for Key Stages 1 and 2.

In light of the discussion above concerning 'good' science, where in the National Curriculum are the three elements located? Where are specified skills, such as recording data and interpreting them, found? Where are attitudes, such as perseverance and curiosity, located? Where is science knowledge and understanding situated?

> Within the National Curriculum, how do the three elements of 'good' science relate one with another? For example, how does the knowledge and understanding element interrelate with skills and procedures?
>
> The autogyro activity concerned itself with doing science whereas quite clearly the National Curriculum is, in addition, concerned with the teaching and learning of science. Given this difference of intention, are there aspects of the Science National Curriculum (what might be termed 'good' science education) which at the moment are absent from our definition of 'good' science? Where, for example, do the general requirements, outlined in the preface to each Key Stage, fit in with 'good' science?

During the last enquiry task you may have discovered that the affective element of science is given little apparent emphasis in the National Curriculum. Why do you think this is? Consider, for example, the difficulty of assessing personal qualities like open-mindedness or respect for evidence on a ten-point scale, yet alone any consideration of the difficulty of assessing such qualities validly and reliably. Does this apparent lack of emphasis regarding assessment of the affective aspect of science follow through as a direct consequence of there being little emphasis during teaching? By giving children direct experience of the other two elements of science (which of course are assessed), will you, of necessity, expose children to, and thus enhance development of, the third, affective, element?

As you will no doubt be aware, a National Curriculum for Science is a relatively recent (post-1988) development in primary schools. Before then, science, like most other subjects, was 'optional' and many primary schools chose to give it little, even no, direct emphasis in their curriculum. In those schools where science did get an airing it was the skills (especially general skills such as observing and recording) and attitudes aspects of science which tended to be stressed: only rarely was much attention paid to developing children's knowledge and understanding of science concepts. It will come as no surprise, therefore, to learn that the introduction of a National Curriculum for science, and the change from a mainly skills-based *optional* curriculum to a *mandatory* one in which knowledge and understanding of science concepts had to be given equal importance as skills and procedures, had a significant impact on virtually all primary schools.

> **Enquiry Task**
>
> For primary schools, what issues have been raised by the Science National Curriculum? Consider this question in terms of:
>
> - curriculum planning and organization;
> - curriculum 'delivery';
> - assessment;
> - the skills, knowledge, understanding and experience needed by teachers.
>
> In terms of the issues identified in the previous paragraph and the need to address these:

- how have individual schools responded?
- what recent changes have taken place in teacher education in science, both initial and in-service?

Given the discussion above concerning the National Curriculum, you might like to consider again the task you undertook at the beginning of this chapter, namely to consider what effects your experiences and views of science will have on how you approach science in your initial teacher training, and in particular your science work in school. How might you address any concerns, for example a lack of science knowledge and understanding, that come to light as a result of this review? (See the bibliography at the end of this chapter for ideas as to how you might do this.)

As has been indicated already in Chapter 1, National Curriculum Programmes of Study do not in themselves constitute a teaching programme or a scheme of work; instead, they constitute a common framework around which individual schools can build *their* scheme of work. How a school translates the framework for science into schemes of work and programmes of work for individual children, and the issues which have to be addressed, constitutes much of the remainder of this chapter. To complete this task successfully requires more than the deployment of a range of general professional skills, knowledge and understanding: it also requires you to have detailed knowledge and understanding of the science concepts which underpin the various statements within the Programmes of Study and how you work with children so that they come to a deeper understanding of science — what is sometimes called *pedagogic content knowledge*.

Children's Ideas and Science Teaching

If teaching science is to be about helping children to develop their understanding and knowledge about key concepts and skills then the pointers given by the typical misconceptions exposed in the 'Draw a Scientist' exercise need to be recognized. Similarly, in the autogyro investigation you will have realized that your interpretation of what was happening and why was clearly affected by what you already understood or had previously experienced. Children come to their science activities with existing ideas and experiences and if you are to be an effective teacher of science then your approach to teaching will need to recognize this. The explanations that *children* give to situations such as the autogyro investigation could well lead you to some disturbing conclusions about the ways in which children's scientific understanding develops. You may well come to the conclusion that:

- what the children have learnt does not match up very well with what they have been taught;
- what the children learnt was not what was intended they should learn;
- the ideas about force that the children use in their explanations were not

the ones you, their teacher, would hope that they would use — some of their ideas may be correct scientifically, but others may not.

When planning work you may find it useful to start from the children's existing understanding. Here are a few ways to do this; some are fairly obvious, since they are used by teachers everyday, others may not be so familiar to you. The six ways that follow can be found in an earlier publication (Marshall and Palacio, 1995) but we have reproduced them here for completeness and because they are central to effective science teaching and learning.

1 You could ask questions, either orally or in writing.

- Who can explain . . . ?
- What do you think will happen when . . . ?, and then,
- Why do you think this will happen?

2 You might ask children to sort (group/classify) everyday objects; for instance, objects made of different materials. This activity can be used with quite young children, and with older children who have difficulty with their writing. Once the children have sorted the objects you will need to ask them why they have grouped them in the way that they have; be careful not to infer the children's reasons simply from the composition of each grouping. You may need to ask the children to sort the objects in more than one way before you get a complete picture of their understanding; if need be, these 'objects' could be pictures of living things.

3 The children might draw what they think is happening during an event. Once again this is a very good activity for children who have difficulty with their writing; with young children, especially, you may experience some difficulty initially interpreting some of their drawings! Older children can annotate their drawings to explain more fully what they think is happening and why they think it is happening. You could ask the children to:

- Draw how to connect up the wires between a bulb and a battery so as to make the bulb light up.

You can also use drawings to probe children's understanding of, for example, night and day, the solar system, and dissolving sugar in water. Here, you might ask your children to make drawings to show:

- Why it is light during the day time and dark at night.
- What they think happens to the sugar when a cube of it is added to a cup of water.

4 You could ask the children to write down their answer. This is an alternative approach to simply asking the children to tell you their answer and, as such, you can use it to best effect with older children, working either singly or in groups of two or three.

- What do you think happens to your food after you have eaten it?
- What do you think happens to the petrol in a car after the engine has been switched on?
- Why do you think a ball comes back to the ground after it has been thrown up into the air?

5 You could organize the class into discussion groups. This is a similar technique to the one mentioned first of all except that here the interaction is not between teacher and pupil(s) but between pupil and pupil(s).

- Why do you think the ball of Plasticine sank when it was placed in the tank of water yet floated when the Plasticine was made into a boat shape?

(Clearly, beforehand, you will need to have provided the children with a tank of water, some Plasticine, and the task of trying to make the Plasticine float. Once the children have discovered that the Plasticine ball sinks you could ask them to discuss ways in which they might get the Plasticine to float.)

6 You could ask the children to draw *concept maps*. The 'concepts' to be explored are expressed as either pictures or words. Therefore, children of all ages, working individually or in small groups, can, very successfully, undertake this type of activity. First of all, you, the children, or best of all, you and the children supply the words/pictures to be used. Then, the children connect up the words/pictures with arrows and, in addition, provide, over their arrows, one or two words of 'explanation'. The children will need to be shown how to complete their map so provide them with some practice beforehand using a completely unrelated set of words or drawings.

You could, for example, find out about children's understanding of force using 'concept' words and phrases such as: movement, balanced forces, push, pull, unbalanced forces, turn, friction. For example:

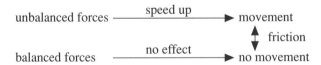

(We suggest that you try this activity yourself before you give it to children to do).

These 'finding out' activities are particularly appropriate at the beginning of a programme of work with a class. Their purpose is to enable you to find out the children's understanding *before* you introduce them to some new work. Equally, these same techniques can be used at the *end* of a scheme of work, that is when you want to find out the gains that the children have made. In other words, these techniques can be used for both planning and assessment purposes.

As the activities we have just considered will show you, regardless of their age, children have their own ideas and understandings about the world. As a teacher of science you will be involved in trying to help children develop their ideas toward the more generally accepted scientific viewpoint. Since many science concepts are quite difficult to understand, you will need to place the work you intend to do in a tangible context. At Key Stage 1, children having sorted out a collection of objects with a magnet to see which are attracted to it are unlikely to be able to use scientific terms to explain what gives rise to the magnetic force. It is sufficient for them to explore the phenomenon and to begin to realize the pattern that emerges: most objects that are attracted to magnets are made of metal. By the end of Key Stage 2, those same children may be able not only to predict which objects are more likely to be attracted to a magnet (those containing iron or steel) but also to be able to talk about magnets exerting *forces of attraction and repulsion.* In addition, they may recognize the usefulness of this idea in relation to finding directions using a compass. The children are moving towards a fuller conceptual understanding yet still need to use their immediate experience of the behaviour of magnets to be able to explain what happens.

Good planning for science teaching should aspire to progressive and developing changes in children's understandings. However, as the structure of the National Curriculum for Science makes clear, it is not just the development of understanding and knowledge about science concepts that constitutes science education. Children also have ideas about what scientific enquiry is, and, as their response to the 'Draw a Scientist' task may show you, some of them may have better formed ideas than others about the processes of science. In planning for science in your classroom, developing understanding of what it is to be scientific, as well as developing science knowledge and understanding, will need to be planned for. Being an active scientist requires the progressive development of key skills and attitudes. The Programme of Study for both Key Stages 1 and 2 emphasizes the attention that you need to give to promoting science process skills. Assessment at the end of both Key Stages places 50 per cent of the weighting on Experimental and Investigative Science (Sc1).

It is important not just to ensure that the lessons you teach are aimed at developing science knowledge and understanding, and skills. It is also vital to appreciate that the demands made by the activities you provide need to be appropriate to the children's learning needs. The biggest challenge facing you is to try to match the lessons you teach to the science and other learning needs of the children. In order to achieve this matching there are a number of factors you will need to try to take into account. These factors are considered, as two sets of questions to be answered, in the enquiry task below.

Enquiry Task

Consider the following scenario. You have been asked to teach a group of 8-year-olds for about four lessons on forces and movement.

Write down the answers to the following questions.

Questions about children and their understanding

- What do I know about children's ideas of force and movement?
- What science skills are they likely to have acquired by this age?
- How proficient are they likely to be at using key skills such as measuring?

Questions about the science curriculum

- What science ideas do I need to teach to enable the children to develop their understanding of force and movement? Whereabouts do these ideas fit in with the Science National Curriculum?
- What skills and attitudes do I need to teach to help the children to develop their ability to investigate force and movement?
- What activities will give experiences that are likely to link into children's current experience and introduce the science ideas effectively?
- Which activities will provide good opportunities to use and develop particular skills?
- Which activity might I use to give the children the opportunity to use and develop their skill in carrying out a whole investigation?
- What resources are most likely to be helpful for these activities?
- What will I, as the teacher, need to do to enhance the children's learning?

You may be able to answer some of these questions by making use of the wider resources available to you. Research into children's learning in science in recent years, such as the Science Processes and Concepts Exploration (SPACE) project (1990, 1991, 1992), has led to a number of useful sources of knowledge about the way children think about key ideas. Published resources for science are beginning to draw on these findings and provide one way to identify activities that are well focused on the appropriateness of their content and demand; for example, Nuffield (1993).

There is no order laid down in the National Curriculum to determine when different aspects and ideas in science should be taught. The overall approach to curriculum planning in a school may specify that science is approached through the use of cross-curricular themes or topics. The themes chosen should ensure that there is a progressive coverage of the curriculum in general. On the other hand, science may be identified as a subject on the timetable with a science-specific programme of topics designed to achieve the coverage of all of the relevant Key Stage Programmes of Study. Finally, some of the questions in the previous enquiry task may lead to the need to identify the science demands of particular activities in order to decide if they are right for the children you have in mind. These questions can be seen as arising from a 'model' of the science teaching and learning process which emphasizes the rôles of the teacher and the pupil in the classroom setting (Marshall and Palacio, 1995). This 'model' is shown in Figure 5.1.

Science learning occurs successfully if the learning activity leads to new ideas and skills that are more scientifically 'acceptable'. If your awareness of the children's ideas and skills is not well developed, the chances are that your teaching

Figure 5.1: A 'model' of science teaching and learning

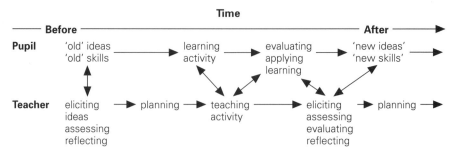

The upper 'line of action' shows the pupil's activities while the lower line tries to summarize your activities as the teacher. (Source: Marshall and Palacio, 1995)

activity, your lessons and how you teach them, will not lead to productive learning activity. In other words, however exciting and interesting your lesson was, the child's ideas may not have changed or, perhaps, they may have changed to take a new form which is no more acceptable scientifically than before. Unproductive learning activity is an example of a mismatch occurring between learning needs and learning activity. Clearly, what is needed ideally is a close interaction between the teacher's and the child's line of action — see the 'model' above. The two lines of action need to progress together so that the child's understanding and skills progressively develop as you and your colleagues provide a programme of work that meets both the needs of the children and those of the science curriculum. If the lines drift apart it may be possible for your lessons to have little real effect on the child's science learning — in spite of all your efforts, he or she retains the old (non-scientific) ideas and level of skill.

We have already explored some of the ways you might try to elicit children's ideas and we need now to turn to that vitally important next step; the planning and achievement of good lessons in science. As we have seen, good lessons will be those which enable children, through effective teaching, to engage in productive learning activity. We have identified some of the important questions that you need to try to answer as you plan. Amongst these are specific questions which relate to *what* science ideas and skills are to be covered, *when* such ideas and skills should be introduced, and *how* these ideas and skills may be taught. It is to these three sets of questions that we now need to turn, and, in particular, to consider them in relation to the National Curriculum for Science.

What Are the Key Ideas and Skills?

The Order for Science (DFE/WO, 1995) has a structure to the Programme of Study that is intended to make clear the important ideas and skills that you need to teach. The accent too is on teaching rather than learning, the Programme of Study attempts to clearly identify teaching objectives; for example,

Pupils should be taught . . . that both pushes and pulls are examples of forces. (KS 1, Physical Processes, 2. Forces and Motion)

Enquiry Task

Look at the Programmes of Study for Key Stages 1 and 2 including the overall statements at the beginning of each Key Stage. List the section headings:

> Life Processes and Living Things
> > Life Processes;
> > Humans as Organisms;
> > Green Plants as Organisms;
> > Variation and Classification;
> > Living Things in Their Environment; and so on.

Remember to look at the 'Common Requirements'; the overall section at the start of each Key Stage; and at Sc 1, Experimental and Investigative Science.

The lists you have compiled give you the key science skill and conceptual areas that are identified as appropriate for study at Key Stages 1 and 2. Another useful way to get a general overview is to look at the statements made in the 'box' at the head of each section of the Programme of Study.

(See the next enquiry task for the concluding part of this activity.)

Scrutiny of the lists of what should be taught, what might be called teaching objectives, within each of the numbered sections of the Programmes of Study will show you the range of study within each skill or conceptual area. You may find that some of these statements challenge your own understanding. The planning of successful lessons will depend on your confidence and knowledge in the area of science you are teaching. As you gradually work through the science curriculum you may need to refresh your own understanding so that you can appreciate the learning that the children are trying to achieve.

Many people feel unsure about some of the ideas of physical science. For example, take a look at the Key Stage 2 Programme of Study for Physical Processes and see how you feel about the statements made about forces. Reflect on what you thought about the helicopter activity. Different people will have uncertainties about different science concepts; we are as individual in our ideas as the children we teach. Research into primary teachers' ideas in science has indicated that teachers can develop their understanding by identifying and reflecting on their own and children's ideas (see, for example, PSTS, 1991, 1992, 1993), and there are a variety of resources available to help you develop your own understanding about science concepts and skills (NCC, 1992, 1993a, 1993b, 1993c; SCAA, 1994a, 1994b).

In planning a particular lesson you will need to consider many factors, but one of the most important issues will be the focus the lesson brings to bear on the ideas and skills of science. The more general the lesson's focus, the less likely you are to challenge and develop ideas. The degree of emphasis you place on ideas and skills in any particular lesson will affect the possibilities for learning. If you wish the children to think about, say, the idea that some substances dissolve in water and some do not, the activity you provide will need to focus on this with a structured experiment to test the idea. This experiment would be an *illustrative activity*. The demands on the children's investigative skills should be low, enabling learning to centre on the dissolving issue. This activity might be followed up by another where the notion of soluble substances is already known but now the activity focuses on skills more centrally. New substances might be presented and the children asked to predict if the substances will dissolve and then given the chance to decide some of the important factors; which factors to keep the same, which one to change and which one to 'measure'. This activity can be seen as more *investigative*, enabling the children to consider variables, identifying the independent (changing) and dependent (measured) variables. As a teacher of science, you need to plan consciously for both illustrative and investigative activities. This will involve you in analysing and developing activities to achieve the purpose of enabling learning about ideas and skills to take place. We shall return to this issue later when we consider in greater depth *how* to approach teaching science.

When Should Ideas and Skills Be Taught?

In seeking to answer this query, two main interconnected issues need to be addressed. A school's policy for science will determine the particular approach to overall science curriculum coverage to be used. Many schools adopt a 'spiralling curriculum' for science topics or for wider themes within which science is covered. Typically, each of the three content aspects of the Programme of Study (Sc2, Sc3 and Sc4) will be touched on twice in each Key Stage. Published teaching materials and schemes will normally seek to achieve a balanced coverage.

Enquiry Task

Select a set of published guidelines for science. Look carefully at the materials for one Key Stage. Match the themes or topics identified in the published materials or guidelines to the National Curriculum Programme of Study headings and the list you drew up for the key ideas in the previous enquiry task.

- Is there a good match?
- Would the published guidelines be a sound basis for planning a scheme of work that covered the whole science curriculum?
- What are the strengths and weaknesses of these materials in assisting such planning?

The way in which different authors present their suggested structuring of the science curriculum can vary considerably and yet still be useful. As we noted earlier, the National Curriculum does not specify the order in which you teach the different concepts. However, if the children's learning in science is to build up progressively, there is a need to discern the development of ideas and skills over time. This whole area is fascinating and the focus for much research. Just the deceptively simple teaching objective:

> Pupils should be taught . . . that the Sun, Earth and Moon are approximately spherical. (KS 2, Physical Processes, 4a)

will require children to achieve major conceptual understanding (Nussbaum, 1985) that cannot be based directly on their first-hand experience. Careful thought needs to be given to how this understanding can be achieved; how children can explore the distant phenomena through the use of models. Try to set up an opportunity to elicit the views of a few children in this area of science and compare your findings with those reported in the literature. We gave some ideas about how you might gather this information earlier. It will be interesting to contrast the children's views with those found in the research study.

In a broad sense, the National Curriculum Order provides support in looking for this progression in ideas and skills through both the Programme of Study and the Level Descriptions. The Level Descriptions are useful in this context as they give an indication of how a child's understanding can be envisaged as developing over time.

Enquiry Task

Choose one area of science skills; for example *obtaining evidence*. Note the progression suggested by the teaching objectives from Key Stage 1 to Key Stage 2. Compare with the relevant sentences within the Level Descriptions from Level 1 to Level 6. Note that the quality of the skill goes from simple to more complex, from direct observation to the careful and repeated use of measuring equipment.

Compare this progression with the Mathematics Order and you will get a fuller picture of how a skill like measuring can be developed progressively through practical science activity. Clearly, when planning, you will need to bear in mind both the scientific and the mathematical progression. Similar issues arise in the area of *data handling* and *communication*; try the same exercise with these skills in mind.

Now select some science concept areas and track them in the same way. Try choosing one from each of the three 'content' areas of the Science Programme of Study.

Comparing statements in corresponding parts of the Programme of Study across the two Key Stages enables you to get a sense of how continuity between them can be envisaged. Over a period of time, you need to develop a progressive set of activities in order that you can most effectively aid pupils' understanding of science ideas and skills. Furthermore, real science understanding requires the linking of learning in science with the wider experience of the everyday world. Science is part of life, it is not something that only happens in school or in the laboratory of the stereotypical balding, bespectacled, white-coated male scientist. So your planning for science will need to lead children *on* in their understanding and skill but also *outwards* in their ability to make connections between the central ideas of science and their wider applications.

One way to do this is to look for and to take opportunities offered in other curriculum areas. In Chapter 11 of this book, and in Siraj-Blatchford and Coates (1995), examples are given of several activities that develop design and technology understanding. In some cases the activities draw on quite specific scientific ideas. For example, the work on yoghurt (Siraj-Blatchford and Coates, 1995) is linked to the idea that micro-organisms cause changes in milk. Children involved in this work will be learning about the 'good' uses of micro-organisms and the way milk can undergo a change that cannot be reversed. The work on the construction of effective teacup cosies (Siraj-Blatchford, and Coates, 1995) gives the opportunity to explore the insulation properties of the material of a teacup cosy. Children here will be considering ideas associated with energy transfer and the thermal insulation properties of the materials used. Explicit recognition of the science being used in the technological activity will help pupils both understand the science better *and* help them to be more effective technologists. Such activities may also enable you to assess the children's understanding as you note the way they are able to apply their learning in science to a new situation.

Enquiry Task

Suppose you have been given a Year 3 class and have chosen to do some work on forces. You look at Key Stage 1 and Key Stage 2 Programmes of Study and decide to build on the idea that *both pushes and pulls are examples of forces* (Key Stage 1) by introducing the fact that *forces act in particular directions* (Key Stage 2).

Identify a range of activities that you could use to allow the children to explore these two notions. What everyday situations might you be able to draw on to illustrate these aspects of forces in action?

In thinking about forces you might consider, for example, a building site or a vehicle. Another fruitful area for children to explore is their own world in which their toys, games and leisure pastimes play a large part. A selection of simple mechanical toys provides a good resource to build up for this work on force. Whatever you decide, children need many experiences through which to explore science ideas before they can move on to a higher conceptual level of understanding.

The same is true of the acquisition of science skills. One opportunity to study a flower through a hand lens will not mean the child can use a hand lens correctly, let alone effectively. You will need to provide many opportunities in differing settings for the child to acquire a good understanding of the appropriate and effective use of that particular aid to observation. Furthermore, in planning to try to develop a particular skill you also need to keep in mind the need to identify other opportunities in other areas of scientific learning for reinforcing the skill through practice. Learning of science skills and ideas progresses along a broad front, a factor that the emphasis on Level Descriptions as summary statements of a child's achievement underlines. One attempt at a fair test cannot provide sufficient evidence of a child's real competence as a scientist. You will need more examples of her/his investigative work to help you form a more reliable judgment.

How Should Ideas and Skills Be Taught?

The current National Curriculum Order for Science offers no more guidance on how to teach science than the previous two. The Non-Statutory Guidance which accompanied the original Order (DES/WO, 1989) offered ideas on ways to approach both planning and teaching. Other publications, for example, NCC (1990, 1993d), all provide food for thought — backed by varying kinds of evidence — on the ways you might tackle your science teaching. What is clear in science is that your approach needs to:

- enable the development of science knowledge;
- enable the development of science skills;
- promote science as a systematic means of enquiry;
- enable children to relate their understanding to their own lives and the wider environment in which they live;
- promote the development of key communication, research and IT skills;
- develop the children's ability to consider their own health and safety, and that of others.

Schools are required to establish schemes of work in science and these need to identify the teaching approaches to be used. What is certain is that any work worthy of being called science will have a very significant practical element to it. Your rôle as a teacher will be to plan programmes of work for children that put a school scheme of work into practice. These programmes of work need to identify:

- the Programme of Study elements to be taught;
- the range of activities the children will carry out in your lessons;
- the teaching resources that will be required;
- the way these activities will link to the Programme of Study, to other areas of the curriculum, and to cross-curricular issues such as Health Education or Economic and Industrial Understanding;
- the way these activities will acknowledge the special needs of the children;
- the way these activities may be of use in contributing to the assessment of the children's progress.

At the heart of a good programme of work, though, lies the basic approach you adopt in your individual science lessons. As we have noted earlier, the selection of the actual activities you are going to teach will be governed by their relevance to, and clarity of focus on, the ideas and skills to be taught. They will also be subject to the availability of suitable resources. However, for them to be successful, good lessons still need your skill and knowledge of science *and* your skill and knowledge of working with your pupils. The order you choose to teach the lessons may make the difference between helping the children to progress in their understanding and skill, and enabling them simply to experience a range of interesting but apparently disjointed activities. The balance you strike between the illustrative and the investigative focus will similarly help, or perhaps hinder, the children's growing understanding of science as both a body of knowledge and a set of processes and procedures.

Investigations explore ideas and phenomena — they require particular skills. A programme of work needs to develop both knowledge and understanding and skills to the point where meaningful investigation can occur. This, in turn, will help to extend both skills and knowledge and understanding. Some programmes of work will lend themselves less to full scientific investigation than others: compare, for example, the number and range of opportunities for investigative work on the 'Earth and Beyond' with those in work on 'Changing Materials'.

The way you teach your lessons will determine the effectiveness of the link between the teaching activity and the child's learning activity that we identified earlier. Introductions to lessons that enable the children to feel included and that their views are valued by the questioning you have employed, and teaching that makes clear the way the subject matter is relevant to the real world, will be vital to help the children see the science as *theirs* rather than yours. Activities that enable the children to work at their level because you have thought in advance about their needs, recognizing where the written instruction may pose a barrier or the likely positive interaction of particular groupings of children, will be essential to promote productive work. Providing prompts to assist the children's investigative approaches, either through written planning guides (Qualter, 1995; Platten, 1993), or by your involvement in the process alongside the children, will be important to enhance the likelihood of learning. Using questions to stimulate and guide the children's thinking about ideas and use of skills will not only enhance the likelihood of learning but also enable you to observe and assess the children's achievements. Finally, and importantly, allowing the children the opportunity to try to draw conclusions and communicate what they have found out, to evaluate and relate their findings to what they already know, and their methods to other possible approaches will be essential if their 'old' ideas are to be challenged and replaced where appropriate by 'new' ones.

The purpose of the National Curriculum for Science is to give directions on what you teach in science and how to judge your pupils' progress. As we have indicated, it provides a framework for learning in science through the study of experimental and investigative exploration (Sc1) *and* three key aspects of science knowledge and understanding (Sc2, Sc3, and Sc4). What we have tried to explore in this chapter is the way in which you might make effective use of that curriculum, and the challenges you need to meet, in order to make a reality the enjoyable and constructive learning of science by the children you teach.

References

COATES, D. and RUSSELL, A. (1995) 'BEd students' perceptions of science and their science course', *Primary Science Review*, 37, April, pp. 22–3, Hatfield, Association for Science Education.

DEPARTMENT OF EDUCATION AND SCIENCE/WELSH OFFICE (DES/WO) (1989) *Science in the National Curriculum*, London, HMSO.

DEPARTMENT FOR EDUCATION/WELSH OFFICE (DES/WO) (1995) *Science in the National Curriculum for England and Wales*, London, HMSO.

HARLEN, W. (1983) *Assessment of Performance Unit Science Report for Teachers 1: Science at Age 11*, DES/WO/DENI.

HOBDEN, J. (1993) 'Do children see themselves as real scientists?', *Primary Science Review*, 28, June, pp. 6–7, Hatfield, Association for Science Education.

JANNIKER, M. (1995) 'Images of scientists', *Primary Science Review*, 37, April, pp. 26–8, Hatfield, Association for Science Education.

MARSHALL, C. and PALACIO, D. (1995) 'Science', in ASHCROFT, K. and PALACIO, D. (eds) *The Primary Teacher's Guide to the New National Curriculum*, London, Falmer Press.

NATIONAL CURRICULUM COUNCIL (NCC) (1990) *Investigations Working with Science AT1 in Key Stages 1 and 2*, York, NCC.

NATIONAL CURRICULUM COUNCIL (NCC) (1992) *Knowledge and Understanding of Science: Forces*, York, NCC.

NATIONAL CURRICULUM COUNCIL (NCC) (1993a) *Knowledge and Understanding of Science: Energy*, York, NCC.

NATIONAL CURRICULUM COUNCIL (NCC) (1993b) *Knowledge and Understanding of Science: Electricity and Magnetism*, NCC, York.

NATIONAL CURRICULUM COUNCIL (NCC) (1993c) *Teaching Science at Key Stages 1 and 2*, York, NCC.

NATIONAL CURRICULUM COUNCIL (NCC) (1993d) *Teaching Science at Key Stages 1 and 2*, York, NCC.

NEWTON, L., and NEWTON, D. (1991) 'Child's view of a scientist', *Questions*, **4**, 1, September, pp. 20–1, Birmingham, Questions Publishing Company.

NUFFIELD PRIMARY SCIENCE (SPACE) (1993) 11 Teacher's Guides and 22 Pupils' Books for Key Stage 2, Teacher's Guide for Key Stage 1, Teacher's Handbook and INSET Pack, London, Collins Educational.

NUSSBAUM, J. (1985) 'Earth as a cosmic body', in DRIVER, R., GUESNE, E., and TIBERGHIEN, A. (eds) *Children's Ideas in Science*, Milton Keynes, Open University Press.

PLATTEN, A. (1993) 'Standardised sheets to encourage children's investigations', *Primary Science Review*, 27, April, pp. 10–12, Hatfield, Association for Science Education.

PRESTON, M. (1995) 'Images of scientists', *Primary Science Review*, 37, April, pp. 24–6, Hatfield, Association for Science Education.

PRIMARY SCHOOL TEACHERS AND SCIENCE PROJECT (PSTS) INSET Materials: *1.Understanding Forces* (1991a); *2. Understanding Energy* (1991b); *3. Understanding Plants and the Gases They Need* (1992); *4. Understanding Materials and Why They Change* (1993a); *5. Understanding the Earth's Place in the Universe* (1993b), Oxford University Department of Educational Studies/Westminster College, Oxford. (PSTS INSET Materials are available from Association for Science Education, College Lane, Hatfield, Herts AL10 9AA.)

QUALTER, A. (1995) *Differentiated Primary Science*, Milton Keynes, Open University Press.

RICHARDS, R. and KINCAID, D. (1983) 'Autogyros', *Learning Through Science Project, On the Move*, London, Macdonald Educational.

SCHOOL CURRICULUM AND ASSESSMENT AUTHORITY (SCAA) (1994a) *Knowledge and Understanding of Science: Chemical Changes*, London, SCAA.

SCHOOL CURRICULUM AND ASSESSMENT AUTHORITY (SCAA) (1994b) *Knowledge and Understanding of Science: Genetics and Ecology*, London, SCAA.

SCIENCE PROCESSES AND CONCEPTS EXPLORATION (SPACE) Research Reports, *Evaporation and Condensation* (1990); *Growth* (1990); *Light* (1990); *Sound* (1990); *Electricity* (1991); *Materials* (1991); *Processes of Life* (1992); *Rocks, Soil and Weather* (1992), Liverpool, Liverpool University Press.

SIRAJ-BLATCHFORD, J. and COATES, D. (1995) 'Design and technology', in ASHCROFT, K. and PALACIO, D. (eds) *The Primary Teacher's Guide to the New National Curriculum*, London, Falmer Press.

WARD, A. (1989) 'A child can be a scientist studying paper helicopters', *Primary Science Review*, 10, Summer, pp. 16–17, Hatfield, Association for Science Education.

WRIGHT, D. (1990) 'Teachers' attitudes to primary science', *Primary Science Review*, Summer, pp. 12–13, Hatfield, Association for Science Education.

List of Suggested Reading

DEPARTMENT OF EDUCATION AND SCIENCE/WELSH OFFICE (DES/WO) (1989) *Non-Statutory Guidance* (see above for full reference).

HARLEN, W. (1996) *The Teaching of Science in Primary Schools* (second edition), London, David Fulton.

NATIONAL CURRICULUM COUNCIL AND SCHOOL CURRICULUM AND ASSESSMENT AUTHORITY (NCC and SCAA) *Knowledge and Understanding of Science* series — see above for full references.

OSBORNE, R. and FREYBERG, P. (1985) *Learning in Science: The Implications of Children's Science*, London, Heinemann.

PRIMARY SCHOOL TEACHERS AND SCIENCE PROJECT (PSTS) *Understanding Science Concepts* series (see above for full references).

SCIENCE PROCESSES AND CONCEPTS EXPLORATION PROJECT (SPACE) *Research Reports* (see above for full references).

6 History

Ann Jordan and Paul Taylor

Introduction

The purpose here is to suggest practical ways to approach the planning, teaching, resourcing and assessing of National Curriculum History at Key Stages 1 and 2. The emphasis will be on thinking about, questioning and reflecting on the nature of the subject, with enquiry tasks included for consideration. The way cross-curricular themes can be developed will also be explored and there will be a brief section on history outside the National Curriculum.

Planning National Curriculum History

The revised National Curriculum for History having been in place since August 1995, most schools will now have an overall whole-school framework for the subject. Within this long-term planning, units of work will be starting to be put in place and individual teachers will be in the process of preparing and delivering the detail required. What follows offers some suggestions as to how to approach the planning needs and should compliment the specific planning strategies suggested in Taylor (1995).

Every teacher needs to make themselves aware that what they are planning for their history work should fit within the overall school strategy and develop the requisite knowledge, understanding and skills of the subject. Therefore consideration needs to be given by the teacher to what she/he thinks are the most relevant key elements to be given attention for that particular area or unit of work. In the History National Curriculum there are five Key Elements: chronology; range and depth of historical knowledge and understanding; interpretation; historical enquiry; and organization and communication. Given that pp. 75 and 77 of the National Curriculum document (DFE, 1995) shows these Key Elements as being common to Key Stages 1 and 2 this gives opportunity for teachers to prepare for and build on the same planning ground throughout the primary years. By the end of Key Stage 1, and then Key Stage 2, it is necessary that the Key Elements as a whole have been given appropriate time and attention.

Key Stage 1 Considerations

At Key Stage 1 it may be worth considering how a history-based topic could meaningfully incorporate all the Key Elements without attempting to artificially 'force' them into the planning. For instance, in a wider study of houses and homes you could address the issue of chronology by gathering a collection of photographs of dwellings over time to identify areas of change and to initiate a sequencing activity building up words such as modern, old, and newer. From this you could delve into more specific features of a dwelling, such as the kitchen or bathroom, to enhance children's wider knowledge of how the structure was used. In the case of a bathroom, you could initiate discussion based on the children's own experience of the modern bathroom. These discussions could form the basis of a simple questionnaire that the children would then be encouraged to take home and share with parents, grandparents, relatives and other adults in the family context. This will begin to address aspects of historical enquiry and organization. Bringing their findings back into school and communicating them orally could lead into discussion of why the past is seen from different perspectives, given a likely mixture of previous 'bathrooms'. This activity as a whole touches on all the Key Elements but you, as the teacher, decide which of these you will develop and extend.

The essential interrelatedness of much of the learning that takes place at Key Stage 1 lends itself to seeing history planning as involving taking the pupils' perspective and current awareness and interests, and using these as a vehicle to deliver the more abstract concepts required of the subject, such as time and interpretation. Given that pupils in the early years do not learn things in isolation, it is important in your planning that you make the learning context as integrated as possible. Though p. 74 of the National Curriculum document (DFE, 1995) does not give you much to go on as to which detailed planning to undertake, this should be seen as a favourable feature in that you can interpret the requirements for the fundamental needs of your pupils as you see fit, for example, locality, background, cultural influence.

Arguably, it is easier to start with the Key Elements and think how you will develop them through the Areas of Study, rather than starting with the latter and trying to slot elements in. Apart from specific references to Britain, to which you must give credence, the rest of the requirements and suggestions are the kind of thing you yourself would have been likely to come up with, for example, everyday life, change, people and events. A planning grid, such as the example in Taylor (1995, p. 86), with headings for focus/key questions, concepts, activities and resources could have a fifth column shown for Key Elements, and where you feel that these need highlighting.

Enquiry Task — Key Stage 1: Planning

Given that so much of Key Stage 1 planning involves cross-curricular approaches, but that nevertheless there are specific history requirements whether you teach history-related topics or history as part of a wider focus, you need to be able to identify and show National Curriculum coverage. Therefore you may wish to consider the following:

- Is your topic aiming to be history based or is the history part of a wider project? Does this affect how you perceive the nature of the tasks to be undertaken?

- you need to have a planning grid of some form such as the example in the original non-statutory guidance (NCC, 1991) or as suggested by Taylor (1995, p. 96). The decision needs to be made on whether the component history parts are on a specific grid or are incorporated and/or highlighted as a common grid. This ensures the history is specified and given due credit.
- If the history is on a general grid, is it blocked in terms of time or does it flow through the topics as a whole?
- Is the aim to cover part of the Areas of Study in the topic or touch on them all? If so, how do you ensure breadth and depth respectively? There needs to be a Key Stage 1 overview to ensure no gaps in Areas of Study or Key Elements.
- Have the concepts to be dealt with been given consideration as to their complexity and meaningfulness in the light of the topic work as a whole?
- Where are the learning experiences in the work specifically historical? It is all too easy to have activities with a historical underpinning but which are essentially exercises in English or art, for example.

This planning would hopefully enable the subject to be given clarity and recognition in the overall school system and be available for outside inspection and observation leading to the highlighting of continuity and progression.

Key Stage 2 Considerations

In the Key Stage 2 history study units, the content headings are prescriptive and issues for planning revolve around the five Key Elements within a set context, whether it be the Romans, Anglo-Saxons and Vikings in Britain, Life in Tudor Times, Victorian Britain, Britain Since 1930, Ancient Greece, Local History or a past non-European Society. Although not all five Key Elements must come into every study unit, you do have to identify which are being covered so that by the end of Key Stage 2 all will have been covered. Having said that, it is difficult to envisage any history study unit being taught in which, to a greater or lesser extent, there was not some reference to time, understanding content, and situations, seeing different points of view, using a range of resources, and showing work through a variety of mediums.

It is also a requirement that by the end of Key Stage 2, pupils have seen history in outline and in depth. The very nature of the units means that there will be outline work, and depth in each; for example, Life in Tudor times looks at the way of life of people across that period but it also requires in-depth study of specifics, such as the Spanish Armada. A number of the study units specifically mention Britain in the title and it is important to remember that this includes aspects of England, Ireland, Scotland and Wales, as appropriate.

An issue which requires care is that of incorporating a variety of perspectives into your history planning: that is, political, economic, technological and scientific, social, religious, cultural and aesthetic. These may be referred to as the PESC formula for short. Though it is not a requirement to include PESC in every study unit, it remains a useful way of considering how to capture the imagination and interests of the pupils as a whole in any study unit you teach, knowing that different pupils are obviously stimulated and motivated by different facets of a topic, for example, inventions, laws, music, customs, wars.

PESC can avoid a narrow view of history being put forward in pupils' minds and ensure that any work is not just a litany of 'how people lived' or 'how people worked', for instance. Having a PESC outlook yourself means 'taking the blinkers off' and adopting a lateral view of the subject content. For example, if you were planning a unit of work on Ancient Egypt you might choose one of a number of PESC approaches to introduce the work to the pupils. The list below offers some suggestions.

Area of PESC	*Introducing the Unit*
Political	Role of Pharaoh and power
Economic	Significance of Nile
Technological and scientific	Pyramids and Shaduf
Social	Structure of society; hierarchies
Religious	Worship and gods
Cultural and aesthetic	Impact of discovery of Tutankhamen

Each of these different approaches allows you to phase your initial emphasis in a clear context. You may prefer to emphasize the importance of the monarchical system and, therefore, the place of the Pharaoh. On the other hand, you may wish to begin with a view of the Nile and its influence in allowing Egyptian civilization to flourish along its banks. If you wanted to start by showing the power, greatness and lasting impact of these people, you might begin with some of their leading inventions, innovations and structures, for example, Pyramids. 'Lives of ordinary people' is obviously a different starting point, as is concentrating on their unique and particular belief-systems as being so central to their existence. On the other hand, you could commence with the 1920s discovery of Tutankhamen's tomb by Howard Carter and how this highlighted and developed the significance of the cultural impact of these people. Any of the above would be an appropriate way to focus early planning, you may well have others and certainly the idea can be adopted for any history study unit.

When planning for Key Stage 2 there are a number of useful approaches suggested in the Non-Statutory Guidance for History which came with the Order for the first National Curriculum in History. (For more information on planning, in particular the use of planning grids at Key Stage 2, see Taylor, 1995: these remain pertinent.) Schools use a variety of planning grids and Figure 6.1 shows a set of headings, with an example of a more detailed initial planning strand incorporated, taking into account the Key Elements.

The grid begins with a question because the essence of good history teaching is centred around an investigative approach. Highlighting the essential questions you wish to raise should lead to the pupils acquiring the intended learning outcomes you require. Ideally, the rest of the questions for the topic would flow from

Figure 6.1: Introductory planning strand to unit

Focused Questions	Key Elements	Concepts	Contents and Resources	Learning Experiences
When and why did the Vikings come to Britain?	2b to describe and identify reasons for and results of historical events, situations, and changes in the period studied 4b to ask and answer questions and select and record information relevant to a topic 5b the terms necessary to describe the periods and topics studied	Invasion Conquest Settlement	From a variety of visual and written sources the pupils will be studying the significance of location and motivation in the movement of peoples leading to a greater understanding of migration.	Use a variety of maps and atlases to identify Scandinavia and Britain in the present day. Identify possible routes and distances involved. Discuss appropriate transport. Who came? Motivations? Where would they have been likely to land? From selective resources identify some significant dates of landing and settlement which occurred. Through all of the above pupils to begin to form an opinion as to why the Vikings came.

this and therefore you may go on to complete the first column in its entirety before moving on to the others. In this way your unit planning and focused enquiry are clear from the start. When your questions cover the content required for the study unit, it should be possible to more readily identify which Key Elements are being raised at a given point. Concepts need to be detailed, pinpointed and specific; being chosen carefully to avoid generalizations. By identifying purposeful learning experiences in regard to content and resources this rounds off a sound, structured approach at this stage.

Enquiry Task — Key Stage 2: Planning

Use your planning grid/matrix/formula to set yourself a series of tasks to ensure that the history work meets National Curriculum requirements. If you used the headings in the grid mentioned above, the following might be appropriate.

- How many focused questions do you want? Are they open or closed questions? Can they be delivered in the time available? Do they flow in a logical sequence?
- How many Key Elements do you link to each question? Can you sub-divide the Key Elements? Must there be a Key Element linked to each question?
- How many concepts do you want to specify? Is there an optimum number? Do you rank order them?
- Is the content matched precisely to the question, and are the resources needed available/purchasable/acquirable?
- How far does the previous learning experience of the pupils and the projected future work envisaged underpin the thinking behind your planning?
- Look across the sections/columns of your plan. Does the work as a whole read coherently whether you read the columns vertically or horizontally?
- How would you evaluate the work after it has been undertaken with the pupils?

The place of assessment in planning will feature in a later section.

Teaching and Resourcing National Curriculum History

The importance of questioning means that Key Element 4 of the National Curriculum on historical enquiry and its requirement to use a range of sources of information becomes crucial. It is possible to see it as the gateway to the other Key Elements in that it is through enquiry that aspects of time, discussion of knowledge and understanding, looking at points of view and opportunities for organizing historical work can be undertaken. Resources are either primary, that is from the time (for example, artefacts), or secondary, that is written after the event (for example, textbooks). Obviously, you will be using resources, but the best resource is the teacher providing opportunities, challenges and activities to enhance pupils' learning.

There is no single correct way to teach history in that there are potentially a range of approaches you may adopt. Whole class teaching is a way of disseminating information, either from yourself or a visiting speaker, setting a scene — for example, by using a video and discussion on it — eliciting pupils' initial knowledge, opening-up to the pupils what will be happening in the topic and providing a sense of direction. At its best, this will include open questioning with the pupils, possibly a range of resources to look at — for example, maps, objects, books — and a feeling of shared experience. At its worse, it is a session where the teacher simply recites information verbally and on the board to a largely passive audience: in other words, an overwhelmingly didactic approach which is the antithesis of genuine enquiry.

Group work in history gives the opportunity to cover different aspects of a topic. For instance, if you were studying Henry VIII and wanted an overview of the background of his wives, you could split your class into six groups and give them a limited time to find out some basic information, written and pictorial, about each wife to report back to the class at the end of the session. This would mean an active session in which all pupils were collecting and collating information and sharing their knowledge. You can then fill in any gaps and clarify any misunderstanding. This is learning through enquiry, and if you have developed and explained strategies to avoid pupils simply copying from resources it is a time effective and skill enhancing activity.

There is no reason why Key Stage 1 pupils cannot do the same basic group work activity using a more accessible range of written resources and pictorial images or representations. For instance, if you were looking at forms of transport people used in the past, different groups could search for varying types of motor-vehicles, motor-cycles, bicycles, trains, boats, planes and so on. By sharing the group's chosen images, you could begin to address areas of chronology relating to language development of the pupils, and through simple written description some exploration of changes in transport and why these might have come about.

History gives individual pupils an excellent opportunity to develop smaller scale research tasks within an overall topic to not only enhance the pupils' interest and confidence in the material but to allow this later to be potentially shared with the rest of the class. For more able pupils, the teacher may set more challenging lines of enquiry which extend the skills inherent in the Key Elements, for instance looking at a wider and more complex set of interpretations of an historic event, such as the significance of large-scale urbanization in the Victorian period. For pupils with more specific learning needs, requiring reinforcement and return to past work, the use of a designated set of material to enhance individual confidence may be needed, for example, visual images of the growth of towns and cities in the same period.

Whether it be whole-class, group or individual teaching, careful selection of resources is necessary to ensure pupils have access to as wide a range of varied and appropriate material as possible. Within, and across, each Key Stage there need to be artefacts, pictures, photographs, written sources, and use of buildings and sites. In particular, at Key Stage 1, there should be an opportunity to use adults talking about their own past, while at Key Stage 2, especially, documents and printed sources, along with music, are also specified in the National Curriculum document.

Although not all sources have to be used within every topic the range required means that cost, availability, access and allocation need to be given consideration across the school.

In addition to textbooks and packs from publishers that schools buy, there are a wealth of other types of resources, some of which are either free for educational purposes or relatively inexpensive. Libraries often have a local studies section or access to archives, while museums in many parts of the country continue to provide school support through designated rooms for pupils to work in, and education officers offering workshops and loan collections for use in the classroom. Some County Record Offices allow school parties to use their materials and these can give work a regional focus. A number of towns and cities have active history societies who can provide speakers and there are a number of re-enactment bodies that will work with children; for example, the Sealed Knot on the English Civil War, who portray the military and domestic life of the time. Visual images such as this appeal across the Key Stages. Newspaper offices also have a wealth of collected information. Of course, the local environment with its public buildings, churches and statues allows frequent and free access to a living past. Organizations such as English Heritage provide resources, advice, information and guidance on a variety of sites of national interest.

History can interrelate with a range of cross-curricular themes which can thereby mutually enhance each other. Citizenship, economic and industrial understanding (EIU), and the environment are, for instance, potential avenues for exploring meaning within an historical context. Teaching about citizenship with Key Stage 1 could lead to an examination of school rules over time — for example, Victorian and today — allowing pupils to discuss questions of what is fair and right, and whether people in the past had the same values and attitudes. With Key Stage 2, covering the Greeks, issues of slavery and freedom could lead to a more formal structured debate among the pupils. With EIU, younger pupils can examine the types of occupations people do now and look for similarities and differences with the past, thereby viewing contributions to the life of the community. Older pupils studying the Victorians or Britain since 1930, with their strong emphasis on the economic climate, have ample opportunity to enhance their perceptions in this area, and the history grids (Taylor, 1995) show, particularly through transport developments, activities that can be undertaken in this regard.

The environment has been, and remains, a source of interest and concern, as shown in the publication of a booklet entitled, *Environmental Matters* (SCAA, 1996). This contains approaches to using history to support the teaching of environmental issues. You might consider providing Key Stage 1 pupils with the chance to study how goods were purchased in the past and what happened to the wrappings and containers in which they were sold. This could be compared with methods used now, and whether we are more or less environmentally friendly than in the past, and why this might be. At Key Stage 2, comparing the emphasis on conservation and preservation of scarce resources during the Second World War can be matched with the profligate and 'throw-away nature' of much of society during the 1960s and 1970s leading to a growth in 'green issues' in the 1980s and 1990s. The reasons for this, and the economic and social consequences, can be explored through examination of media coverage, artefacts and pressure groups.

Enquiry Task

- Look at your planning grid for history to ensure that pupils have opportunities through your teaching to work as a whole class, in groups and individually.
- Do your planned learning outcomes allow pupils access to a variety of resources? If not, how could this be achieved?
- Are you providing activities that cater for differentiation by specifically chosen tasks, appropriate resources to match pupil ability or open-ended enquiry opportunity?
- Is your work balanced over the week/month/unit to allow progression in terms of knowledge and skills?
- In what ways does the organization of your classroom allow pupils to engage in the kind of activity set?

Assessment in National Curriculum History

There are a number of purposes to assessment in history. Your self-evaluation is critical to determining the validity of the overall planned task as you set it and the specifics of particular sessions. Making judgments on pupil progress across the study area/unit as a whole, while on-going and at the end, in terms of selected criteria, is crucial. In history, with so much emphasis on continuity and progression, it can only be through an agreed form of assessment that credible statements can be made. There are four fundamental questions to be addressed in terms of assessment in history — Why? When? What? and How? — and each is therefore deserving of attention.

Without assessment, it is difficult to make informed judgments about whether or not the aims behind your scheme of work and its associated lesson planning were met, and specifically how far the learning objectives for the pupils were attained. This assessment will be the bedrock for future planning and is integral to the whole concept of being a reflective practitioner.

There are a number of people who have the right to be assured that you are meeting the History National Curriculum requirements. For instance, your school's history/humanities coordinator, the deputy and/or headteacher, the governors, the County Advisor, Office for Standards in Education (OFSTED), local secondary/ middle schools and parents. There is much work to be done, as is made clear in OFSTED's review of inspection findings in history published in 1995, which stated that, '. . . schools should seek to develop their understanding of assessment in history' (p. 5) and that, 'Assessment remained under-developed in Key Stages 1 and 2' (p. 11) (DFE, 1995).

In practice, teachers make informal assessments all the time, but we believe that there should be designated points where you feel best able to gather the required information to make positive statements. You need to show where this is taking place between R/Year 1 and Year 6 for you and your colleagues to build on. When initial planning of history work is taking place you may need to build in 'mid-points', 'check-ins' or, if you like, to use a motor-racing analogy, 'pit-stops', to ascertain how well pupils are developing their skills in the five Key Elements. This gives you more flexibility in the overall direction of the work.

At the end of the Key Stage, or indeed at the end of teaching a unit of study, there are the Level Descriptions which are statements of characteristic pupil performance in the subject at that point. Waiting until the end of the work is like buying a new car and not bothering to assess it until the MOT three years later. Most people prefer to have a regular service to check if all is well and avoid further problems. Therefore, assessing part way through is as useful as assessing at the end.

Assessment can include a variety of outcomes, for example, topic books, projects, displays, exhibitions, timeline work. It is worth remembering that, 'often insufficient attention was given to the particular needs of children of different abilities, and especially of those who found reading and writing difficult' (DFE, 1995, p. 14). This is a crucial area for consideration for all children, not just those with special educational needs. Written and oral work allows you to see how pupils are developing their understanding of the five Key Elements, which are the criteria to be judged in the areas and units of work.

In practice, it is unrealistic, and unnecessary, to expect that each Key Element must be individually assessed at various points in five different ways. It does mean looking for opportunities to see where more than one Key Element can be displayed during the process of a particular pupil task. For instance, if pupils were using artefacts (Key Element 4 — Enquiry) to elicit interpretation of their use and by whom — for example, a set of irons or a collection of World War II memorabilia such as ration books and identity cards (Key Element 3 — Interpretation) — and reporting back through group discussion of their findings (Key Element 5 — Organization and communication), it is possible to have assessed these three Key Elements in one activity.

This formative assessment allows you to plan on the basis of on-going development, and from it you can identify more clearly those pupils who have specific problems and those pupils who need additional stimulation; in other words diagnostic assessment. Summative assessment is inevitable, and if the school is large enough and/or the history coordinator in the school keen enough, an evaluative assessment of pupil performance across the school and within the year groups can provide a picture to enhance curriculum development.

In essence you will often assess by outcome, where all the pupils do the same work and a range of expectations are allowed for; or by task, whereby certain individuals/groups are doing work specifically aimed at their expected level of ability and development. Keeping evidence of pupil responses helps you to decide ultimately where a pupil is in relation to the features outlined in the Level Descriptions. How you record and report that information will depend on whether or not the school has a set pattern for recording pupil progress across the subjects of the curriculum as a whole or for history specifically. If it does not, then you will need to devise such a system. Figure 6.2 shows a possible observation schedule for use at Key Stage 1 or 2.

The grid (shown in Figure 6.2) is designed to be straightforward, easy to store and allows you to survey across a class by individual pupil, but also by Key Element. It would allow a newly qualified teacher, a new appointment, a supply teacher, a student or a specialist teacher assistant to access the type of work done in history, give examples to guide them and allow them to play a part in assessment.

If you keep evidence of assessment in terms of a cross-section of pupil tasks/ topic books (perhaps photocopied), photographs of displays, audio and/or visual recordings of drama/assembly productions these can show what has taken place after the actual work has been done. Much good work has been 'lost' in the fatigue of the end of term, the run-up to the Christmas play and the preparations for the summer fair. If the requirement to keep samples become a systematic policy, the likelihood of a lack of evidence is lessened, even more so if history subject portfolios are kept, and replacement work put in to update them.

With the basic Level Descriptions, you may need to be wary of 'pushing' your pupils up the Levels simply to 'do the best you can for them' or through feeling that you have 'failed' if they have not moved up a Level. It can distort the true picture and leave you and other teachers, particularly the Year 6 staff, little room for manoeuvre and real progression.

Without agreed and understood assessment strategies there can be no effective development of a subject grounded in progressive skill enhancement.

Enquiry Task

- Having considered all other aspects for your study unit/area, look for opportunities regarding assessment.
- Decide how often you wish to assess during the unit and which of the Key Elements are to be specifically chosen.
- How are the assessment opportunities to be linked into your planning; for example, will you build it in as part of your normal teaching unit or will you choose to evaluate at certain points?
- You will need to list specific success criteria, that is, what indicators you are looking for in pupils, and decide what evidence will be required, such as pupil's written work, oral observation, teacher's notes following handling of sources or artefacts.
- You need to decide how you will cater for pupils who, after having been assessed, need to revisit certain elements. For more able pupils, you may need to increase the content and/or knowledge/skill level to develop their potential.

History Outside the National Curriculum

In addition to the existing National Curriculum, schools have flexibility to use up to 20 per cent of time for issues, projects and themes outside the statutory requirements. Each school needs to show its justification for use of non-National Curriculum

Figure 6.2: Observation schedule for Key Stage 1/2 History

Pupil's Name: **Year:**

Title of area of study/unit:

Key Element 1	Key Element 2	Key Element 3	Key Element 4	Key Element 5
Task and date undertaken:	Task and date undertaken:	Task and date undertaken:	Task and date undertaken:	Task and date undertaken:
Evidence of Level Description as shown by:				

time, therefore how you select and plan is critical. Given this opportunity, history would allow you to develop your own topics within the subject or in conjunction with other areas.

A number of schools have made the decision to continue teaching previous National Curriculum history work for reasons such as prior resourcing, interest and enjoyment, and the practical availability of local sites. Therefore, for example, the role of myths and legends, and the appreciation of music in different historical contexts continue to feature in the early years, whilst, with older pupils, themes such as food and farming or writing and printing continue to be profitably explored.

You are likely to want to develop your own ideas for appropriate history work. This may be a specific history topic, such as World War II in a wider European setting, or Settlement and Early Man. There are a wealth of potential topics, providing you have, or can acquire, the necessary practical resources. It may be that you wish to have a historical focus to support an issue, such as equal opportunities, looking at the rôles of men and women over time in a domestic and political setting. This could involve looking at the changing nature of people at work during the nineteenth century, and the arguments for equal voting rights coming to the fore in the early twentieth century.

History can be seen as a tool in that it can be used to shape, form and construct the pathways to a wider understanding of other subject areas. For instance, in geography, if you are looking at rivers and their significance for human habitation in terms of location, direction and impact — for example, flooding — then the evidence from maps, written accounts and printed evidence, such as newspapers, informs children's understanding of the present through the past. In science, if you were exploring aspects of health and the importance of various substances, such as tobacco or alcohol, perceptions of these have altered significantly over time; for example, cigarettes being seen as harmless, relaxing and soothing until at least the 1950s. History could explore why these perceptions came to be so ingrained and how they began to change.

This is only a snap-shot of how history may play a rôle beyond the strict confines of the National Curriculum. There are a number of issues you would want to consider and then argue for if you felt the time was to be justified.

Enquiry Task
- Clarify to what extent the non-National Curriculum time as a whole is being allocated within the whole school policy and the justification for it.
- Discuss with colleagues how and where history might enhance and inform existing and proposed work.
- Draw up a proposal for making use of history in non-National Curriculum time, incorporating aims, objectives, content and learning outcomes. This ideally would link the tasks not only to the enhancement of the subject and its inherent skills but also clarify how it develops other areas of the curriculum and matches with the whole school plan.

References

DFE (1995) *Key Stages 1 and 2 of the National Curriculum*, London, HMSO.

English Heritage Educational Service, PO Box 1BB London W1A 1BB.

NCC (1991) *History Non-Statutory Guidance*, York, NCC.

NCC (1990) *Curriculum Guidance Series*, York, NCC.

OFFICE FOR STANDARDS IN EDUCATION (OFSTED) (1995) *A Review of Inspection Findings in History*, London, HMSO.

SCAA (1996) *Teaching Environmental Matters through the National Curriculum*, London, SCAA.

TAYLOR, P. (1995) 'History', in ASHCROFT, K. and PALACIO, D. (eds) *The Primary Teacher's Guide to the New National Curriculum*, London, Falmer Press.

TAYLOR, P. (1996) 'History and technology at Key Stage Two: A practical partnership', *Teaching History*, 84, June.

List of Suggested Reading

Blyth, J. (1994) *History 5 to 11*, London, Hodder and Stoughton.

Cooper, H. (1995) *The Teaching of History in Primary Schools* (second edition), London, David Fulton Publishers.

Lomas, T. (ed.) (1996) *Planning Primary History*, London, John Murray (Publishers) Ltd.

7   Geography

John Halocha and Maureen Roberts

Introduction

In this chapter, we will first look at how you might familiarize yourself with the local environment around your school, as the National Curriculum for Geography takes the local area as one of the starting points for developing and teaching geographical understanding. We will introduce ways of planning lessons which build on the locality, and other National Curriculum requirements. We will also include the integral rôle of information technology and assessment. Further important features of planning lessons will be included; for example, how to utilize fieldwork in both Key Stages 1 and 2. The concepts, issues and progression of skills and overall ideas will be discussed using practical examples. This will involve looking at the integration of *skills, places* and *thematic studies*. We shall conclude by considering other practical ideas and guidance.

The *Locality* and the National Curriculum

Wherever your school is located, it will provide opportunities for children to investigate both the school's immediate environment (Key Stage 1) and, at Key Stage 2, the slightly wider locality (DFE, 1995). It is, therefore, essential for you to familiarize yourself with the area you will be using with your children. This may already have been undertaken by your colleagues so you may find it useful to check with staff and the school policy documents. If it has not already been done, the following enquiry task will guide you in what to look for.

Enquiry Task — Locality Audit

- Together with at least one other colleague and/or a parent, carry out an audit of your locality from a geographical perspective.
- What would you use at Key Stage 1? What would you use at Key Stage 2?

The aim is to list what is available and to note what is not. Eventually, this list will help you to select your contrasting locality.

Examples of things to include:

---

streams;

slopes;

any small place with a microclimate — for example, a wind tunnel between tower blocks;

types of buildings;

services;

street furniture;

quality of the environment.

On your walks, you may have noticed a number of interesting features which can be of use in your geographical planning. For example, even an unpromising litter-strewn street offers a starting point for children to express their opinions about the attractiveness of the local environment. As you move around, try to notice the different noises, both their levels and sources. This is an aspect of *environment* which is worth bringing to children's attention, as it directly relates to the quality of life in the area.

Because schools are located in such varied places, you will need to consider what you found nearby as a starting point for your planning. However, it is likely that a number of features will be missing that are needed to teach fully the National Curriculum. This is where you might begin to think about identifying a contrasting UK locality to complement your children's understanding of geography; for example, if your school is in the middle of a large city, you will probably need to look for a rural area. Another point to think about is whether or not your locality might be especially good for planning work on one of the thematic studies: at Key Stage 1, it may be the topic of 'Town and Country' or 'Homes' (either of which forms a good foundation for progression to the 'Settlement' theme when the children are older); at Key Stage 2, your own area may offer a good diversity of settlement patterns, while your contrasting UK locality may be more suitable for teaching 'Rivers'. Later, when considering your choice of distant place, you may want to think about how this locality extends and develops your pupils' understanding of their UK-based studies.

Teaching Geography — Topic or Subject Approach?

Schools are at various stages in developing their approach to the teaching of geography. In some, you will find geography taught through a topic approach, whilst other schools have adopted a more subject-based approach. Many schools are in the process of revising their geography planning to meet the 1995 changes to the Geography Order (for more details, see Halocha and Roberts, 1995). You may find that your school is already well advanced and has chosen its contrasting localities; links may already have been established with teachers in other areas. However, should you find that your school is in the early stages of such planning, you can find some good examples of twinning with other schools (to share information and resources) in Morron and Taylor (1992). Alternatively, the Central Bureau for Educational Visits and Exchanges will help you with world-wide introductions. If your school has access to the Internet, web sites may be another starting point. You may also choose to establish links with other teachers or friends who can provide you with the necessary information to make an interesting locality study. There are several published packs which could also be used; for instance, 'Rural Locality Pack: An Upland Village' (Harrison, Harrison, Lancaster and Lancaster, 1995).

Planning and Assessment at Key Stages 1 and 2

> The post-Dearing version of the Order covering Geography looks deceptively simple . . . However, it is still not in a form that will enable teachers to make school plans straight from the Order. (Morgan, 1995)

As we were discussing above, geography plans will need to be customized for your school. Schools are using a range of planning methods. Blocked and continuing units of work (SCAA, 1995) are being developed taking either a topic (e.g., 'Homes') or a subject-based approach. These represent the long-term planning of the school. Also, incorporated at this level are decisions about the scope and opportunities for fieldwork. You may be involved at this level of planning, but it is more likely that you will be working from medium-term planning to make the short-term plans for your class.

Medium-term planning looks at the programme of work to be taught to each year group of pupils and identifies opportunities for assessment. The Order states that:

> . . . pupils should be given opportunities, where appropriate, to develop and apply their information technology capability in the study of National Curriculum subjects. (DFE, 1995)

Consequently, the place of IT should be considered at this level of the planning process.

Short-term planning is what you will be doing for your class. However, you need to understand how your schemes link with the school plans and build progression for the children across the primary phase. As a reflective practitioner, when working with maps, for example, you will wish to make yourself aware of children's previous experiences in making and using maps so that you can continue to build up progression in their geographical understanding.

Enquiry Task — Investigating Your School's Approach to Planning

- Locate your school's geography policy.
- Have a look at the date. Has it been updated to match the 1995 Order?
- Identify the approach taken: is it topic-based or more subject-focused?

- What method of planning is used by your school — is it using the blocked and/or continuing method?
- Imagine you are tracking a child's progress through the school.
    Which localities will she/he study?
    How and where in the plans will the child gain knowledge about weather?
    How often is information technology clearly identified in the planning?
    What stages of environmental awareness are the children encouraged to develop?
    In the plans, are there a variety of methods and opportunities for assessment?

Specific Planning Strategies

In this section, ways of designing tasks to fit the learning objectives specified in the 1995 Order will be considered. Within both blocked and continuing styles of planning, an investigative focus is recommended to encourage children to ask questions about the world. In many books and journals this is called the *enquiry* approach. For teachers, this approach fits well with the notion of reflective practice. It is often based on children's first-hand experience. For example, if your school is on a busy main road, children may develop an enquiry encompassing which types of vehicle pass the school, changes in the traffic flow during the day, pollution levels, and the origins of the lorries and also the loads they are carrying. A discussion of ethical issues may flow from this. This will help children at Key Stage 1 to handle data and begin to see how their locality links with the wider world. Key Stage 2 children may be looking at *settlement* or *environmental change*, whilst becoming aware of how *places* fit into the wider geographical and social context. You may notice that this example does not follow the main headings in the Geography Order. Instead, it draws on the overall aims, combines *geographical skills, places* and a *theme* as defined by the Programme of Study for Key Stage 2.

This interrelationship between *values*, *skills*, *places* and *themes* cannot be overemphasized. It is not intended that you 'deliver' skills separately, without reference to places and thematic studies. Values are a continuing concern for the reflective teacher across the whole curriculum.

Bearing these underlying points in mind, we come to the design of your particular scheme of work. Schools have many different formats for planning children's work. You may wish to investigate the extent to which long- and medium-term plans provide features listed in the following enquiry task.

Enquiry Task — Schemes of Work

For the age group that you teach, look at your school's schemes of work for geography.

- Are all units of work the same length — for example, half a term — or are they varied to suit the content?

- Does the scheme have a clear rationale?
- If topic based, can you clearly define the geographical content?
- Is there a series of well-developed enquiry questions to guide the children's learning?
- Are a variety of teaching methods used where appropriate; for example, whole class, group and individual activities?
- Does the scheme make effective use of, or link back to, the locality of the school?
- Is fieldwork part of the programme?
- Are assessment points built into the planning?
- Can you see how children's knowledge and skills will progress? Is it a logical sequence?
- What range of resources may be used to encourage active learning?
- Is information technology planned effectively into the scheme?

The Integral Role of Assessment

In the enquiry task above, you were asked to look for assessment opportunities within the scheme of work. Ideally, you should have found them because schools have been given a lot of advice on the necessity of having assessment procedures which are integral to schemes of work. SCAA emphasizes that assessment should not be a bolt-on activity. Perhaps the reasons for this can be best seen by considering the guidance from the Geographical Association (Butt, Lambert and Telfer, 1995). They list the following reasons for assessment:

- to enhance pupils' learning;
- to measure (or possibly raise) standards;
- to check teaching objectives against learning outcomes;
- to recognize and plan for pupils' learning needs;
- to place pupils against different descriptors of achievement;
- to discover what pupils know, understand and can do;
- to help plan future learning objectives;
- to help pupils to devise personal targets;
- to evaluate teacher effectiveness/performance;
- to motivate both pupils and teachers.

They are not listed in order of importance. Your priorities will vary depending on how well you know the children, the time of year, and what you hope to achieve through assessment. Assuming that you have clear aims for your assessment then it becomes relatively easy to devise an appropriate programme of assessment. Eventually, you will be ready to conduct summative assessment by matching evidence from your collection of the children's work to the Level Descriptions.

Enquiry Task

Choose three or four of the reasons for assessment listed above. For each one devise an appropriate and different assessment task. Some possible methods include: observational notes; closed tasks; audio taping; collecting samples of work.

Check with the schools' assessment coordinator to see if the tasks are valid: are they giving you the information needed? Also check the reliability: are they consistent and fair, and would another teacher get the same results?

Below, we outline some of the aspects that, as a reflective practitioner, you are likely to consider in your planning.

Progression

We have emphasized the importance of planned progression. Each scheme of work needs to build on children's existing skill levels whilst adding new subject knowledge and concepts. Sometimes, you may choose to re-visit topics: a good example of this is the study of 'Weather'. In the reception class, children keep simple wall-charts of daily weather; later they can record the actual temperatures, cloud cover and rainfall; by Year 6, pupils should have built up a range of weather recording skills so they can access and compare data from various places around the world, possibly via e-mail or the Internet.

Differentiation and Special Needs

A responsibility of the reflective practitioner is to ensure access to a stimulating and challenging curriculum for children of all abilities. One of the many advantages of the geographical enquiry approach is that activities can easily be planned at a variety of levels of complexity. The way you structure the focused questions leads children off in either easy or complicated activities and thinking. Even on a fieldtrip, there can be a substantial difference in the range of work undertaken by different groups. Remember the access statement (DFE, 1995, p. 85) and its implication, namely that children with special needs have a right to be included in fieldwork in ways appropriate to their abilities. These and related issues deserve detailed attention beyond the scope available in this chapter: Sebba (1995) discusses these issues in depth and offers practical advice and examples; see also Chapter 16 in this book.

Information Technology

The use of information technology is at the present time still patchy. Some good practice exists but it is rarely linked well in progression across all subjects. This may well be an area where you can work with your colleagues to build up good practice. You need to spend some time finding out what levels of experience and skill your children have; for instance, to see where information technology is used at the moment in the curriculum. Where could IT be used in a relevant way within the geography curriculum? For example, a simple data handling package could be used to keep and ask questions about weather data collected by the children. You may need to explore which CD-ROMs may help children with their work on other localities. Perhaps even more important with this example are the questions, 'How is this use of IT really developing children's research skills?' and 'How will they make use of the information when they have it?' You may need to consider information technology which extends beyond a computer on a trolley: some of the many types of IT you may plan to use in your geographical enquiries include a programmable robot used in the early years to develop spatial and directional skills; a temperature probe for recording weather data; and a camcorder used to record, for example, people's views on a local environmental question. Once this is done there are very good opportunities to build IT into geography planning.

Flexibility

Although schemes of work are the most developed form of planning, you may need to be aware that the most effective whole school plans expect you to include wider geographical awareness throughout the curriculum. At Key Stage 1, the home corner may become an airport with many world-wide destinations: at Key Stage 2, globes and atlases may be used in historical studies to locate places where events occurred. Best practice manages to include reference to significant global events as they occur: this would include volcanic eruptions, floods, population movements, and locating other topical world events. Even though these brief discussions about global events may not have been planned into the formal curriculum for the time when they occur, they have two benefits. First, they help bring real world events into the classroom and give children the chance to ask questions. Second, they can be used to re-visit values, skills and concepts developed in geographical topics at times when geography is not the main focus of interest; for example, you might use an inflatable globe to locate the hurricane reported on the news, and use the opportunity to reinforce the skills and vocabulary of maps, atlases and globes and also to consider the hurricane's effects on people in the area.

At Key Stage 1, *communicating and handling information* might involve children using a concept keyboard overlay designed by you so as to use geographical vocabulary appropriate to their topic. A traffic survey can easily be put on a database from which children can ask further enquiry questions; for example, 'Which types of vehicles most frequently use the road?' *Controlling and modelling* might include giving instructions to a simple programmable robot to go on a journey. An example might be a Roamer transformed into a bus that has been programmed to collect passengers through a village marked out on the floor.

At Key Stage 2, in *communicating and handling information* children might use a desktop publishing package to create a newspaper which includes factual and ethical discussion about local environmental issues. Data handling can be extended (by the addition of 'monitoring') to handle more complex variables; for example, using an automatic weather station. Commercial simulations on geographical topics, such as rainforests, can be built into your planning to develop the *controlling and modelling* aspects of IT, whilst at the same time improving the children's subject knowledge and awareness of problematic environmental issues.

A good example of planning with a range of issues and flexibility in mind can be found in Mansfield (1996): this quite short article contains three medium-term plans for the study of rivers as well as considering issues such as progression, information technology and differentiation.

Fieldwork

Fieldwork is an important and enjoyable part of geography in primary schools. Fieldwork has to be part of your work if all the National Curriculum requirements are to be met. In this section, we will guide you into the planning process for effective and safe fieldwork, as well as introducing some curriculum considerations.

At its most local, fieldwork means planning for your children to work in the school and its grounds. The most distant fieldwork you are likely to find in primary schools may involve a residential visit to another European country. Many schools have looked closely at their range of visits to see how they enhance the curriculum and allow children to experience opportunities which reinforce progress and continuity in their learning. As a reflective teacher, you may wish to enquire further into the purposes and evaluation of school visits, and the degree of autonomy given to individual teachers in planning such visits.

All schools must have a policy about the practical arrangements for visits. This will have been agreed with your school's governing body. You may need to ask your headteacher to give you copies of the relevant paperwork, or to guide you to where it is kept in the school. This paperwork should include guidelines for staff on obtaining parental permission for children to take part in visits. Also, the school should have a policy in respect to asking parents for contributions towards the costs of fieldwork visits. Most schools now have prepared letters and forms which can easily be adapted for particular visits. Ask about your school's policy — reading this document should prevent you reinventing the wheel or going against existing agreements. Local Education Authorities and schools vary on their rules about matters such as pupil/teacher ratios for visits, so don't assume that your previous experience applies when you move to a new job.

The basis for high quality fieldwork is thorough planning. You need to know the location well, from both content and safety perspectives. This is now called 'risk assessment' by the Health and Safety Executive. Work out in detail the equipment you will need, and plan for large and small emergencies; for example, accidents or papers which take off in the wind!

Most teachers discuss the practical arrangements of a fieldtrip with their adult helpers; for example, who takes first responsibility for which children, and where you will have lunch. One of the easiest ways of enhancing your fieldwork is to brief your helpers on the educational aims of the visit and how they can enhance this work. For example, you may ask them to use a particular range of geographical vocabulary when they are talking with the children during a walk in the locality.

The *Fieldwork in Action* series of booklets edited by Stuart May and published by the Geographical Association (May, 1993, 1994, 1995, 1996) offers excellent detailed advice on planning and carrying out safe and interesting fieldwork. Teaching unions also publish useful leaflets on fieldwork. Your Local Education Authority may well have guidance papers, but the first place to seek advice is in the documents produced by the school and the experience of your colleagues. If you are a student teacher organizing a visit, it is essential that you, your classteacher, and your headteacher are fully aware of the legal position.

Integrating Skills, Places and Themes with Special Reference to Studying Distant Localities

Effective planning of units of study will be based on the relevant integration of skills, places and themes. At first, this process may appear to be complex. However, the integrated result has great possibilities for a strong knowledge component, development of skills and concepts: in addition, the result is likely to lead to a high interest factor amongst the children. It is worthwhile persevering so you start from a high quality base. This section will look at some examples from both Key Stages.

Key Stage 1

Since the Order allows you to choose a locality in an overseas location, it provides an excellent opportunity for children, at an early age, to broaden their awareness of the wider world. If you have been involved in studying local services or traffic problems, you could choose a place overseas which offers a rich contrast. This can introduce children to other cultures and other ways of doing things. If you have chosen a small village in Africa, for example, children can ask how their counterparts get to school, what their village is like, what they learn, and what a typical day is like. Remember that this locality should be of similar size to your own school locality, and that your children will need to avoid stereotyping people from another culture. Within this 'Overseas Location' topic, there is ample opportunity to develop geographical skills. The children will need to locate the place on a globe and to look at simple local maps; for example, one showing the buildings in the village. This may involve descriptions using simple geographical terms.

You may be fortunate in having links with a school of the type mentioned in the previous paragraph. If not, there are now a variety of excellent secondary sources with appropriate photographs, maps, house plans, daily routines, school timetables and menus which allow you to bring the other place to life. This can also be enhanced by the purchase of some foods grown in the other locality. Artefacts, videos and TV programmes may also be available. Depending on the environmental issues in that locality, the possibility exists to develop some aspects of the thematic study. Your children may have studied traffic pollution and looked at how they travel to school: it would be valuable to look at the same issues in Africa. This enquiry may offer contrasts and similarities, with the possibility of developing understanding and empathy.

Key Stage 2

The Key Stage 1 issues described above apply also to Key Stage 2 but now, in order to cover the whole Programme of Study, you have four thematic studies which will need integrating with geographical skills and places. The locality of the school is now wider than at Key Stage 1. Both an overseas location *and* a contrasting UK locality must be studied. The Order also encourages you to include examples from the European Union. You do need to choose places which help to develop the themes and enhance the skills: although you can introduce these in isolation, this neglects a real chance to study the interrelationships between various communities and places.

You may decide to choose a distant locality which helps develop work within the theme 'Environmental Change'. An example could be one which includes a river affected by pollution. The reasons for this pollution could be examined, and then the children could make comparisons between this river and a local river or stream. This can help the children understand that people around the world share similar environmental concerns but that there may be varying causes and effects. Map work on the two rivers will help children see the patterns in physical geography and reinforce their geographical vocabulary. They will begin to learn that all rivers share certain features; for instance, that they have a source and that humans interact with them in a range of ways. In this way, you can plan relevant activities which will help children study a place and themes found within it, and through these activities enable the children to develop geographical skills. Different topics will contain, in varying amounts, *skills*, *places* and *themes*, but good planning will ensure they are linked in ways which reinforce the strength of each one of them. We feel this point should be made clearly because the layout of the Geography Order gives an impression that skills, places and themes are separate sections.

Resources

As a reflective practitioner you will wish to evaluate the geography resources in your school. Some of the best materials are likely to be made in the school and relate directly to the school's locality and planned topics; for example, a wide range of local maps and photographs can be more useful than a set of textbooks with little meaning to the children. Some useful geography resources may be linked to other subjects; for example, you might look through the fiction library for stories linked to journeys or rivers.

You may also learn a great deal from talking to other teachers and the wide range of adults who come into school. One small conversation can make a huge difference to the quality of the work you do. The authors recently came across the following exciting example in a school. Work was well developed with the Ancient Greek part of the History Order and the staff had made contact with a school in Greece to develop the geographical work. Language might have been a problem, but on hearing of the proposed link, the school classroom assistant announced she spoke fluent Greek. The link has gone from strength to strength thanks to her skills!

Finally, and perhaps most importantly, every one of your children will bring to their geography work a great variety of experience, knowledge and understanding about both the locality and the wider world. If you can begin to appreciate your children's backgrounds, you will not only gain a fascinating insight into their thinking, but also have a valuable foundation upon which to extend and deepen their understanding of *our* world.

Sources of Help and Guidance

We have already mentioned ways in which your school and colleagues can help with your geography teaching. So that you do not feel you are working alone in a subject with which you may want some help, here is a list of a number of other places to look.

The Geographical Association

You may need to find out if your school is a member of the Association. If they have corporate membership, there should be materials in the school. You can also become a personal member. The Association can help you in a number of ways: with school or personal membership you receive four issues of the journal *Primary Geographer* annually. This journal contains practical articles and ideas, as well as up-to-date information on developments in primary geography. The Association publishes many booklets and teaching resources for primary geography. Members can buy these at reduced rates. Regional and national conferences are held frequently, and all teachers and people connected with schools are most welcome. You can make contact with them at: The Geographical Association, 343 Fulwood Road, Sheffield S10 3BP, telephone: 0114 267 0666.

The Local Education Authority

You could find out if your Local Educational Authority (LEA) has advisors or inspectors with responsibility for primary geography. Resources to support geography teaching may be available, and courses may be advertised. Different LEAs organize their support for schools in various ways, so find out what your Authority can offer. Many County Councils have an officer designated to develop European initiatives. If this interests you, find out who does this work and how they can help you.

The Times Educational Supplement

There are regular supplements devoted to geography and educational visits. It may be worth looking out for these as they contain many ideas and sources of up-to-date information.

Development Education Centres

These are located in many places around the country, so there may be one close to your school that you could contact. Most Centres have an excellent collection of resources, staffed by people who are keen to help you. However, there may be a charge for some services.

Field Study Centres

These may be run by LEA staff, or they may be independent organizations. You might find out from colleagues how they are used and the facilities they can offer. Some Centres are located locally whilst others are to be found further afield: the latter type give children the chance to experience a time away from home in another part of the country.

Urban Studies Centres

These are fewer in number but can often be excellent places to obtain resources and discuss your needs with experienced people.

Local Universities and Colleges

If you are teaching in a school, you may have students from a nearby university or college. It could be worthwhile asking visiting tutors how you can contact geography and humanities staff at their institution: the research and teaching interests of these staff may link with work you are doing, and they often have a range of contacts; for example, with schools in other European countries.

Your Local Secondary School

It is often valuable to talk with the member of staff in your school who is responsible for primary/secondary liaison work. He/she may be able to guide you into making contact with the geography staff in the secondary school.

Other Sources in Your School

Many documents have been produced in the last few years. In addition to the current National Curriculum Order, see if you can locate the grey National Curriculum Council *Curriculum Guidance* booklets, which include useful ideas on a number of issues including Environmental Education (NCC, 1990). The non-statutory guidance in the 1991 National Curriculum Geography Order (DES/WO, 1991) has some helpful ideas. The two booklets *Planning the Curriculum at Key Stages 1 and 2* (SCAA, 1995a) and *Consistency in Teacher Assessment* (SCAA, 1995b) are also helpful. Even if you cannot locate these, the activity might help you learn where and how information for staff is organized in your new school.

References

BUTT, G., LAMBERT, D. and TELFER, S. (1995) *Assessment Works*, Sheffield, Geographical Association.

DES/WO (1991) *Geography in the National Curriculum*, London, HMSO.

DFE (1995) *Key Stages 1 and 2 of the National Curriculum England*, London, HMSO.

HALOCHA, J. and ROBERTS, M. (1995) 'Geography', in ASHCROFT, K. and PALACIO, D. (eds) *The Primary Teacher's Guide to the New National Curriculum*, London, Falmer Press.

HARRISON, P., HARRISON, S., LANCASTER, J. and LANCASTER, L. (1995) *Rural Locality Pack: An Upland Village*, Dunstable, Folens.

MANSFIELD, K. (1996) 'Progression within the Rivers theme', *Primary Geographer*, 25, April, pp. 23–5, Sheffield, Geographical Association.

MAY, S. (ed.) (1993) *Fieldwork in Action 2: An Enquiry Approach*, Sheffield, Geographical Association.

MAY, S. (ed.) (1994) *Fieldwork in Action 3: Managing Out of Classroom Activities*, Sheffield, Geographical Association.

MAY, S. (ed.) (1995) *Fieldwork in Action: Planning Fieldwork*, Sheffield, Geographical Association.

MAY, S. (ed.) (1996) *Fieldwork in Action 4: Primary Fieldwork Projects*, Sheffield, Geographical Association.

MORGAN, W. (1995) *Plans for Primary Geography*, Sheffield, Geographical Association.

MORRON, M. and TAYLOR, B. (1992) *Cheshire Twinning*, Cheshire Education Services, Cheshire County Council.

NCC (1990) *Curriculum Guidance 7: Environmental Education*, York, NCC.

SCAA (1995a) *Planning the Curriculum at Key Stages 1 and 2*, London, SCAA.

SCAA (1995b) *Consistency in Teacher Assessment*, London, SCAA.

SEBBA, J. (1995) *Geography for All*, London, David Fulton Publishing.

8   Art

Jackie Chapman

Introduction

The teaching of art in schools has undergone many changes. In the 1960s and 1970s, educationalists rejected the formal, prescriptive, skills-based instruction of earlier times and instead concentrated on allowing children free expression through (some would say, largely unguided) experimentation. Teacher intervention was actively discouraged and a belief developed that skills teaching was something best left to craft lessons. Art was about 'spontaneity', 'freedom from constraints', and 'creativity', which should not be interfered with.

Since the introduction of the National Curriculum, we have almost turned full circle. It is now recognized that it is important not to simply 'facilitate' or to 'allow access to' art but to *teach* art. However, this doesn't mean that we must revert to the vocational emphasis of Victorian times, but rather that we can now employ the very best of all previous knowledge and methods in order to teach art in such a way that children are able to *investigate*, *make*, and *understand* art through *knowledge*, experimentation, creativity and skills development.

Angela Rumbold, then Minister of State for Education, in her speech to the National Association for Education in the Arts (NAEA) Conference in 1987 said:

> Education in the Arts is a fundamental part of our educational proposals for the curriculum. Without it we would be allowing our children to have missed a huge area of enrichment . . . and an essential preparation for all that lies before them in their adult life.

Art teaching in schools is open to much criticism. Part of the problem lies in the fact that there is a world full of art, which is seen by many as being quite separate from the art carried out in school. The task before us is to bring the two closer together, to establish some correlation between them. From time to time the media 'have a go' at art teaching (along with education standards in general); for example, British children's apparent inability to draw and paint when compared with Chinese children. It is sometimes difficult to cope with this sort of superficial criticism and to be sure that what we are doing as teachers is based upon sound educational theory and philosophy.

Another difficulty that new and inexperienced teachers may have to face is that of the nature of art knowledge itself. By this, I mean that there is a question you must ask yourself concerning the source of your knowledge about the teaching of art. Is it received wisdom? Is it based on your own art education? Is it based on current thinking and practice? There is a danger in basing your teaching style on that which you witnessed as a child in that you might perpetuate a cycle of poor, or outdated, practice.

Starting Points

You really need to start by deciding what your own philosophy of art is. This is not as daunting as it sounds: I mean simply that you need to decide what art *is*, what it means to you, where you can find it, and how you recognize it. There have been many attempts to define art and as many variations as a result.

> Art is the creation of forms symbolic of human feeling (Suzanne Langer)
>
> Art . . . in which we encode and share our response to experience. (Herbert Read)
>
> A real and true definition of art is logically impossible. (Morris Weite)

You may decide that art has to do with beauty or aesthetics; that it is about human endeavour and expression; or that it is a purely personal perception or response, *in the eye of the beholder*, as a student of mine once put it. Whatever you decide, you need to be as clear in your own mind about this as you are about what the concept of number is, or the elements of language are. If asked, we are quite comfortable about saying why we teach, say, reading. We may talk about developing literacy, providing children with a basic skill to equip them for the future, to enable them to deal with other subjects in the curriculum, to enable them to grow into literate adults thus avoiding the stigma of illiteracy, and to foster a love or appreciation of literature. *All* of these reasons can be attributed to teaching art and about art. On the other hand, I believe that filling up Friday afternoons, illustrating topic work, keeping children 'busy' when they have finished other work or to make a change from the more 'academic' subjects are *not* acceptable reasons for teaching art.

Enquiry Task

Draw two columns and head one 'Why teach reading?' and the other 'Why teach art?' In the first column, list all the reasons you can think of for teaching children to read.

Then do the same in the second column for art.

What parallels between the two lists can you draw?

Approaching the Teaching of Art

It is important to remember that *children* are at the centre of learning in art and this has important implications for the way art is taught. Teacher-centred or knowledge-centred approaches, therefore, are generally inappropriate because they do not allow for each child's unique experience. Instead, art teaching should:

- support, encourage and stimulate;
- focus on achievement rather than failure;
- ensure progression;
- ensure learning in, through, and about, art;
- provide direct and practical experience;
- allow for exploration, experimentation and the taking of appropriate expressive risks;
- value personal expression and response; and
- allow children to be involved in negotiating the direction their art experience takes.

However, the role of the teacher is not simply to provide resources and then to stand back and watch the results happen. Instead, the teacher's role is to take the *major responsibility* for planning the programme of work, to develop specific skills, to broaden the range of art experience and knowledge, and to maintain a high profile for art in the classroom and the wider community of the school.

You may find it helpful to consider teaching art like teaching any other curriculum subject. It takes no more 'God-given talent' to teach art *well* than it requires an eminent physicist to teach science. In other words, you do not have to be 'good at art' yourself in order to teach it. What it *does* require is a thorough grounding in pedagogy — planning for progression, development of knowledge, understanding, skills and concepts — and the ability to assess and evaluate these elements accordingly.

The learning sequence may be divided into four processes. **Perceiving** (sensing, receiving, experiencing); **transforming** (thinking, feeling, imagination, intuition and problem-solving); **expressing** (revealing thoughts, feelings and understandings in artistic form); and **appreciating** (reflecting, analysing, criticizing and valuing art). These processes are interconnected and interact with each other as the model in Figure 8.1 attempts to show. Here's a simple example of how the model may be applied to painting:

> When painting a landscape (**expressing**), a child is observing and absorbing a scene in the natural environment (**perceiving**); thinking about the way the scene might be interpreted or changed to achieve the desired effect (**transforming**); and standing back to view, analyse, criticize and reflect upon the work as it progresses and when it is completed (**appreciating**).

So, how do you start? I strongly suggest that you do not start by skimming through books of 'bright ideas for art activities' or 'a hundred arty things to make' and then, armed with fragments of ideas for finished products, to trawl through the National Curriculum document to find ways in which these prescribed activities fit the statutory requirements.

So, let's start again. Try starting with the National Curriculum document and the Key Stage requirements appropriate to your class. If you don't understand any of the terminology, you may find it helpful to do what you would do in any other circumstance — find out the meaning, perhaps by looking it up in a book (there are

Figure 8.1: The learning sequence

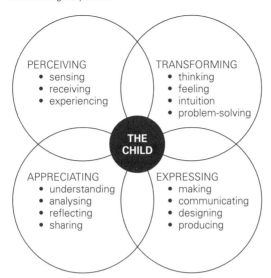

lots to choose from and some are listed in the bibliography at end of this chapter) and/or ask someone who knows (the art coordinator in your school, course tutor, local advisory service, etc). To help you make a start, there is a short glossary of terms at the end of this chapter, p. 129.

The next step is to decide how best to provide the children with a scheme of work which will enable them to meet these requirements.

Resources for Effective Art Teaching

It is very important to know what resources you have to work with. It may be helpful to start a new term/new teaching practice with an audit of resources to ensure that you have in stock at least basic drawing, painting, printing and modelling materials. These resources include a good range of drawing pencils (HB through to at least 4B), charcoal, coloured pencils, chalks, pastels and, perhaps, coloured inks. Paints are best kept in one form — water-based powder, blocks or ready mixed — and the range of colours kept to this simple formula:

Two reds —	one purple/red	(often called crimson or brilliant red)
	and one orange/red	(often called vermilion)
Two blues —	one purple/blue	(often called ultramarine or brilliant)
	and one green/blue	(often called sky blue or cyan blue)
Two yellows —	one orange/yellow	(often called brilliant yellow)
	and one green/yellow	(often called lemon yellow)
Black		
White		

From these basic colours, the children can mix all the others they are likely to need. Be cautious about buying lots of extra colours which look nice, but may not be suitable for mixing, and do not encourage children to experiment and mix for themselves. However, you may find it an advantage to buy some brilliant green as this is a secondary colour which is difficult to mix from the blues and yellows generally available to schools. Also, I have found that it is advisable to buy greater quantities of yellow and white than other colours as these are the ones which generally get used up the fastest. There is a case to be argued for withholding black from the children's palettes in the early stages of painting as it can destroy other colours and therefore needs to be used with care.

Printing, modelling and other materials should also be kept simple to avoid expensive, but little-used, luxuries.

I advise that you start planning the children's artwork from the point of view of what they will learn **in, through** and **about** art, not just what they will learn about a topic say, the Romans or the Victorians. You could start with one or more of the *elements* of art, as listed in the National Curriculum for Art document (DFE, 1995), and make these the basis of your topic work. After all, the world is, and always has been, made up of lines, shapes, colours, and forms, etc. Or you could start with an artist — there are enough to choose from without having to resort to the rather over-used Monet or Van Gogh. Whatever artist you choose, he or she will have worked in a time and place, and will have been influenced by, or will have had influence on, other artists, designers and craftspeople. If you don't know about any artists, you may need to do some homework and find out about some, or use the evidence which is all around you — the clothes you wear, the furniture you live with, the building you live in. Often these are created by artists, designers and craftspeople unknown to you.

Try the practical activity below for yourself, and then use the second part of the enquiry task to help you evaluate its value in the classroom.

Enquiry Task

Carefully study each garment you are wearing today (including socks, shoes, and hair decorations — even jewellery). Make a colour 'swatch' (a small piece of paper) to match as exactly as you can the colour, texture and pattern of each item. You can use any suitable medium — pencils, paints, crayons, pastels, etc. Make a particular detailed study of logos or patterns. Pin the 'swatches' together to make an overall 'picture' of what you are wearing.

Identify the areas of the Programme of Study for art which you have addressed during the above activity. You may find it helpful to think about the **strands** which are explained later in this chapter.

As you can see, this example does not require any more than basic resources of drawing and painting media. The 'swatches' can be made on scrap paper and need not take up a lot of space. The main resource for this lesson is the clothing the children themselves are wearing!

'I can't draw, so how can I teach?' — Exploding the Myth

This common misconception refers to visual art, but is also applied to the Arts in general, which is seen by some as requiring God-given talents, little understood, let alone practised by most people. We may appreciate music but not be able to perform at Symphony Hall; similarly, we may enjoy the artwork of others but not feel able to create a 'masterpiece' which sells for millions of pounds.

> Creativity is not a special faculty with which some children are endowed and others are not. It is a form of intelligence and as such can be developed and trained like any other mode of thinking. (Gulbenkian, 1982)

So, neither are we all Einstein, Pythagoras nor Shakespeare, yet the majority of primary teachers are happy to teach science, maths and English. Why? Because, I suggest, there is a recognized need to study the pedagogy of a subject, especially if there is a perceived weakness in personal knowledge or expertise, and we are prepared to read, research and practise in preparation for our science lessons, for example, and to make use of relevant literature and/or colleagues' strengths. So, the same applies to art. It is certainly not necessary to demonstrate your own art ability in order to facilitate children's learning in art; it *is*, however, necessary to know what, how, and *why* you are teaching the children in and through art and to know *how* to encourage their development (for instance, by providing good source materials, resources, and helping them to communicate and express themselves through their artwork).

Should personal research fail to provide the support you need, then there are other avenues to explore — tutors in your local college; colleagues in your own school, in the area or school cluster; and through inservice courses and/or professional organizations.

Cross-curricular Issues

> Art is a subject discipline in its own right and, like a primary colour, nothing else can stand in its stead, although it can be a key component in some interesting and valuable mixtures. (Morgan, 1993)

Many schools plan all or most curriculum areas around a central theme or topic. There is nothing wrong with this approach to teaching art (unless this is the only experience of art the children ever get). There are many opportunities to link art with other subjects.

Occasionally, you may find that you will further your objectives in art teaching more if you plan a term's work from an art standpoint. This does not mean teaching art to the exclusion of other subjects — indeed, many curricular areas can be incorporated into Arts-led topics. Here are just a few examples of the most obvious links to which you could add some of your own ideas.

Art-based topic	Main curriculum area links
Colour	Science
Design	Maths/Technology
The Pre-Raphaelite Movement	Literature and Poetry
The Art and Craft Movement	History (the Victorians)
Gill, Robertson, and the Heidelberg School	Geography
Architecture	Maths/History
Icons and Artefacts	RE

In the appendix, I have listed some more, perhaps less obvious, titles together with a short brainstorm of ideas connected with each one.

Starting points for an art programme could include the following:

- an artist — for example, Lowry, Hokusai, Pissaro, Richard Long, Mary Cassatt, Richard Hamilton, Bridget Riley, Beryl Cook;
- or a school or group of artists — for example, the Pre-Raphaelites, Australian Aborigines, Cubists, Minimalists, War Artists;
- or a technique — for example, printmaking, computer art, batik, pottery;
- or a concept — for example, portraits, boxes, holes, gaps and cavities, buildings, poppies, Rousseau's Tiger, movement and animation, letter forms, baskets and other containers.

Enquiry Task

Look up any of the names or concepts you do not recognize from the lists above. Add some more of your own.

Draw up a list of ideas associated with each one, identifying cross-curricular links where appropriate.

Having identified some starting points, you're now ready to start planning in more detail. You will need to find ways of avoiding having a fixed outcome in mind (a collage of a Norman village, a collection of butterfly mobiles, a wall display of . . . , etc), so that you do not stifle the children's creativity by expecting them to provide you with the means of realizing your finished mental picture. The outcome of such a prescriptive approach is at best a pretty display, at worst, thirty near-identical versions of your 'model'. In either case, the question you *must* ask is, 'What have the children learned in and about art?'

So, instead of a finished *product*, have the *process* in your mind when you plan. This does not necessarily mean a 'skill' (which is not in itself teaching the children anything about art) but a progression of understanding.

You may be comforted by the thought that your aim in teaching art to primary school children is not to train them for a professional career, but rather to help them to an understanding of the central rôle art plays in life. Your important concern is not how to measure progress on a rigid scale, but how to evaluate each child's aims in relation to individual intent.

Identifying Progression

Progression can be ensured by:

INCREASING THE RANGE OF EXPERIENCE
e.g.   recording from experience, imagination and observation; exploring a range of two and three dimensional media.

INCREASING THE DEMAND
e.g.   the stimulus; the task or brief; complexity of process; challenge of artists', craftspersons' or designers' work.

INCREASING THE QUALITY OF PERFORMANCE
e.g.   confidence in undertaking task; expression; awareness and insight in applying knowledge to own work. (SCAA, 1994)

At the beginning of each Key Stage Programme of Study there are six statements which relate to general balance, range and scope at each Level. The statements, which do not change from Key Stage to Key Stage, are about the balance of art work:

Pupils should be given opportunities to experience approaches to art, craft and design, including those that involve working individually, in groups and as a whole class. (DFE, 1995)

The fourth statement is concerned with the central role of art and what is called *artistic elements*. At Key Stage 1, children are *introduced* to concepts of visual form; at Key Stage 2, activities should *extend* children's understanding; at Key Stage 3, children's understanding is extended even further to include how *meaning* is communicated in making images and artefacts. From an *exploration* of artistic elements at Key Stage 1, children are encouraged to *investigate*, then at Key Stage 2 and at Key Stage 3 they are expected to *interpret* them. You may ask, 'What is the difference?' Try this short task for yourself:

Lines/mark marking
- Fill a piece of paper with lines. How many different lines can you make? Describe them.
- Carefully draw the lines in a selection of leaves — the angle and position of the veins, etc. How do these relate to the outline shape of the leaf and the stem? Compare your drawing with those of artists such as Henry Moore — or look in a biology text book to see how and what these drawings tell us about the leaves.

- Collect some Henry Moore drawings of sleeping figures in the air-raid shelters during World War II. Look for the *outline* of the figures — are there any? How did Moore show the rounded form of his figures with the use of line?

Enquiry Task

Match each of the activities above to the appropriate section of the National Curriculum for Art.

For each activity, identify at least one planned learning objective. Can you identify the progression?

The fifth statement at the beginning of each Key Stage Programme of Study is about the range and scope of the art curriculum: the implication of this statement for schools ensures that not just *artists*, but also *craftworkers* and *designers*, are included in the art curriculum. A short list of examples is provided in the document, but as with any list it is not exhaustive, including, as it does, graphic design and architecture but omitting, for example, computer design. This highlights the danger of providing a list of examples as, often, something or somebody will be missed out.

You may wish to make use of secondary source material to familiarize yourself with the wide range of art-related activities. In order to help you choose, there is a short list of useful books at the end of this chapter, p. 128.

You are also encouraged to ensure that works of art, craft and design are introduced from the *locality* as well as a variety of cultures, and that *contemporary* work is experienced alongside historical examples.

There is a fairly simple way of checking progression from Key Stage to Key Stage. Not only does the General Programme of Study remain the same, but the Key Stage-specific Programmes of Study are arranged with an alphabetical system, with each one matching with the next Key Stage, thus providing *strands* which can be followed through systematically. These strands are central to providing a comprehensive art curriculum throughout the three Key Stages.

Strand 1: Record responses to direct experience, memory and imagination. It is important to realize that direct experience, memory and imagination are three different sources. To record a scene or an object, a feeling, a sound, a taste, or any other sort of direct experience, may take a variety of forms; for instance, verbal, written, drawn, a mixture of all three, a rubbing, a print or a photograph. On the other hand, recording from *memory* requires recall of a past experience and the ability to relate or retell it visually or in some other form. *Imagination*, of course, requires no direct experience and it has been said knows no bounds. Memory and imagination can become linked and it may be necessary to untangle one from the other — especially given the wealth of imaginative stimulus provided by the media. Often children will 'make up' something which was, in fact, the creation of an animator or a TV director. Similarly, young children in particular will tend to draw what they think or imagine is there, and you may want them to focus on close observation for their drawing.

Strand 2: Gather and use source material to stimulate and develop ideas. Source material can be either *primary* (i.e., using direct observation) or *secondary* (using books, reproductions, photographs, etc). You can create sketches, make notes, take photographs and so on which can then be used to design a finished piece of art work or stand in their own right.

Strand 3: Explore and use materials, tools and techniques in practical work on a variety of scales. The exploration of materials, tools and techniques can result in the creation of work: conversely, planned work may require specific skills and use of materials which need to be practised. There will certainly be a degree of overlap here with design and technology. Providing children with the opportunity to work on a variety of scales is important too — perhaps with a magnifying glass and a sharp pencil or biro on one occasion and with broad, flat brushes on a large class mural on the next.

Strand 4: Review and modify work as it progresses. This involves you in talking about the children's work; asking questions about it, get them to say how they might continue their work.

The four strands outlined above are all concerned with Investigating and Making, the area with which most teachers are familiar. The following two strands are concerned with Knowledge and Understanding.

Strand 5: Develop understanding of art, craft and design, and

Strand 6: Respond to and evaluate different kinds of art, including their own and others' work. (DFE, 1995)

It is these two areas of 'expertise' (Knowledge and Understanding) which many teachers worry about. There are an increasing number of books and resource packs available which will help you. However, one of the most important aspects of Knowledge and Understanding is the realization that art, craft and design is all around us; that it is not confined to framed images on the walls of art galleries. Another important aspect is that responding to art works is not the exclusive right of erudite 'professionals', art historians and the like, but is the right of us all. Thirdly, it is quite acceptable to respond to artwork in a *negative* way — you don't have to like it! Personal preferences about art are just that — personal. What is important is awareness and the ability to make informed judgments.

It is not important to know the biographical details of artists — although they can help to set the geographical and historical context of a piece of work. What is important is to try and find out where their ideas stem from. It might be quite straightforward to look at a landscape and understand that the artist was clearly inspired by the beauty of the scene (not all landscapes fall into this category). However, to appreciate the work of contemporary artists such as Andy Goldsworthy or Tony Cragg, for example, you may need to look back at their earlier work to follow the progression which has led to their latest pieces. Very few artists will set out to make art unless there has been some preparatory work and development of a theme or idea. Often, when you are aware of this development, it is easier to understand the piece itself.

Lastly, children cannot make art in a visual vacuum — after all, you can't learn a language without hearing it spoken or seeing it written. When we make art we make meanings as well as marks. There are no fixed rules, only shared values and beliefs, and children need regular opportunities to share their developing ideas about art. Lewis Carroll's heroine, Alice, said, 'How do I know what I think till I hear what I say?' Language is so important when sharing artworks with children. Initially, children may base their judgments on personal preference — I like it, so it's good. Good art teaching will help them make informed judgments.

Relationships between Art, and Design and Technology

Because the National Curriculum Order for Art calls for art, craft, and design to be covered within the title 'art' there are many obvious connections to be made with design and technology. You may find it helpful to not only recognize these similarities, but also the important differences. The Non-Statutory Guidance (NCC, 1992), provides a useful section on this issue and lists the 'unique characteristics of art in the National Curriculum' which include:

- the emphasis on visual literacy;
- specific technical skills;
- harnessing observation, memory and feelings in order to express and communicate ideas in visual form;
- a distinct body of knowledge (of artists and of art itself);
- response to the work of artists.

Enquiry Task

Have in front of you the Programme of Study for Art and the Programme of Study for Design and Technology for whichever Key Stage you teach.

Go through and highlight the similarities between the two. Now, pick out the differences.

Check what you have identified with those set out in the Non-Statutory Guidelines.

A Word about IT

Computer art is a fast growing and ever-changing area which would be impossible to address adequately in this short chapter. There are dozens of art programs suitable for primary children and too many variables in terms of software/hardware compatibility to cover here. There are, however, some good books available to help you; see, for example, Mathieson (1993) on the list of suggested reading at the end of this chapter. Alternatively, you could turn to the chapter on information technology in this book.

IT is not simply concerned with computers. There are many other slightly 'lower-tech' possibilities to consider using, such as overhead projectors (for enlarging drawings, making silhouettes, etc); photocopiers (for making multiple images or distorting images); cameras (both still and video); audio equipment (for initial stimulus or for multi-media presentations); slide projectors, and so on.

Equal Opportunities and Special Needs

It is a statutory requirement (as for other curriculum subjects) to teach art 'to the great majority of pupils in ways appropriate to their abilities' (DFE, 1995). Appropriate provision should, therefore, be made for pupils who have particular needs, such as visual impairment. In the case of art, it maybe helpful to plan for children with a particular need of this nature to have more tactile experiences, such as working in bas relief, clay or textured materials. It is also necessary to ensure that you teach a broad and balanced curriculum across and within each curriculum subject too. The Art Order calls for pupils:

> . . . to be introduced to the work of artists, craftspeople and designers in order to develop their appreciation of the richness of our diverse cultural heritage. The selection should include work in a variety of genres and styles . . . from a variety of cultures, Western and non-Western. (DFE, 1995)

There is a wealth of resource material made by artists, craftspeople and designers who do not fall into the category of 'dead, white, European males'. So, instead of concentrating on the well-known Monet, Van Gogh, Constable, or Picasso, you could extend your personal knowledge by finding some examples of art, or craft or design made by:

- a black woman painter;
- a potter who currently works in your locality;
- a Japanese designer;
- a disabled artist.

It doesn't matter if you can't find out any biographical details of these art makers. What is important is that you find ways of introducing them to the children. In the case of a local artist, invite him or her into school, or arrange a visit to his/her studio.

Evaluation and Assessment

The most important question you must ask yourself is, '**What are the children learning *in* and *through* art?**' You can use this question to check your planning in advance as well as to evaluate your lessons afterwards. If you can't answer this question honestly it could mean that your children are learning little or nothing in or through art. They may have 'made things'; they may have 'cut out and stuck down materials'; they may have 'learned about working with others and sharing resources', but they may not have reached the objectives you had for teaching art.

If you ask the children to work to a set pattern — for example, 'make a shape like this and stick it here' . . . or 'cut around the template to make your puppet/ Christmas decorations/funny animal . . .' — all they are learning is to follow directions to make a predetermined outcome. This is the sort of approach to making things that popular children's television programmes like *Blue Peter* take. It *may* be fun, it *may* look nice, but are the children experimenting, exploring or interpreting art media? Where is the *creative* element? This sort of pastime is best left to the *Blue Peter* presenters.

Enquiry Task

Take a good, long look at a classroom. It may be your own room, or that of a colleague's, or be one in a school which you are visiting. If this is not your own classroom, you may not be able to answer some of the questions which follow, so it would be most valuable if you could enquire further from the classteacher about his/her methods of teaching art.

The overall impression may be one of bright, cheerful displays, lots of children's artwork, colourful patterns, carefully executed drawings, and so on. Now look very closely at each display of artwork and ask yourself some of these questions.

- Which *specific* aspect of the National Curriculum for Art has been addressed?
- What have the children been learning *in* or *about* art? Did they learn a new *skill* in art, and did this skill extend their *understanding* or *perception* of art?
- Can you identify any of the elements of art which may have been taught and, if so, to what *depth* have they been investigated?
- Is the work genuinely that of the children, or do you think it was teacher-led, or teacher-finished? Can you see evidence of the use of pre-drawn templates, for example?
- Are all the pieces of work *individual responses* or do they all look alike?
- Is the work art-based or is it illustrated topic work, or is it the result of a maths or a science lesson?
- Do the children ever help the teacher mount and display their art work and do they ever themselves mount and display their work?
- How does the teacher ensure that each child's work is represented at some time in the displays?
- Are experimental pieces ever displayed no matter how 'unfinished' or 'messy' they may look?
- Do the displays tell you anything about the methods employed in making the art?
- Are there labels on the displays and, if so, do they tell you anything of the method or progression of work?

If you manage to obtain answers to all or some of these questions, you need now to think critically about the artwork which is going on in this classroom.

Figure 8.2: The learning cycle

Figure 8.2: The learning cycle

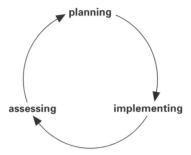

The questions provided in the enquiry task above should not be confrontational or challenging; indeed, teachers are constantly being encouraged to question their own practice in the interest of professional development.

Assessment

Assessing children's artwork is something which appears to many teachers to be very difficult. You will need to consider how you might measure a child's 'artistic ability' when factors like creativity, personal expression and aesthetics are involved.

If your planned learning objectives are clear (and have been based on the requirements of the National Curriculum for Art), then you should be able to implement your plans and then assess whether or not, and to what extent, each child has achieved those objectives. This, in turn, should help you to plan your next objectives. In other words, following the cycle of planning, implementation and assessment, as Figure 8.2 illustrates.

Although formal (SAT) assessment in art is not a statutory requirement, on-going teacher assessment in all subjects, including art, is. Children's progress in art, therefore, like any other subject, is determined through observation, listening, discussing work with the children, and occasional assessment tasks which I will say a little more about later in this section. To back up your own professional judgment you will need to collect *evidence* in the form of notes, a small sample of annotated work and, perhaps, photographs of larger scale or three dimensional work. This evidence can then be used to enable you or your colleagues to plan for the next stage of the children's artistic development.

It may be helpful to think of assessment in art as comprising three elements:

Creative ability (for example, has the composition been well thought out? have line, tone, colour, pattern, or shape been used to increase visual interest?);
Technical ability (for example, is the drawing accurate? has line been used in a variety of ways? have colours been mixed carefully? have the tools been used effectively/safely?);

Contextual ability (for example, has the source material been reflected in the work?).

The pervading question is, '**Have your planned learning objectives been met and to what degree?**'

In order to help teachers with the process of assessment and to ensure progression, many schools suggest that their teachers set a similar task at the beginning (or end) of each term, half year, or year. In this way, it is possible for the teacher, and the children, to see how, for example, drawing ability, handling paint or modelling skills have developed. The sort of tasks which are suitable for this type of assessment could include: a self portrait; an observational drawing of a plant; a painting from memory of 'my house'; a clay or Plasticine model of an animal. There are many other examples, of course, but you need to ensure two things: (i) that the task can be easily repeated by others in the future; (ii) that there is an opportunity for children who may be better at one kind of task than another to succeed (for example, some children are better handing two dimensional materials than three dimensional ones and vice-versa).

Margaret Morgan (1993), suggested approaching assessment via three basics, the child, the teacher and the work. In summary:

The Child	*The Teacher*	*The Work*
• as a maker • as an assessor (of own development) • as evaluator (taking in account what is or has been useful and valuable)	• as assessor (of the child's performance and outcomes) • as evaluator (measuring the educational value based on evidence and observations; also own performance) • as catalyst, provider and planner (planning developmentally, organizing environment, providing resources and support, materials etc.)	• looked at in sequence (accumulated evidence)

As stated elsewhere in this chapter, it is essential to link planning with assessment, and it is important to check on the balance of art activities covered. Realistically, it is not possible to cover everything in the space of a term or even a year, but you may find the following check list helpful. For example, draw a connecting line between each of the practical activities the children have been engaged in and the methods used. It may be possible to connect each one with every other but this single example shows how it works with printmaking as an example:

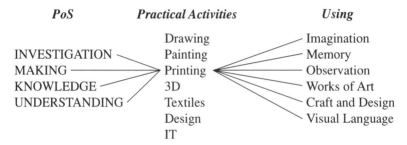

PoS	Practical Activities	Using
INVESTIGATION	Drawing	Imagination
MAKING	Painting	Memory
KNOWLEDGE	Printing	Observation
UNDERSTANDING	3D	Works of Art
	Textiles	Craft and Design
	Design	Visual Language
	IT	

In this example, prints were made using purely imaginary images, images made from what the children remembered seeing, or images derived from observational drawings made of leaves and plants. The children were introduced to the work of William Morris, a designer who often used natural forms as inspiration for his work, and to Paula Rego, who made a series of prints based on the imaginary characters in nursery rhymes. The children then made some initial designs using the computer to experiment with the effects of changing colours, and with repeating patterns using the photocopier to help speed up the process. The children discussed the differences between prints and paintings, and started to learn some of the specialist vocabulary associated with printing. During this project the children investigated an area of art, made art themselves, gained knowledge about art and artists, and understanding of some art concepts (i.e., part of the Programme of Study).

In addition, you may find it useful to keep records along these lines:

Artists' work used _____	Male/Female ☐
_____	Western/non-Western ☐
_____	Contemporary/Historic ☐

Art topics covered	Other topic-related art

Large-scale work	2D/3D

Finally, ask yourself, or your colleagues, *when* art is taught and the message this might convey. Traditionally maths or language work is taught first thing in the morning, while the children are fresh and alert, but art is so often left until the end of the day when the children are inclined to be tired, and we all know that Friday afternoon can be a difficult time. There is, of course, a need to ensure balance in your curriculum planning, but it may be worth considering this example of quite the opposite approach taken by a Sheffield school situated in an area of particular social deprivation. Some years ago, the staff made a conscious decision to start every day with an art lesson in order to stimulate the children's creativity and to 'set the tone' for the day. In this school, every child's work is valued, with the resulting growth in self-esteem especially noticeable in those children who are frequently affected by unsettled home circumstances.

A Final Word

Remember, you don't have to be good at art in order to teach it well — you just need to be a good teacher.

References

DFE (1995) *Key Stages 1 and 2 of the National Curriculum*, London, HMSO.

CALOUTE GULBENKIAN FOUNDATION (1982) *The Arts in Schools — Principles, Practice and Provision*, London, Caloute Gulbenkian Foundation.

MORGAN, M. (1993) *Art in Practice — Motivation and Development 3–12 Years*, Oxford, Nash Pollock.

NCC (1992) *Non-Statutory Guidance*, London, HMSO.

SCAA (1994) *The National Curriculum and its Assessment*, London, SCAA.

SWANWICK, K. (ed.) (1990) *Papers from NAEA 1983–1990*, London, National Association for Education in the Arts.

Suggested reading

BERGER, J. (1972) *Ways of Seeing*, London, Penguin.

CENTRE FOR THE STUDY OF THE ARTS (1994) *The Censape Tapes*, comprising *Understanding Progression in Primary Art*; *Planning for Progression in Primary Art*; *Reviewing Progression in Primary Art*, Plymouth, Plymouth University.

CLEMENT, R. and PAGE, S. (1992) *Primary Art Series*, comprising *Principles and Practice in Art*; *Investigating and Making in Art*; *Knowledge and Understanding in Art*; *Picture Resource Pack* and *Teacher's Book*, Harlow, Oliver and Boyd.

MEAGER, N. (1993) *Teaching Art at Key Stage 1*, Corsham, National Society for Education in Art and Design.

MEAGER, N. and ASHFIELD, J. (1995) *Teaching Art at Key Stage 2*, Corsham, National Society for Education in Art and Design.

MATHIESON, K. (1993) *Children's Art and the Computer*, London, Hodder and Stoughton.

MORGAN, M. in association with SUFFOLK COUNTY COUNCIL (1988) *Art 4–11: Art in the Early Years of Schooling*, Oxford, Blackwell.

PEPPIN, A., SMITH, R. and TURNER, A. (1992) *Approaches to Art*, London, Ginn.

Appendix

Some titles for art-based topics with a short collection of ideas associated with each one. I am indebted to colleagues in Australia for some of them.

Barriers	edges, frames, borders, boundaries, x-ray vision and things in cages and boxes; walls, fences and gates; mazes.
Camouflage	animals, plants, building designs and eye sores; make-up and body paint; war machines and soldiers, teapots in disguise; fakes and things that pretend to be what they're not.
Changes	changing fashions, changing pictures, drawing changes; things that do not change; aging and immortality.
Dirt	what kind of stuff, what we like to do with it and in it; dyes, stains, pigments; buried treasure, fossils and buildings made from mud; tunnels.
Faces	portraits, family resemblances, Identikit portraits, caricatures, one-line face drawings, face painting, masks and decoration.
Flags	and Trademarks — national flags, company logos, advertisements, trademark colours, personal identity marks, signatures, initials and symbols as trademarks.
Inside–Outside	holes, openings, gaps and cavities; doorways, secret places, hollow things; open and closed shapes; inside looking out, outside looking in; pop-up pictures.
Layers	and cross-sections; x-rays, mosaics, glazes, skeletons and bones; layers of paint, rock strata, sawing things in half.
Looking	optical illusions, telescopes, magnifying glasses, drawing from memory, different points of view, creating depth and perspective.
Miniatures	small things, replicas, aerial views, scale models; size relationships; working small; giant ants, mini elephants, baby giants and giant babies.
Reflections	mirrors, distorting mirrors, reflections in water, building with mirrors, matt and glossy surfaces and what Monet painted for the last 20 years of his life (clue: ponds!).
Shadows	making shadows, drawing shadows, silhouettes, shadow puppets, col-oured shadows, shadows in pictures, shadows at night.
Wear and decay	how things age, wear down, erode or rot; the preservation of art, food and people; old age; temporary art, glyptic sculptures; mummies and tombs.
Wet and dry	melting, splashing, fountains, water falls, the colours of water, paint-ing wet paper; liquid containers, glasses, cups, mugs and teapots.

A Short Glossary of Art Terms

Abstract Non-representational (*not* to be confused with 'modern' or 'contemporary').

Bas relief Sculpture in which the subject does not stand far out from the ground on which it is formed.

Batik Designs are made by making a resist

with hot wax painted or dripped onto fabric, which is then allowed to cool before being dyed.

Biscuit firing (or 'Bisque') Firing clay work in a kiln to a temperature (at least 900°C) which produces porous, but durable ceramic.

Block printing Printing on to paper or fabric with a block cut from lino, potato, polystyrene, etc.

Ceramics Clay objects that have been fired in a kiln.

Collage Making pictures by sticking miscellaneous items to a backing sheet or board.

Complementary colours Colours that are directly opposite to one another in the colour wheel.

Composition Putting together all or some of the basic elements of art (line, colour, tone, texture, form, pattern, shape) so that there is a satisfactory relationship between them.

Contemporary (or 'modern') Art of the present time (not to be confused with 'Abstract' — see above).

Earthenware Pottery which has been fired to 1040–1140°C.

Elements of art Colour, tone, line, shape, pattern, texture, form.

Fixative Colourless liquid that is sprayed onto charcoal and chalk drawings to prevent smudging. (Hair lacquer works quite well too!)

Glazing Method by which ceramic pieces are made waterproof. Glazes are made up of chemicals which turn to liquid at a very high temperature and cool to a glass-like finish. Can be coloured or transparent.

Glyptic sculpture The process of carving a shape from a solid mass (as opposed to moulding or joining pieces together).

Hue Another name for colour.

Intensity The degree or depth of colour (e.g., pale to bright red on the petals of a poppy).

Kiln An oven that reaches very high temperatures (800°C plus) and turns clay to pottery.

Kinetic art Artwork which moves in some way e.g., a mobile.

Laminating An alternative to papier mâché

in which strips of paper are dipped in glue and pasted on to a framework to build up solid shapes which can then be painted. If PVA glue is used, the resulting structure is very strong.

Medium The material used to produce art e.g., paint, clay, charcoal.

Monoprinting A shiny surface is rolled with printing ink. A design is made by scratching into the ink. Paper is placed on top and rubbed gently to transfer the design.

Mosaic Pictures and designs made by embedding small pieces of tile, stones, or shells into plaster or cement.

Mural A painting made straight on to a wall.

Neutral colours Usually refers to white, grey and black.

Papier mâché Made by soaking shredded newspaper in a bucket of water, then stirring in paste powder until the mixture reaches the consistency of dough. See also **Laminating**.

Pencils Pencil leads come in grades of hardness and softness. The hard (grey) leads are in the H range; the soft (black) leads in the B range. The higher the prefix number the more striking the difference – e.g., 4B is softer and blacker than 2B and 2H is harder and greyer than an H. The mid point is HB which has all-round uses, but the B range is more suitable for drawing.

Press printing Pictures are made by pressing small objects (corks, bottle tops, etc) on to paper after being charged with ink or paint.

Primary colours Yellow, red, blue. Colours that cannot be made from mixing other colours (not to be confused with science primary colours).

Proportion The relative size of one shape to another, or amount of one colour to another.

PVA A Poly-Vinyl Acetate solution of plastic-like particles in water which evaporates leaving a transparent film. Can be used as an adhesive or can be mixed with paint or water.

Sawdust kiln Clay work is dried and loaded into a metal dustbin or suitable container, packed with sawdust, which is then set alight. It is slow burning but can reach temperatures sufficient to biscuit-fire and even glaze.

Scale   The relative size of a drawing or painting to the actual subject being studied.

Secondary colours   A mixture of two of the primary colours.

Shade   When black is added to a primary or secondary colour, a shade of the original colour is produced.

Template   A shape which serves as a guide for reproducing that shape, e.g., a saucer could be used as a template for drawing a circle.

Three-dimensional   Forms which have depth or are surrounded by space, as opposed to being flat.

Tie dye   Material is bound with string or elastic bands and dipped into dye.

Tint   When white is added to a primary or secondary colour, a tint of the original colour is produced.

Tone   A way of referring to the lightness or darkness or colour.

Transfer printing   Printing ink is applied to a surface and then transferred to paper.

Two-dimensional   On a flat plane.

Viewfinder   A piece of paper or card with a hole (usually rectangular) cut in it. Useful for sketching to isolate a subject or part of a subject.

Wax resist   Thin water-based paint or dye is washed over a wax crayon drawing or rubbing.

9   Music

Patricia Thompson

Introduction

As John Keats wrote in the opening lines of his poem *Endymion*[*]

> A thing of beauty is a joy forever:
> Its loveliness increases; it will never
> Pass into nothingness; but still will keep
> A bower quiet for us, and a sleep
> Full of sweet dreams, and health, and quiet breathing.

Music is a thing of beauty. It can bring joy into the lives of those who experience it, both presently and long after the moment has passed. How often do we try to find out the name and composer of an appealing piece of music to enable us to re-live that primary aesthetic experience over and over again? Often it is the shyest child in the class who loiters with intent at the end of a session to ask you about the music just heard. It is your responsibility to enrich and bring alive those experiences for pupils of all ages, abilities, backgrounds and situations. This may appear a daunting task to those who feel that their own knowledge, skills and understanding of music leave much to be desired. But music is a very sociable art. It is best enjoyed in the presence of others, and the voyage of discovery undertaken together, with the key emphasis being on the word *enjoyment* — a word used for the first time in the 1995 Statutory Order for Music (DFE, 1995). This is a wonderful opportunity for you to capitalize on the fun element in learning through enjoying making and experiencing music with others.

The National Curriculum for Music was the first time in the United Kingdom that statutory provision had indicated the need for every child to be able to play a musical instrument so as to fulfil the requirements of the Programme of Study for each Key Stage. This obviously has considerable implications for a class teacher trying to follow the Programmes of Study for music, if they feel they do not possess basic levels of musical knowledge, understanding or skills.

---

[*] Reproduced with permission from Book I of Endymion, Billy Bembo Ltd.

The most successful music lessons in school are likely to be those where you engage children in music making, not necessarily where you display your own high level of attainment. The emphasis is on practical participation: direct, first-hand experience of the elements of music through active and participatory music making. The seven main elements, or characteristics of music — pitch, duration, dynamics, tempo, timbre, texture and structure — are conveniently listed and enumerated in the Programme of Study for each Key Stage, a recurrent theme like a *leitmotif* or *ostinato* (please see glossary of musical terms at the end of the chapter for definitions, p. 145). Practically, these seven musical elements can provide a most useful planning outline, providing you with a framework on which to place lesson planning.

In the opening statement to the Programme of Study for each Key Stage, you are exhorted to 'bring together requirements from both **Performing and Composing** and **Listening and Appraising** wherever possible'. A cycle of activities may be planned, involving the critical faculties of listening and appraising at every stage of the process. For example, it is important when either performing or composing to bring into play listening and appraising skills to develop necessary critical faculties which enhance the final musical product.

The educational benefits of being in direct contact with music are well understood — the quality of being *in the moment*, of being totally absorbed in what is happening musically at that moment of time. Music has the gift to influence physical, emotional, and intellectual aspects of life, developing musical and social skills, physical coordination and language acquisition, to name but some of the main advantages. Many of us have been fortunate to have seen and heard music produced by children in the classroom for whom the act of composing or improvising has been a vital cathartic experience, maybe stimulated by a feeling or an experience that they felt unable to verbalize. For example, I observed a child with a difficult home life who found school equally difficult, but who unexpectedly produced an impressive musical composition. The teacher persuaded him to perform the piece to his classmates, earning their considerable respect along with a new sense of confidence and self-worth. The process had obviously provided a much needed positive channel for release of emotions: we hear daily of less positive results of outpouring of emotion. At the 1996 Music for Youth South Bank conference on Key Stage 2 music, part of the Music for Youth's National Festival, Gavin Henderson, Principal of Trinity College of Music, said in his opening address that, music was more beneficial than team games in promoting qualities of enthusiasm, confidence, appreciation of excellence and sensitivity to others. 'We who teach music are relegated to a role of frivolous optional extra,' he said. 'Yet it is we who unquestionably hold the means to the prevention of crime and to a vista of hope for many whose lives are deprived of purpose and achievement.'

Enquiry Task

- Identify which children in your class especially benefit from music.
- Observe them during various musical activities.
- Identify what they have learned.
- Develop a system for recording this learning.

Hidden Curriculum

So, how to provide that vista of hope for all children, with varying degrees of musical experience, and in all kinds of situations, whilst meeting statutory requirements? *Music in the National Curriculum* (DFE, 1995) is a slight, slim document. This is liberating as it does not prescribe specific music to be studied, nor particular pedagogic methods of teaching and learning. There is a whole, exciting, diverse world of music out there, waiting to be explored and discovered. The best educational experiences will occur where you are enthusiastic about a particular piece of music, and bring that passion, enthusiasm, and sense of exploration and discovery when introducing it to children. Whether you choose Javanese Gamelan music, piano music by Schumann, a film score by Michael Nyman or a Scottish Folk Song, the main accompanying ingredient must be your enthusiasm for that particular music. This will transmit wonderfully to children: enthusiasm is as contagious as measles!

It is interesting to note that what is omitted from the statutory document appears to be more pertinent than what has been included. The hidden message of the interlinking of the two Attainment Targets — AT1 *Performing and Composing* and AT2 *Listening and Appraising* — throughout the Programmes of Study is that you should not plan in isolation, but rather choose activities that will involve both Attainment Targets simultaneously in a seamless circle of activities. For example, you might find an appropriate extract of music for the children to listen to and appraise. Through careful questioning about the extract, focus their attention on a particular aspect of music, and use that musical element as the basis for the children's compositions. After some time these compositions may be performed, even recorded onto cassette, requiring development of listening and appraising skills to achieve both the best possible performance and the most musically satisfying end product, the composition.

The range of opportunities listed down the left-hand column on the second page of each Programme of Study (DFE, 1995) has the telling ratio of two-to-one in favour of AT1 *Performing and Composing*. The implication here is to spend twice as much time involved in *Performing and Composing* activities as on *Listening and*

Appraising, emphasizing the essentially practical, 'doing' nature of music making compared with the more reflective, less physical, often thought of as passive, listening and appraising skills.

An excellent precis, succinctly summarizing the specific knowledge, understanding and skills for each attainment target can be found in *A Guide to the National Curriculum* (SCAA/CAAW, 1996, p. 55):

Performing and Composing
Pupils should be taught to sing and play instruments with awareness of other performers, to share their music making, to improvise and explore sounds, resources and structures with awareness of the intended effect, and to use notations.

Listening and Appraising
Pupils should be taught to identify resources and musical elements and how they are used, to recognise how music reflects when and where it was created, to develop understanding of musical traditions and to express ideas and opinions about music.

Progressive Ideas

A useful starting point, especially to help a new teacher become quickly acquainted with the children, is to use the children's names in a rhythmic way. Begin by clapping the rhythm of your name, explaining this is how it sounds in music. Ask the children how many claps for each part of your name:

Mrs   Thompson

Key Stage 2 children may even realize that you are clapping one sound for each syllable! Ask the children to think about how to clap the rhythm of their own name: first names only at Key Stage 1, surnames included for Key Stage 2. Practise clapping some as examples, especially names with only one syllable e.g.:

Kate   Ashcroft

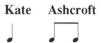

Ask the children questions to check that all has been understood:

Whose name has four claps like mine?
Whose name has more than four claps?
Whose name has three claps?

When all appears clear, go round the class individually to hear each child simultaneously clap the rhythm whilst saying their name, asking them all to listen to each other very carefully. Ask the children:

- Who spoke in a high voice? Who spoke in a low voice? (**pitch**)
- Whose names have the same rhythm? (**duration** and **structure**)
- Who clapped/spoke loudly? Who clapped/spoke quietly? (**dynamics**)
- Who clapped/spoke quickly? Who clapped/spoke slowly? (**tempo**)
- Who clapped with hands flat? Who clapped with hands cupped? (**timbre**)

In this climate of non-competitive participation, gently encourage every child to join in the activity, but you may not wish to insist if they appear shy at first. Also you may decide to allow a child to say and clap their name how they want: it is after all *their* name and quite precious to them. For example, the name **Barbara** could be clapped with two or three syllables depending on how it is pronounced:

This activity can be developed in short bursts over a period of time, ensuring progression and continuity in children's knowledge, understanding and skills. A more advanced form can be introduced using a steady **pulse** played on the tambour by the teacher. This involves the concept of accent. For example, my first name has the accent or emphasis on the second syllable:

compared with the name **David** where the accent is on the first syllable:

You might demonstrate for the children how the start of some names synchronizes with a tambour pulse, whilst those with the emphasis not on the first syllable have to begin before the pulse so that the accented syllable fits with the pulse. Combining the steady pulse on the tambour with the individual clapping of each name, one after another, brings in the remaining musical element of **texture**. After quite a few sessions of this activity, you could try a variation, where, prompted by the tambour pulse, each child in turn claps the rhythm of their name against a partner's name, thus involving independence of thought and action:

Child:

Patricia

Partner:

David

This is excellent preparation for pupils singing and playing different parts in ensemble, as described in the End of Key Stage Descriptions for Key Stage 2 Attainment Target 1: Performing and Composing: 'They sing songs and rounds that have two parts, and maintain independent instrumental lines with awareness of the other performers' (DFE, 1995).

   This introductory activity can form the central core of a scheme of work, linking with creative activities using body sounds emanating from listening and appraising, even practising, for example Steve Reich's *Clapping Piece for Two Performers* (1972). Maybe continue the theme by practising and performing the song, 'If you're happy and you know it, clap your hands' simultaneously with its partner song, 'If you clap, when you're feeling sad' (Song Nos 79 and 80 in *Flying a Round*, Gadsby, Harrop, Bannister and Cheese, 1982). Songs provide excellent opportunities to be recreative, that is to perform the song adding the children's own improvised and composed accompaniments, both rhythmic and pitched, allowing opportunities to use the imagination, both musically and literary. Thus the scheme of work not only meets the requirements of Music in the National Curriculum, but also derives from reflective practice, and its underpinning qualities of open mindedness, responsibility and commitment. The children can be directly engaged in exploring the elements of music, with a good balance achieved between progressive skill acquisition, creative work and the enjoyment of music making, in a relaxed atmosphere where every child can participate at whatever level they are able to, and, most importantly, feel a sense of achievement.

Enquiry Task

- Choose a musical activity that builds progressively over a period of time; for example, exploring the story of *The Sorcerer's Apprentice* by Dukas.
- Match this activity to the musical elements listed in the National Curriculum.
- How might you resource and organize the activity with a class of children?
- Identify the knowledge, understanding and skills developed by the activity.

Orchestral Manoeuvres

Below, I outline an activity that begins with a song, 'The Orchestra Song', No 61 in *The Jolly Herring* (Bush and Bentley, 1980). This is a song in five parts with words which describe the timbre and type of music played by each of five instruments — violin, clarinet, horn, trumpet and kettle drum. If children in your class play any of these instruments, you might encourage them to bring their instruments into lessons to demonstrate. It may take a few lessons to learn each part, to build up eventually to sing in a five-part texture, as there is plenty of scope to improve vocal articulation, tonguing, good breath control and support to reach high notes. The original words of the clarinet part:

The clarinet, the clarinet
goes doo-wah, doo-wah, doo-wah, doo-wah, day, (Bush and Bentley, 1980)

are useful practice for the tongue withdrawing from touching the back of the upper teeth. This is an important technique for recorder and all woodwind instrumental playing, as well as articulating words like *kettle, little*, and *bottle* when singing. A baby says *kekkle*, a 7-year-old with newly emerging front teeth says *kettul*, whereas an adult withdraws the tongue from touching the back of the upper front teeth, making the *t* almost disappear, like a glottal stop. Decisions also have to be made about where to take a breath so as not to interrupt the sense of the words. There are many opportunities to add expressive elements to the performance: the words of the horn part encourage! '. . . can murmer low and loudly blast (sic)' (Bush and Bentley, 1980). The technique needed to play each of these melodies on the recorder shows wide differentiation, as the horn part uses one note only, G, whilst the remaining parts increase in difficulty gradually — kettle drum, clarinet, trumpet and violin. Later, after some associated listening, the children can compose their own words describing other instruments, making up new melodies within the written chord structure using C and G. All these activities clearly meet the requirements of Key Stage 2 Performing and Composing:

> 5. a
> sing songs, developing control of diction and musical elements, particularly phrasing, *e.g., giving shape to a song by breathing at the end of a phrase*;
> 5. c
> sing songs, including songs and rounds in two parts, and play pieces which have several parts, developing the ability to listen to the other performers;
> 5. e
> improvise rhythmic and melodic ideas, *e.g., add a percussion part to a song.*
> (DFE, 1995)

Along the way, 5. b, d, f, g and h are likely to be covered, but the scheme of work links well with Key Stage 2 Listening and Appraising:

> 6. a
> identify the sounds made by a variety of instruments individually and in combination, *e.g., classroom instruments and families of instruments.* (DFE, 1995)

To balance the performing and composing element, listening to a brief extract — for example, the introductory theme from *The Young Person's Guide to the Orchestra* (Britten, 1947) (also known as Variations and Fugue on a theme of Purcell) by Benjamin Britten — provides a complementary activity. Discussion may be stimulated by the words of the song regarding the names of the families of instruments in the orchestra: strings, woodwind, brass and percussion. You can ask the children to identify aurally which family is playing as you point to numbers 1 to 6, synchronized with each family's performance of the theme. Further listening can develop recognition of the timbre of individual instruments. For example, Variation A is played by a piccolo and two flutes accompanied by the harp. You may wish to find time near the end of the project to play the fugue to the children: it is wonderfully exciting and exhilarating. Britten first composed the piece to be performed with narration, as it was originally written for an educational documentary film, *The*

Instruments of the Orchestra, a product of post-war pedagogy. This version is especially useful when introducing the music to children in the early stages. Eric Crozier's marvellous words describing the grand finale cannot be improved upon:

> We have taken the whole Orchestra to pieces. Now let us put it together in a Fugue. The instruments come in one after another, in the same order as before — beginning with the Piccolo. At the end, the Brass will play Henry Purcell's fine melody, while the others go on playing Benjamin Britten's Fugue. (Britten, 1947)

There are also recordings without the narration, which would provide a stimulating contrast for the children to listen and appraise:

> 6. e
> express ideas and opinions about music, developing a musical vocabulary and the ability to use musical knowledge to support views. (DFE, 1995)

To summarize the process, children will have been stimulated to perform and compose, listen and appraise in a closely woven web of practical, musical activities, encouraged to participate and work at whatever level they are able to achieve.

Enquiry Task

- Ask the children to write about their favourite part of the activities described so far.
- Analyse their responses into four categories: performing, composing, listening and appraising.
- Consider if the results are commensurate with the observed participation and involvement of the children during these activities.

Current Issues and Concerns

Two recent studies have produced interesting findings about the development of children's musical abilities. One study, conducted in Switzerland (Spychiger and Patry, 1996), showed that those who had extra music lessons made better progress in language and social skills than those who had not. The other study in the USA by Gardiner, Fox, Knowles and Jeffrey (1996) demonstrated that when children enjoy the arts, this motivates them to acquire arts skills which can result in an improved attitude towards learning and school generally. Also the learning of arts skills stretches mental abilities useful to other areas of learning; for example, ordering skills in mathematics.

Whilst this kind of reporting and research can only strengthen and improve the place of music, often regarded as a so-called *Cinderella* subject, in the curriculum, we must keep in mind the very special qualities music alone possesses, and not devalue its particular role in the total learning experience of children. Links with other subject areas, especially other performing arts subjects, can enhance and enrich, but we must not lose sight of the necessity to provide vital and regular opportunities to develop musical knowledge, understanding and skills for those able to achieve the very highest standards of musical excellence. There is no substitute, nor alternative, to regular practice.

Debate often focuses on what kind of music we should choose to introduce for children. The answer to this important question should be *all kinds of music*, but with the qualifying statement added, *but of the very best quality*. Much is talked about concerning how we attend to pupils' spiritual, moral, cultural, mental and physical development. Music can play a key role in all these aspects. Indeed, each Key Stage states that, 'the repertoire chosen for performing and listening should extend pupils' musical experience and knowledge, and develop their appreciation of the richness of our diverse cultural heritage. It should include music in a variety of styles:

a)   from different times and cultures;
b)   by well-known composers and performers, past and present. (DFE, 1995)

It is an opportunity to give children a sense of a well-crafted composition, a performance which excels and communicates totally to the audience, an ensemble which truly gels together in practice, to introduce them to music with artistic integrity.

Another area of considerable discussion is the passing on of a cultural heritage. The Statutory Order uses the phrase, 'our diverse cultural heritage', demonstrating acknowledgment of the multicultural nature of this country. You may wish to ask, 'Whose cultural heritage?' There is a veritable cornucopia to be explored. The important lesson here is the one of valuing a musical work whatever its cultural origins, and the process of composition which brought it into existence.

You may need to be mindful, when using instruments in the classroom, not to confirm the stereotype of girls playing small, quiet instruments, and boys playing larger, noisier instruments. You might decide to ensure that all instruments are equally used and played, operating a visible rota if this is more practical. Some children do have a strong sense of which orchestral instruments should be played by whom: flute for a girl and trumpet for a boy. You may need to develop strategies to ensure equality of opportunity to try an instrument for size, but obviously embouchure, teeth formation, and physical size in the early years are important factors which need to be considered.

Resources for Learning

Teachers often feel a heavy burden of responsibility to have to deliver the Statutory Order for Music, especially if they are less than confident about their own musical abilities. The class teacher, especially for Key Stage 1, *is* best placed to develop the necessary skills, knowledge and understanding in their pupils, as they can provide the most suitable conditions for skill acquisition and musical understanding through timely opportunities of 'little but often'. One of the strongest influences in successful musical progress is encouragement, and again the class teacher is ideally placed to provide that as they already have a strong rapport with each child in their care.

There are many ways for you to find help and support. Until the advent of the radio station, Classic FM, its accompanying monthly magazine with choice of Cover CD or cassette, and its *Countdown Top 10*, Alan Keith's *Your Hundred Best Tunes* broadcast on BBC Radio 2 on Sunday evenings was an education in itself. Since then there has been a proliferation of radio programmes like BBC Radio 4's *Classics with Kay* on Saturday evenings playing short extracts of classical music with excellent, brief introductory comments by avuncular Brian Kay, formerly of The King's Singers.

The WOMAD (World of Music, Arts and Dance) Foundation publish a wide variety of music, including recordings on CD and cassette, from around the globe. Some of these have been produced in conjunction with Heinemann Educational.

Local music shop and record shop staff can provide useful information, whilst a browse in either shop may repay time and effort spent, not least because the latest, fashionable album may be playing gently in the background: an obvious marketing ploy. The medium may well be the message: the simple truth is to stay current and aware.

You may wish to make use of the skills of parents, relations, friends, musicians in the local community. They may be especially helpful in providing opportunities for pupils to 'respond to, and evaluate, live performances', whilst perhaps simultaneously comparing 'music from contrasting musical traditions'. In the classroom we mostly have to rely on cassette, CD or CD-ROM for providing listening experiences for children, but the very best kind of aural experience may be reinforced by use of the visual sense, and is live, of the moment. Perhaps it is this unique, shared experience of being in the audience, and the opportunity for the unexpected in performance that makes it so special and magical.

Local musicians may be helpful in your own skill acquisition, even if it is 'teach yourself recorder', using a published tutor and cassette to play along to. The most enjoyable and quickest way to learn to play an instrument, is to learn in a group. There are many adult education classes, Saturday morning music schools, and residential summer schools dedicated to this end. Many local piano teachers, often reputed to be quite conservative in teaching methods, now organize at least one group session a week.

Enquiry Task

- Carry out an audit of all the musical help available from parents, relations, friends, musicians in the local community.
- Draw up a plan as to how a visit by any of these musicians could fit in with the current scheme of work for your class.
- Consult with them over ways to prepare for the visit and to develop the work after it.
- List the benefits for the children of having visiting musicians in the classroom.

Assessment Practice

As with art and physical education, music has single End of Key Stage Descriptions instead of a progression of Level Descriptions. These describe the standard of attainment in music expected of the majority of pupils at the end of each Key Stage. These expectations match the level of demand in other subjects and are broadly equivalent to Level 2 at Key Stage 1, and Level 4 at Key Stage 2.

The statements in the End of Key Stage Descriptions are qualified by qualitative terms like *confidently, attentively, accurately, make expressive use of*. To help you differentiate exceptional performance, additional descriptions are provided at Key Stage 3. Since music is often taught across a very wide ability range in the same class, these additional descriptions may prove of use if you are attending to the requirements of an earlier Key Stage. Some children will have had the advantage of instrumental lessons from an early age, and may have reached an impressive standard of technical competence accompanied by considerable expressive and interpretative qualities. You should not feel frightened or threatened by this level of achievement: you may need to think about how to use it to best advantage by organizing children such as these to lead activities, play a special part in the music to be performed, or to compose pieces especially for the class or for an occasion.

Because of the subjective nature of the arts, teachers are often reluctant to classify a musical response as being wrong or right. The aim is to have fun and enjoy the activities in an atmosphere of genuine encouragement. This makes it hard to write statements about the achievements of each child, but you must attend to sound record keeping and assessment practices to inform your planning and teaching. Informal note keeping, with a page for each child to be added to after musical activities as and when appropriate, may be useful when writing the annual report or talking to parents about their child's progress. When assessing children's musical development and planning future work, it may be helpful to carry out the following activities:

- discuss work with the children individually or together;
- listen to children's discussion;
- observe participation in group or class activities;
- listen to children's compositions and performances, live or recorded.

During the early years of music making, we tend to value the process of the activity somewhat more than the end product, but we may need to be mindful to give due credit to a good performance or impressive composition when they happen.

Enquiry Task
- Choose a cross-section of children of varying musical knowledge, understanding and skills.
- Write descriptions of musical progress and achievement for each one, using qualitative terms to illumine progress.

- Compose additional descriptions of exceptional performance at Key Stage 1 and at Key Stage 2.

References

BRITTEN, B. (1947) *The Young Person's Guide to the Orchestra*, London, Boosey and Hawkes.

BUSH, R. and BENTLEY, R. (1980) *The Jolly Herring*, London, A & C Black.

DEPARTMENT FOR EDUCATION (DFE) (1995) *Music in the National Curriculum (England)*, London, HMSO.

GADSBY, D., HARROP, B., BANNISTER, J., and CHEESE, B. (1982) *Flying a Round*, London, A & C Black.

GARDINER, M., FOX, A., KNOWLES, F., and JEFFREY, D. (1996) 'Learning improved by arts training' *Nature*, **381**, 23 May, p. 284, London, MacMillan Magazines.

PARKER, G. (1969) *Poems of John Keats*, Saffron Walden, Geoffrey Parker.

SCHOOL CURRICULUM AND ASSESSMENT AUTHORITY/CURRICULUM AND ASSESSMENT AUTHORITY FOR WALES (SCAA/CAAW) (1996) *A Guide to the National Curriculum*, London, SCAA.

SPYCHIGER, M. and PATRY, J. (1996) 'Children learn faster to the sound of music', *New Scientist*, **150**, 2030, 18 May, p. 6, IPC Magazines.

THOMPSON, P. (1995) 'Music', in ASHCROFT, K. and PALACIO, D. (eds) *The Primary Teacher's Guide to the New National Curriculum*, London, Falmer Press.

Annotated List of Suggested Reading

BAXTER, K. (1994) *Fundamental Activities*, Nottingham, Fundamental Activities.
(An interesting pack, full of good, practical ideas, consisting of video, video notes and accompanying handbook of activities undertaken with pupils and teachers in England and Romania.)

BURNISTON, C. (1975) *Speech in Practice*, Southport, The English Speaking Board.
(A useful reference work for assisting clear articulation, and appropriate use of tongue, teeth and lips when singing.)

BUSH, R. and BENTLEY, R. (1980) *The Jolly Herring*, London, A & C Black.
(A wide-ranging collection of songs for Key Stage 2 and beyond.)

CHILDS, J. (1996) *Making Music Special*, London, David Fulton Publishers.
(An essentially practical book of ways to create music.)

GADSBY, D., HARROP, B., BANNISTER, J. and CHEESE, B. (1982) *Flying a Round*, London, A & C Black.
(An immensely useful and greatly enjoyable collection of rounds and partner songs, many with actions.)

HINCKLEY, P. and HINCKLEY, M. (1992) *Let's Make Music: Music for All: 1*, London and Sevenoaks, Novello.
(Based on topics for Key Stage 2, this book with accompanying cassette has a helpful and supportive reference section detailing untuned and tuned percussion instruments, questions to use when appraising music with children, and ideas for making graphic scores.)

JONES, G. (1994) *Exploring the Music of the World: Music of Indonesia*, Oxford, Heinemann Educational.

(Although this series of world music packs including cassettes is written with Key Stage 3 pupils in mind, it serves as a comprehensive introduction to world musics for teachers wishing to widen their own musical knowledge and understanding.)

SMITH, P. (1985) *Playtape Ten Toe Tappers*, Milton Keynes, Creeth Publications.

(Children — and adults! — love to play recorder along with the rhythmically lively accompaniments on cassette for these ten pieces, including reggae, rock'n roll and tango.)

WIGGINS, T. (1993) *Exploring the Music of the World: Music of West Africa*, Oxford, Heinemann Educational.

(As with *Music of Indonesia*, this is well researched, and visually and aurally stimulating.)

WILLS, P. and PETER, M. (1996) *Music for All*, London, David Fulton Publishers.

(Although this excellent book is about developing music in the curriculum with pupils with special educational needs, it is aimed at the musically challenged teacher, and is consequently very useful when working with all children.)

Glossary of Musical Terms (with special reference to Music in the National Curriculum)

Duration Basically, how long a sound is held on for; but this also includes pulse or beat, and rhythm.

Dynamics All the different levels of volume, ranging from very loud to very soft; and also including silence and accent.

Embouchure The muscle system around the mouth.

Leitmotif A recurring musical phrase characterizing the personalities of the drama, as in the operas of Wagner.

Ostinato A musical pattern repeated many times. This could be rhythmic, melodic or harmonic.

Pitch High or low sounds, and their letter names, e.g., C, G or tonic solfa names, e.g., doh, soh.

Tempo The speed of the music, e.g., fast/slow, and any changes occurring.

Texture One sound on its own, e.g., melody, or several sounds heard together, e.g., chords.

Timbre The quality of a sound that makes it identifiable, e.g., harsh or mellow.

Structure How a piece is composed, e.g., beginning, middle, end.

10   Physical Education

Jennifer Gray

Introduction

The terms *sport* and *physical education* have often been used synonymously. Physical education has developed from a games tradition where it (games) was thought to train the moral qualities of the individual. In the nineteenth century, only boys were taught games, with the aim of developing the qualities of self-control, vigour and decision of character. It was only after the Education Act of 1870 that physical education for girls was considered.

This historical background is not without its influence on the current curriculum; for example, although six different areas of study are included in the Key Stage 2 Programme of Study, there is a major emphasis on games. The current political interest in games arises in part because games is seen by some politicians as a means to channel the energy, high spirits, competitiveness and aggression of the young in a socially beneficial way as well as providing lessons for life which young people are unlikely to learn so well in any other way (Department of National Heritage, 1995, p. 6). At the same time, there has been a decline in the time devoted to physical education in schools and a reduction in 'out-of-school' activity. This lack of physical education in our schools is also currently blamed for our inability to win gold medals at the 1996 Olympic Games, as well as the lack of fitness of school-aged children.

Although it is essential that, through physical education, teachers enthusiastically introduce pupils to major games and also encourage activities which facilitate a healthy lifestyle, these are not the only aims of the physical education programme within the National Curriculum (DFE, 1995). It is through the physical education programme that a contribution is made to the social, moral, cultural and spiritual development of the individual. It is hoped that through the physical education programme, the unique characteristics of the individual can be developed, thus allowing him/her to make a positive contribution to life.

The teaching of the physical education programme is likely to present to you with many challenges and this chapter will seek to suggest possible ways of addressing these. Physical education is not just about skill learning, but is also about adding to pupils' total development. The point to bear in mind is that PE is not just what children learn *in* PE: what the children learn *through* your physical education programme is of more importance.

Misconceptions

In many schools, physical education lessons have been, and even today are often still used as a time for the children to let off steam, to have a rest from their lessons or just to have a good run around. In schools such as these, there has been little planning and very little assessment other than 'tries hard'! It has been thought sufficient to give a group a ball and let them 'get on with it'.

Often, I am asked how soccer can be taught with only one ball. This is indeed very difficult, especially if physical education is not to be seen simply as getting some fresh air, stretching one's legs and enjoying oneself. In this chapter I will argue that physical education is much more than this: PE is concerned with skill learning in a variety of interesting and challenging activities and is about developing one's personal capabilities and strengths (and coming to terms with one's weaknesses) in challenging situations. PE is concerned with:

- learning about fair play and respect for opponents;
- learning to win and lose and cope with the consequences of both;
- learning to work with others;
- appreciating team spirit and the strengths and weaknesses of other team members;
- working cooperatively to get the best from group effort;
- learning about cultural similarities and differences, especially through dance.

Dance is part of the National Curriculum for Physical Education although in this book it is discussed separately in Chapter 15. It is also about keeping fit and providing a philosophy and lifestyle which will encourage lifetime participation. It is also about enjoyment, but it is only through carefully planned lessons that this enjoyment and all the other points mentioned above will be achieved.

Teacher Concerns

Teachers approach the teaching of physical education with varying degrees of ability and confidence. All are likely to relate closely to their previous experience which may, or may not, have been positive; this previous experience may lead them to equate the teaching of physical education with personal performance or, as already stated, the coaching of games.

Contrary to popular belief, especially amongst primary school and prospective primary school teachers, it is not essential to be proficient in the performance of an activity to be able to teach it effectively. You will not have to vault a box in gymnastics, or score the winning try in rugby, but you will have to assist children in safe PE activities, and teach them the skills and tactics of a game to enable them to score the winning goal or try. It is knowledge of the discrete subject areas, together with a sound educational philosophy and enthusiasm, which will allow you to be able to teach the physical education programme with confidence.

The lack of adequate facilities is often given as another major concern and this will be discussed later.

Enquiry Task

- Look at the National Curriculum Order for PE for the Key Stage appropriate to your work.
- Identify your own strengths.
- Identify your own weaknesses.
- Develop an action plan that demonstrates how you intend to build on your strengths and reduce the impact of your weaknesses.

Once you have identified your personal strengths and weaknesses, it will be necessary to build a personal development plan to enable you to 'deliver' those aspects of the PE National Curriculum appropriate to your class. In many schools, parts of the curriculum are delivered exceptionally well; for example, the teaching of games, but other parts are often paid lip-service or ignored completely; for example, dance, and outdoor and adventurous activities. Undoubtedly, the National Curriculum Order for PE does present concerns for many teachers. There are few teachers who see themselves as strong in all areas of the curriculum, and physical education is one area where many teachers feel they have inadequate knowledge to devise or deliver programmes of work which are progressive and valid. For the whole curriculum to be delivered effectively, you will need to seek, and effectively utilize, the expertise of others. You may be able to get help from within your school or from within your school cluster. It may be possible to use other staff as part of a staff development programme: you may need to organize some teaching on a shared basis. Some of your individual weaknesses, for example, a perceived lack of subject knowledge, may be met by individual reading — see bibliography at the end of the chapter for books which might help you here. There are many excellent new publications which should help with subject knowledge and lesson planning. (Lesson planning will be dealt with later in this chapter.)

You may find it helpful to attend a local inservice course or a National Governing Body (NGB) teaching course to acquire any necessary discrete subject knowledge which you feel you might lack. To meet the demands of the practising teacher, sport-specific governing bodies have seen the need to provide for *teaching* rather than the traditional *coaching* courses. For example, in the case of swimming, the Amateur Swimming Association has traditionally filled this role: however, the Association has now recognized the unique needs of primary school teachers and is introducing a course specifically to meet these needs. Similarly, the British Amateur Gymnastics Association has introduced a teacher's qualification, and the Football Association and the Rugby Football Association have both introduced teaching qualifications which require mentored teaching experience with children. Such courses are an ideal way for you to acquire discrete subject knowledge taught in a variety of teaching styles.

Facilities

Lack of adequate facilities will often present you with problems. Space in primary schools is often limited and usually shared. Whenever possible, games and athletics lessons should be taken outside. Our climate should not be an excuse and you may need to consider your planning in order to ensure that pupils are kept active and that 'the cold' is not a problem. You may also need to consider appropriate dress for your pupils since they are likely to find it difficult to concentrate and participate fully if they are cold. Consideration of both the appropriateness of activities and the clothing may result in more effective teaching in PE. If there are no suitable changing facilities then you may need to consider discussing this problem with your headteacher. There are ways of overcoming this very real problem. The adverse weather conditions and the shared use of the facilities gives the less enthusiastic teacher a perfect excuse to cancel PE lessons.

Providing an appropriate swimming programme has presented a problem for many schools since you not only have to find a pool but also staff who are qualified to teach the programme safely. Local safety requirements will vary, but you will need to be aware of these requirements and ensure that they are adhered to. If in doubt, contact your school's PE coordinator. You may consider gaining knowledge of resuscitation — courses are available through the Red Cross, the St Johns Ambulance Brigade and through the Royal Life Saving Society. Details of courses are usually displayed on swimming pool noticeboards. Techniques do vary and it's important to be up to date. Remember, any qualifications you gain will need to be renewed frequently. If you already have a qualification, is it still valid?

Swimming techniques also change and the current strokes may not be the same as the ones you were taught, assuming, that is, that you were taught some! You may need to consider how to obtain up-to-date knowledge, if only to prevent you 'correcting' a stroke that a child's swimming coach has taken hours to perfect. One way of gaining this knowledge is to ask at your local swimming club. Coaches or teachers will usually allow you to observe sessions which will enable you to see the current strokes. Consulting reference books is another way to gain knowledge of 'modern' strokes; the bibliography at the end of this chapter includes a list of suitable titles.

School swimming is expensive and you will have to be very organized and employ the most effective teaching methods in order to make best use of the time in the water. As a responsible, reflective practitioner you will wish to plan this time as effectively as possible to ensure that no time is wasted, especially through inappropriate teaching methods.

Inclusion of All Pupils

In some schools, pupils are excluded from PE if they have not finished other work or if they have exhibited unsatisfactory behaviour. You may wish to consider whether this is acceptable. The PE National Curriculum does state that all pupils are entitled to participate in physical education, but you may also wish to consider the message non-participation gives pupils about the importance of physical education within the whole curriculum. You should also consider whether you would exclude children from maths or English if they behaved badly in PE, or if you would consider lengthening the games lesson if pupils had not completed the tasks you had set. You may also wish to consider the message given to the pupils if you continually cancel PE lessons.

Organization

Effective teaching will only be possible when you are completely happy with the organization of the whole learning environment. Teachers often worry about moving children around the school and control of the children in practical situations, especially where large apparatus is concerned. Safety must always be paramount: you may wish to reconsider your organization and teaching strategies in light of this, bearing in mind the need to allow the children to participate fully and thereby enable them to reach their full potential. Safety can be seen as a reason for not allowing children to take some responsibility for their own progress. In order to gain confidence in organization you may find it helpful to observe good practice.

Enquiry Task

Observe a teacher working with a class in PE.

- How does he/she line the children up to move to the PE area?
- What noise level does the teacher accept when moving children around the school? How is this noise level maintained?
- How and when do the pupils enter the PE area?
- What is their first activity?
- How does the teacher select pairs and groups?
- How is apparatus organized?
- How do pupils get out and put away apparatus?
- How are pupils dismissed from the lesson?
- How do the children move back to their changing area?
- How is changing organized?
- How do children move to their next lesson?

Now, consider how the time and facilities have been used to good effect by the teacher. Based on this evaluation, plan your own strategies for the effective organization of your pupils.

There are likely to be many more questions that you still need to ask, so further careful observation of effective practice may be necessary. Do evaluate other teachers' practice. Decide whether or not the organization made best use of time and facilities, and allowed effective teaching and learning to take place. Your confidence will only be enhanced when you have developed safe teaching routines that give you and your pupils stability.

Planning

The Programme of Study for Key Stage 2 comprises six Areas of Activity: games, gymnastic activities, dance, athletic activities, outdoor and adventurous activities, and swimming. During each year of the Key Stage, the PE programme should include games, gymnastic activities and dance. The other three areas should be taught at some points during the Key Stage, and it is recommended that they need to take approximately one quarter of the total amount of time available, i.e., about half an hour per week. Your first planning task may be to decide when these specific Areas of Activity will be taught: what year and at what time of the year. In many schools, this will have been decided already, but your task is likely to be the detailed planning of schemes of work and individual lessons for your class.

It may be worth considering whether it is more advantageous to organize activities as a single block of work or whether it is better to organize them on a rotational carousel basis. In a rotational carousel, pupils may change activity on a weekly basis and it may be a few sessions before the same activity is revisited. I know a teacher who works her swimming programme as a block in which all non-swimmers experience two weeks of swimming. The children go every day for the two weeks and she says that the improvement in each child's swimming ability is incredible. Such blocks of teaching require considerable organization; for example, what provision needs to be made for pupils who, for whatever reason, have missed this two-week block of work?

Enquiry Task

Examine the Key Stage 2 PE programme of work of a school that you know.

- Are all six Areas of Activity included?
- When are they included?
- How much time is allocated to each Area of Activity?
- Is about one quarter of the total time allocated to Areas other than games, dance and gymnastic activities? (You may need to estimate here.)
- What provision is made for swimming?
- How are outdoor and adventurous activities presented in your school?
- Consider the advantages and disadvantages of the arrangements for the whole programme of work.
    - What model of teaching and learning is implied by these arrangements?
    - What alternative models could be used?

When planning your schemes of work, you will need to consider how to make the work progressive and build on the children's prior experience.

Progression in physical education is identified in two ways:

by increasing the difficulty of **what** a pupil is doing (matching capability with a pupil's physical, cognitive, social and emotional development); by making increasing demands on **how** activities are planned, performed and evaluated by pupils. (DFE, 1996, p. 6)

Games is included at both Key Stages, and, therefore, the children may be involved in soccer activities throughout their primary school career. We would hope to see improvement in their soccer skills from Year 1 to Year 6. For this improvement to come about, you may need to develop an understanding of the requirements of the game and how the skills within it vary in difficulty. Pupils should not work against an opponent until they have learnt individual ball skills. Skill learning must be progressive: this is best achieved with pupils working first on their own, then working in cooperation with a partner, moving into small sided one-to-one or two-on-two games, before finally moving into mini-games. You may need to make the rules of the game more complex. In gymnastics, you may plan for the pupils to first learn to control their own body before working on apparatus or with partners. In a theme such as balance, balances may be initially on large body parts with pupils working on their own on the floor. They may progress to similar balances on the apparatus, and then work towards reducing the size of the points of balance. As children become more proficient, the apparatus may become more challenging. They may then progress to working with partners, and finally onto group work.

You may find that if your work is not progressive in the ways outlined in the previous paragraph then one outcome may be a lack of challenge with the result that the children become disruptive because they are disinterested and bored. As a reflective teacher you will want to ensure that your lessons are carefully planned with each unit of work and each lesson having clear learning objectives. Activities will be included, using a variety of appropriate teaching styles, which allow these objectives to be realized. Although planning by pupils plays a less dominant role now than it has done in the past, you might wish to experiment by including pupils in the planning process. They enjoy the planning process and value the opportunity to contribute.

Planning and assessment need to be intertwined. As stated already, you must always have clear learning objectives with tasks set which cover these objectives. In any one lesson it may be impossible for you to assess in detail every pupil against these objectives, but through observation and questioning, you may be able to create a general impression of achievement. You may find it useful to identify those pupils not achieving the set learning objectives and, in future lessons, plan your work so that these pupils are given further opportunity to succeed. It may be better not to provide the same activities but rather to use a variety of teaching styles and different activities to try to attain the objectives.

Assessment

Assessment must be at the heart of the process of children's learning. The End of Key Stage Descriptors against which attainment should be judged are very general, but if the physical education programme is going to be effective, you will need to develop strategies for continuous assessment.

Assessment in PE is difficult as you are assessing bodily actions which may occur only for a few seconds. You are often making qualitative judgments which depend on your own *knowledge of the subject*. Assessment must influence all your planning, but at the same time, your assessment process must not be so unwieldy that it prevents you teaching. The very nature of the physical activity and the contexts in which it takes place makes recording difficult. The use of observational tick sheets which may involve you in continually filling in forms rather than observing and paying due regard to safety may need to be considered. Assessment requires setting tasks which cover the learning objectives followed by careful observation and judgment of pupils' achievements set against these objectives.

You can record times and distances which will give you a record of measurable achievement, but bear in mind that the assessment criteria are that the children can plan, practise, improve and remember more complex sequences of movement. However, you can assess skills by asking the question: Has the pupil developed her/his skills through practice? Your measurement will give you an indication of skill development, but you will need to remember to measure improvement from the individual pupil's base level, and not compare pupil against pupil. Remember, the least able child may have made the most improvement.

If you are making quantitative measurements of children's achievements, consider their display. Records of such achievement are often displayed on public boards. You may wish to consider what positive and negative effects this may have on pupils, and whether you would display results of other tests such as reading ages on public boards. Other judgments will need to be qualitative; for example, a pupil throws the ball a certain distance, and, in addition to recording this distance, you will need to make judgments concerning the throwing action. Does it conform to the 'correct' throw? For you to make such judgments in any of the discrete areas you will need specific subject knowledge.

The National Curriculum Order asks you to assess pupils' swimming competence in terms of their water confidence and their ability to swim 25 metres. However, you may have more competent swimmers in your class and may, therefore, wish to assess these pupils against nationally recognized awards. In such awards, it may be necessary for the pupils to swim a given stroke according to ASA (Amateur Swimming Association) law. It will be necessary for you to know the ASA law and also how to judge your observations against that specific law. So, to make informed qualitative judgments, you will have to have specific knowledge.

The third assessment situation is that made in the aesthetic areas of PE, particularly dance. You will have to create your own assessment model for aesthetic assessment. There is no set model, and every teacher will have their own experience to bring to this model. Although there is no set model, the End of Key Stage

Descriptors specifically ask you to assess pupils' ability to *explore and present different responses to a variety of situations*. This will include the pupils' response to a variety of stimuli in dance.

Enquiry Task

- Interview other teachers to find out what criteria they use for aesthetic assessment.
- Consult the dance and gymnastic literature to find aesthetic assessment criteria.
- Draw up a list of your own assessment criteria for aesthetic aspects of PE.

You may wish to involve pupils in their own assessment: for example, they might assess their work against set criteria and then evaluate their own progress. At the end of each Programme of Study, pupils might complete a record of achievement. Pupils could be asked to identify their own skill strengths and weaknesses: they might assess what they have learnt in a unit of work and maybe any qualities they have gained as a result.

You may wish to ensure that you use different forms of assessment; formative, diagnostic, summative and evaluative. How might the information gained from this assessment influence your future practice?

Enquiry Task

Consider a PE lesson — it could be one of your own or one that you have observed another teacher teach.

- How were specific learning objectives met within lesson activities?
- What assessment opportunities were used during the lesson?
- Were the tasks/activities modified, and in what way(s), in the light of feedback?
- How could your analysis of this lesson be reflected in your future planning?

Reporting to Parents

When writing your reports to parents, it will be essential that you address all the criteria set out in the End of Key Stage Descriptors (EKSD). It will be necessary, of course, for you to relate your comments to the specific aspects of the Programme of Study which you have covered.

> Pupil reports to parents are to be a commentary in relation to the EKSD. (Spode and Whitlam, 1996, p. 29)

Safety

The general requirements of the National Curriculum Order indicate that the teacher must ensure safe practice. Safe Practice in Physical Education (BAALPE, 1990) gives very explicit guidelines on safety in PE. Many of the sections are specifically for work at Key Stages 3 and 4, but much is very relevant to the primary school teacher. You act in *loco parentis*, exercising the same degree of responsibility that any reasonable and careful parent would exercise. This does not mean that you have to wrap the children up in cotton wool and not allow them to participate in any activity which is in any way challenging. In your planning, it will be necessary to undertake risk assessments, to anticipate the possible actions of the children, and the possible dangers arising from the activity itself and how these might be minimized. You may need to consider how the children's attention may be brought to issues relating to safety; you may also need to assess what constitutes appropriate clothing and footwear (see earlier discussion on outdoor activities), and to ensure that adequate checks on equipment takes place. If you are a student teacher remember that 'the regular class teacher retains the duty-of-care responsibility for the pupils' safety' (BAALPE, 1990).

Special Needs

In most classes, you are likely to have pupils with special educational needs in respect of physical education. The PE National Curriculum states that:

> ... appropriate provision should be made for those pupils who need activities to be adapted in order to participate in physical education. (DFE, 1994a, p. 113)

Although the Code of Practice on the Identification and Assessment of Special Education Needs (DFE, 1994b) concentrates on pupils who lack ability, it must be remembered that the term 'special needs' refers to not only those pupils who have disabilities but also those pupils who have greater ability — the physically gifted child. If you have an able pupil in your class you may feel that you can not teach them anything since they know more about the subject than you. This may be the case, but if the subject was maths, you would provide extension work to cater for their individual needs. In PE, able pupils are often ignored or are asked to teach other pupils instead of expanding their own particular skill level. *The Guide to the National Curriculum* states that:

> A small number of pupils will be gifted in one or more subjects. In such cases, class teachers will need to work with colleagues in their own school and support services, and occasionally with other schools, to ensure suitable provision is made for gifted children. (DFE, 1996, p. 14)

Your pupils may be gifted in some areas of the PE curriculum and you may need to obtain specialist help to extend their knowledge or ability in this specific area.

Remember, physical education is not only about skill development and the curriculum is not designed to just extend expertise in a specific area, if you are considering additional help for such gifted pupils then consider their ability not just in isolation but together with their social and emotional development.

You may believe that the PE programme for children with special needs, should, if possible, be integrated into the whole school programme. That is, the programme should be *inclusive* for all pupils and not be *exclusive* for individual pupils. For this to happen, you will need a sound understanding of differentiation and be in a position to treat all pupils as individuals. You may need to find ways to look for and understand the abilities of your pupils and not to focus on their disabilities. As with all children, you will need to develop strategies to build on the ability of pupils with special needs rather than just allowing them to take part and do those aspects of lessons they are able to do. Putting this into practice is not easy: considerable planning and detailed knowledge of individual pupils' capabilities will be needed to ensure that all pupils are welcomed into the programme, given equal access to the activities, and their work given equal status as that of the able-bodied child. Achieving this may take time, patience and experience.

Before planning for a child's individual needs, you may decide to look at the current capabilities and the potential of all pupils in your class. The special needs coordinator in your school should have specific information concerning individual pupils but it may be necessary to gain additional information from parents. You may wish to make it clear to parents that you are not seeking this information in order to make the programme different but only to assess their child's capabilities and also for reasons of safety. You need to have an understanding of the disability, and the likely effect of that disability for the child concerned and the rest of the class. In the case of asthma, you must ascertain under what condition the child is likely to be affected. If the disability is degenerative — as in the case of muscular dystrophy — close contact with the child concerned will be necessary for you to ensure that the activities will continue to be appropriate for a weakening body. If medication is required, then you must have sound knowledge of how, and the conditions under which, this should be administered, and for signs which may make administration necessary. You will also need to check on your school's policy regarding the administration of medication. These points must also be considered in the classroom, but very often physical education may require special considerations.

As with classroom activities, your pupils may require, and have access to, learning support during PE lessons. This support may be required to help the child get changed, to provide physical or emotional support, or simply to repeat instructions. Support may also be needed to give the child stability and/or as a motivating factor. Many pupils with special needs require only limited support, and you and the learning assistant must be careful not to give so much support that it stops the child being integrated into the programme and stifles independent movement.

A major consideration for you is how to integrate children with special needs into pair and group work. Individual work is relatively easy, but work incorporating more than one child becomes more difficult. You will often hear pupils say, 'I don't want him/her in my team?' — especially where competition is an essential and significant element. Activities which require pupils to produce a sequence of movement, such as in gymnastics or dance, may be best achieved if the pupils are of a similar ability. Neither pupil will feel frustrated or feel that they are letting down the other one. In games skills, you may consider using the learning support assistant as the partner or a more able child. It is pointless trying to get a child to catch if their partner has no control over the direction of the throw. The more able child will gain in social skills rather than physical skills, and the pupil with special needs will benefit from their competence. Remember the education of the whole child, including their social skills, is the main aim of the physical education programme.

Teachers are often concerned about selection of groups when some pupils have restricted movement. 'Random' selection of pupils by the teacher can ensure that groups are relatively even in ability; ensuring that frequent changes are made to the composition of groups also helps. In team games it may be necessary for you to adapt rules, such as tackling rules, and the distance that pupils have to travel. You will also have to make other pupils aware of the physical problems, but at the same time ensure that they realize that all pupils have the right to participate and that sometimes allowances have to be made.

Hidden Disabilities

Physical education is an area of the National Curriculum where it is very difficult to hide weaknesses. For some pupils in your class, physical education lessons, like other lessons, may be a cause of distress. You may observe pupils who appear to be clumsy or awkward. They may suffer from some form of developmental coordination disorder and as such have difficulty in planning the physical movements that other children acquire naturally.

Enquiry Task

- Ask the children about their likes and dislikes in PE.
- Find out why they have particular likes and dislikes. Is there a consensus of opinion?
- Consider how these feelings might influence what you teach in PE and how you teach it.

Although it is beyond the scope of this chapter to look at ways of overcoming these developmental problems, you should be aware that such difficulties exist and that you, therefore, must create a secure environment which enables pupils with physical and/or other disabilities to participate actively during PE lessons. Details of a programme to help pupils with developmental coordination disorder are provided in the bibliography. My own research has shown that considerable improvement in coordination can be gained by giving children a carefully planned programme which allows repetition of simple skills. I also found that integrating these skills to music to be very beneficial.

Pupils may often try to hide their disabilities by always forgetting their PE kit, by being ill on PE days, or fooling around and making a joke of their inability. Pupils whom teachers suspect may have this problem should be monitored carefully and, where necessary, referred to an occupational therapist for help. Lack of help may cause the child considerable psychological stress. Pupils who display clumsy movements will need to have all skills broken down into very simple sub-skills. Remember, you will have to work very slowly, and give your pupils continual encouragement and praise. Slow but steady progression is essential.

There may also be pupils in your class who are, or perceive themselves to be, excessively fat or thin, those who have knock knees or flat feet. Pupils who are over- or under-weight will need careful consideration, and also encouragement to participate. To encourage participation, it will be necessary for you to provide an environment which is secure and which values the work of all pupils, including the physically least able.

Apparatus for Special Needs Pupils

You may need to ask pupils what makes particular apparatus user-friendly and then incorporate their answers into your criteria for selection. It may be not only necessary to adapt the activity for pupils, but also to consider the appropriateness of the size, shape or weight of the equipment. Beanbags or large, soft balls might be more appropriate than tennis balls for catching practice. Most manufacturers make balls which are designed to be easier to catch. Davies of Nottingham sell a 'sensi-ball' which is soft and lightweight, and is made of a highly tactile material. The ball's outer surface consists of 'gentle stimulating bumps' which provide a resilient bounce and make grip easier. Their spider ball, with its tentacles, makes it easier to catch; when rolled the 'tentacles' act as brakes. For the child who frequently misses the ball, such balls are ideal as they don't roll far when dropped and the child avoids having to run a great distance to retrieve it. For children with limited sight, balls are available which make a noise. The thickness of mats may need to be considered, especially for children who bruise or hurt themselves easily and also for those who lack confidence.

Whenever possible, you may wish to offer to your pupils a variety of suitable apparatus. The excellent variety of apparatus which is now available gives children the opportunity to choose the apparatus they think will offer them success. Remember, decision making is embedded in PE Programme of Study. Such decision making includes choice of suitable apparatus.

Equal Opportunity Issues

The previous paragraphs have looked at the general requirement to 'provide for all' within the context of pupils with special needs. You must also consider gender issues. In most primary schools, PE is organized in mixed gender groups: even so, in some schools, the old traditions of football (soccer) for boys and netball for girls still holds. Provision should be made for *all* pupils to participate in *all* activities, including rugby, soccer and dance: however, the question of whether these activities should be organized in single sex groups or whether the group should be integrated needs to be considered carefully. By working in mixed gender groups, you should consider whether all the pupils have equal opportunity to progress to their full capabilities. In a mixed football game, the boys may always dominate, with the effect that the girls feel inferior and give up. In gymnastics, the boys may be criticized for a lack of poise and extension. Within a mixed gender approach, do your ability groups mean that boys play together and, separately, girls play together? If your existing practice is restricting pupils, it may be better to work in single sex groups. You may need to carefully consider whether your equal opportunity policy really means equal opportunity for all the pupils.

You will also need to consider making provision for the variety of cultural and religious beliefs that exist within your class. Certain children may need to be 'segregated'; for example, in swimming lessons Muslim children may need to be taught in single sex groups, with girls being taught by female teachers and boys by male teachers. Swimwear may need to comply with Islamic modesty, and girls may need to be allowed to wear full leotards.

For Muslim parents, creative dance may also cause concern and jazz dance and dance including pop music may be frowned upon. This last point not withstanding, you should try to include dance from a variety of cultures within your programme of work. You may find it helpful to call upon local expertise to provide some of this knowledge. Such links will foster positive relationships between ethnic groups and will show minority groups that you are valuing their culture. Consideration should be given to clothing, with Muslim girls being allowed to wear clothes which are loose and fully cover the body. You must also consider facilities for changing and/or showering, and how to provide facilities that allow privacy. You should also consider the intensity of work given to Muslim children during the month of Ramadan. Many Muslim children are likely to fast, and remember this means abstaining from not only food but all liquid, from dawn to sunset. You should take care not to over exhaust such pupils, especially during hot weather.

Enquiry Task

Examine your schools' Equal Opportunity Policy.

- In what ways does it allow for full provision of opportunity for all pupils?
- What aspects, if any, are missing from your policy?
- Are pupils and parents aware of the policy?

Examine how implementation of the policy is monitored at school, and in the individual class level.

- What specialized apparatus is available for use by pupils with special needs?

- In what ways are special needs pupils given additional support?
- In what ways does your own planning allow for equal opportunity?
- Does your planning encourage input from a variety of cultures?

Write an action plan to improve equality of provision in your own PE lessons.

References

BRITISH ASSOCIATION OF ADVISERS AND LECTURERS IN PHYSICAL EDUCATION (BAALPE), (1990) *Safe Practice in Physical Education*, Oxford, Alden Press.

DEPARTMENT FOR EDUCATION (DFE) (1994a) *Key Stages 1 and 2 of the National Curriculum England*, London, HMSO.

DEPARTMENT FOR EDUCATION (DFE) (1994b) *The Code of Practice on the Identification and Assessment of Special Educational Needs*, London, HMSO.

DEPARTMENT FOR EDUCATION (DFE) (1995) *Key Stages 1 and 2 of the National Curriculum England*, London, HMSO.

DEPARTMENT FOR EDUCATION (DFE) (1996) *A Guide to the National Curriculum*, London, HMSO.

DEPARTMENT OF NATIONAL HERITAGE (DNH) (1995) *Sport: Raising the Game*, London, HMSO.

RUSSELL, J. (1988) *Graded Activities for Children with Motor Difficulties*, Cambridge, Cambridge University Press.

SPODE, I. and WHITLAM, P. (1996) *Physical Education, Assessment, Recording and Reporting*, Dudley, Dudley Physical Education Advisory Service.

List of Suggested Reading

General

MANNERS, H. and CARROLL, M. (1995) *A Framework for Physical Education in the Early Years*, London, Falmer Press.
(An excellent book which gives sound practice for the teaching of all areas of the Physical Education Programme at Key Stage 1.)

SPODE, I. and WHITLAM, P. (1996) *Physical Education, Assessment, Recording and Reporting*, Dudley, Dudley Advisory Service.
(This booklet gives a practical guide to the assessment of physical education and also includes a sample report document.)

Gymnastics

CARROLL, M. and GARNER, D. (1984) *Gymnastics 7–11*, London, Falmer Press.

MANNERS, H. and CARROLL, M. (1991) *Gymnastics 4–7*, London, Falmer Press.
(Both of these books give details of how to plan programmes of work using a thematic approach.)

Jennifer Gray

Games

READ, B. and EDWARDS, P. (1992) *Teaching Children to Play Games*, London, The Sports
    Council.
    (A most comprehensive loose leaf book which gives examples of practices for all areas
    of games teaching; it includes work cards.)

Dance

EVANS, J. and POWELL, H. (1994) *Inspirations for Dance and Movement*, Leamington Spa,
    Scholastic.
HARRISON, K. (1986) *Look, Look What I Can Do*, London, BBC Publications.
HARRISON, K. (1993) *Let's Dance: The Place of Dance in the Primary School*, London,
    Hodder and Stoughton.
    (These books give very practical ideas for the inexperienced dance teacher. The dances
    are based on themes and classroom projects.)
WIGNALL, D. and GARGRAVE, B. (1995) *Dance in the Primary School*, Wheathampstead,
    Hertfordshire Education Services.
    (This excellent publication includes practical ideas to interpret the National Curriculum.
    It stresses the need for progression through schemes of work and also gives very
    practical ideas to help planning.)

Swimming

LAWTON, J. (1995) *Introduction to Swimming Teaching and Coaching*, Loughborough,
    Amateur Swimming Association.
    (A very well-presented publication which includes photographs of the strokes and skills.
    The user-friendly layout gives instant access to progressive practices and appropriate
    teaching points.)

11 Design and Technology

David Coates and Jean Harding

Introduction

This chapter introduces you to the subject of design and technology. For many people, this was a new subject that had not been in the school curriculum prior to the introduction of the National Curriculum. Its introduction raised many fears in teachers in primary schools. In reality, many of the activities involved in design and technology were already in place in craft, art and science lessons. The subject required a shift in emphasis, presentation and control by the teacher. The teacher became more of an enabler, allowing children to express their ideas in a non-threatening environment. This chapter sets out to show you that there is much that is familiar about technology.

Design and technology capability lies at the heart of the subject and the basis of this is to *design* and *make* things for a *purpose*. The subject reflects what happens in the wider world. In the chapter, we discuss technology in this wider context and then go on to discuss how you can implement and develop the subject in school. There are two examples of units of work that demonstrate how design and technology can work. We address some of the issues that might inhibit the development of design and technology and how these might be overcome.

Enquiry Task

Discuss with teachers/children what they understand by the term 'technology', and what sort of school activities they associate with the subject, 'Design and Technology'.

Identify any concerns that you have about teaching design and technology. Discuss these with a colleague.

What is Design and Technology Capability?

Since our earliest days, when we used pointed sticks to dig up roots to eat, people have been technologists. Technology is an essential human activity. Technology has developed our capability to build homes, grow food, travel to the Moon and talk to someone at the other side of the world. It is a purposeful activity, which allows human beings to use materials, tools and systems to improve their environment

(APU, 1987). Technology is, therefore, a practical activity in which products are created to solve problems and meet people's needs and wants. Products can be viewed in different ways, depending on the need that is met. A car can be considered as a single object (*artefact*) that is attractive when compared with other cars. It is also a collection of objects (*system*) — for example, engine, steering wheel and so on — which together produce movement in the car. It can carry a group of people safely (*an environment*) (NCC, 1990).

Different people have a variety of needs and wants, all of which have to be taken into consideration for a product to be successful; for example, is the car attractive? is the price reasonable? what type of engine and gear box does the car have? does it have air bags and side impact bars? Therefore, we make value judgments about the worth of something, and evaluate it to see if it might be improved. This is an integral part of the technological process. Technological developments can occur when products are evaluated to see if they can be improved to better meet the need and solve the original problem. Early car wheels were made of wood with solid rubber tyres. These have evolved into the steel with its pneumatic tyre.

Many technologists today are concerned that technology should have a 'human face', and that environmental and social issues should be uppermost in any considerations of the values of technology. Most new cars now burn unleaded petrol and many are fitted with catalytic convertors to cut down on air pollution. Technologists do not work in isolation when attempting to find solutions to problems, they utilize and apply knowledge and skills and appropriate resources. Technology is not simply 'the appliance of science', it utilizes and applies knowledge gained from the arts and mathematics, and includes knowledge of similar products and suitable materials.

Design and technology capability is essentially a creative and critical process whereby products are designed and made to solve particular problems. These may be on a large scale — for example, the Severn Bridge — or small scale — for example, a plastic clothes peg. Solutions need to be workable, suitable and fully researched, taking into consideration the constraints set by the original problem. Technology often involves teamwork which develops and utilizes the strengths of all of the team members.

Developing Design and Technology Capability in Children

The Design and Technology Order states:

> Pupils should be taught to develop their design & technology capability through combining their designing and making skills with knowledge and understanding in order to design and make products. (DFE, 1995, p. 58)

Design and technology is, therefore, a subject concerned with practical action, and with a body of knowledge and skills that can be taught. The knowledge gained should not be for its own sake but should act as a resource to be used where it is needed. The skills needed to solve technological problems are both practical, for example, cutting wood; and intellectual, for example, generating ideas. Therefore, design and technology embraces the process whereby children use their knowledge, concepts, skills and creativity to formulate solutions to relevant practical tasks. There is a close link between technology in the wider world and design and technology in schools.

The Programmes of Study detail what you need to teach, and have five sections. The first two parts concern the nature and range of the tasks, activities and assignments to be provided, and the variety of materials, skills and understandings to be applied. The third and fourth parts detail the designing and making skills, and the fifth the knowledge and understanding that needs to be taught for children to design and make in a meaningful way. Children will need to undertake a variety of activities in order to develop their capability: focused practical tasks (FPTs); investigate, disassemble and evaluate activities (IDEAs); and design and make assignments (DMAs). DMAs are the ultimate aim of design and technology teaching; they are at the heart of the process and indicate the capability that the child has developed.

Children, like all other technologists, cannot design and make things without the appropriate knowledge and skills.

> . . . in technology, where the processes of designing and making lie at the heart of children's work . . . pupils should be taught the relevant knowledge to support their designing and making . . . (NCC, 1993, p. 15)

Design and technology activities should build on or extend children's knowledge, understanding and skills. This is the basis of the focused practical task, which should also give children the opportunity to use and apply knowledge and skills gained in other curriculum areas, for example science and art. In science, it might be the study of the forces involved in structures: in art, it might be the use of graphic media. Safety and hygiene are particularly important aspects that need to be taught and re-emphasized whenever appropriate (see, for example, NAAIDT, 1992).

Year 1 children may have to be taught how to fold and cut card carefully when making a Christmas card. Year 6 children may be investigating series circuits, and soldering motors and lamps into models. The teaching of design and technology knowledge and skills can be approached in two ways. As a teacher, you may indicate what children need to know and be able to do before they start a particular assignment. Tasks can be set to teach the skills and knowledge that have been identified. At other times, a problem can be set and tasks designed to teach children the skills or knowledge necessary for them to produce their particular solution. Children will be able to apply the knowledge and skills that they already have or will see the need to increase their knowledge and skills, in order to achieve a solution to a problem.

Products that others have made are examined to help technologists develop their ideas. This technique is encouraged through activities where children investigate, disassemble and evaluate simple products (IDEAs). By looking at simple products, children are better able to make products themselves. Children might examine moving toys to find out how they work before making a rubberband-powered toy of their own.

Implicit in the definitions of technology is the idea of 'design'. Designing does not simply mean the production of complex drawings and models. For primary school children it will include an awareness of problems, clarification of ideas and critical evaluation of alternative solutions.

> Children should be given the opportunity to describe and represent (model) their
> ideas in various ways e.g., talking, drawing, using construction kits or 3-D objects.
> (SCAA, 1995, p. 8)

The skills needed to model ideas may be best taught in a systematic way. Young children may design simply by looking at and selecting from materials that you have provided for them; for example, a selection of cardboard boxes and tubes to create a robot. This viewing of resources will help to stimulate children's ideas. Modelling can help children to develop and evaluate their ideas and consider whether they meet the intended need or purpose. Children can still be asked to justify their ideas, perhaps in an oral fashion when discussing their ideas with you. You need to have a clear idea about the purpose(s) of the drawings you want the children to produce; for example, annotated and observational drawings, exploded and sequence diagrams. These purposes should be conveyed to the children to help them in their designing (Anning, 1994). Drawings and diagrams produced by professional designers can act as a stimulus for children's ideas; for example, when working with a Key Stage 1 class, a parent brought in the plans for a large model plane, together with the wooden parts to make the wings. He explained to the children about the plans and placed the wing members onto the 1:1 plan for the children to see. This stimulated much discussion before the children designed their own model planes.

To develop capability, children need to have experience of tackling problems where they identify a need and construct a solution. Children need to feel confident and secure about the value of their contributions and ideas. The ethos of the classroom needs to be positive and responsive to children's solutions to tasks. Children's self-esteem can be enhanced through group work where they share ideas, listen carefully to others, and give and take positive criticism. You need to be willing to spend time to develop this aspect of your teaching, by being prepared to listen to children in your discussions with them, by accepting that children's ideas have value, and by careful questioning to allow children to evaluate their ideas in a non-threatening situation.

A problem that requires a real solution can ensure that the activities are challenging, motivating and relevant. Children should, therefore, identify needs and opportunities, use these ideas to generate a design, and then plan and make their solution to the problem. Evaluation should run throughout the whole process. They can discuss their design proposals to develop and synthesize ideas. Plans can be changed as children realize that what they intended could not be made, and final solutions can be appraised through testing and discussion (Anning, 1994).

Developing Capability in Schools

Planning

> The programmes of study set out what pupils should be taught and provide a basis
> from which you can develop units of work for teaching and everyday assessment.
> These units of work may specify objectives for teaching and assessment and ensure
> that, over the key stage, you give pupils opportunities to show what they know,
> understand and can do. (SCAA, 1996, p. 2)

The development of a child's capability comes through successful planning of
design and technology. Design and technology can be taught as a separate subject
and through themes (NCC, 1990). When taught as a subject you can get a clear
picture of the Programmes of Study to be covered. When taught through themes,
design and technology activities support, and are supported, by other subjects. Both
approaches are appropriate and might be decided on after looking at the long and
medium term plans that the school has in place. Contexts for your teaching should
be selected that are relevant for the children. There needs to be continuity of experience where units of work build on and develop children's designing and making
skills, knowledge and understanding. School plans should indicate the aspects of
the Programmes of Study to be covered in any year. From this, it should be possible
for you to choose the activities that will develop the children's technological knowledge and skills, and the contexts for children's design and make assignments.

You need to consider health and safety issues at an early stage in your planning to identify any risks that might be involved in the work and the strategies
needed to minimize them. Without a broader picture of design and technology
teaching in the school and a knowledge of children's previous experiences, we
cannot ensure balance of experience or progression. Units of work may stand alone,
come out of themes or topics, come from other curriculum areas, result from visits
or visitors, lead from local or national events, or the needs of others.

Design and technology is a good vehicle for teaching time management. The
timing of a unit of work is very important, and children, as well as their teacher,
need to be aware of this to allow them the time necessary for research, brain
storming, designing, making and evaluating their products. The resources that you
have available might be an important constraint on what the children can produce,
and this must be considered in your planning.

The new requirements for Design and Technology (1995) state that all units
for work should include work on:

> . . . designing skills, making skills, materials and components, products and appli-
> cations, quality, health and safety and vocabulary. (SCAA, 1995, p. 30)

The objectives of the unit of work can be established by reference to each aspect
of this list. Once the context and the objectives of the unit of work have been
established, you can decide upon the activities that the children will undertake. The

design and make assignment is at the heart of the subject, and it is here that children exhibit their capability: this, therefore, is likely to be the first type of activity that is planned. There will be a clear link with the focused practical tasks that will develop and enhance children's knowledge, understanding and skills in order to be more effective in their work. Whenever possible, children should investigate, disassemble and evaluate products linked to their DMA in order to enrich their own designing and making, and to increase their knowledge and understanding.

Progression

> Progression is about unpeeling progressive layers of meaning and consequences; like peeling an onion. Whilst a 6 year old can see that a product needs to be safe, a 12 year old might additionally be able to identify a range of risks (fire/cuts/ swallowing etc.) and make proposals to counteract them. (Kimbell, 1994, p. 73)

Children can progress in two main ways; in what they know or are able to do, and in the nature of the assignments that they can tackle. These two aspects of progression can be further subdivided. Children's knowledge and skills can progress in three ways:

- they know more and increase their skills;
- they become more efficient at using the skills and knowledge they have;
- their ability to utilize knowledge and skills from other curriculum areas increases.

Children's progress related to the nature of the assignment moves from:

- contexts which are familiar to them to those which are unfamiliar;
- being directed in their assignments to more open-ended assignments;
- simple tasks, in terms of FPTs, IDEAs, designing and making skills, to complex assignments with many aspects to consider.

Assessment

Assessment can be used to determine your effectiveness in developing children's design and technology capability and to improve their learning. To be effective, assessment needs to be built into your planning. This will mean that you have a clear, broad picture of how each child has performed and of their design and make capability. There are two forms of assessment that you may find useful in your design and technology teaching; formative (or diagnostic) assessment, and summative assessment. Formative assessment is the day-to-day assessment of children's activities which assist you in planning the next tasks and units of work. The planning, teaching and assessment that you undertake will link directly with the Programmes of Study and the Level Descriptions. You may need to assess children's design and make capability and also the knowledge, understanding and skills that they have acquired. Specific concepts and skills are taught through FPTs and IDEAs within a unit of work. Children may utilize these in their designing and making. Therefore, we need a check on these in ongoing formative assessment throughout the year.

Summative assessment can be used at the end of each unit of work, or more properly at the end of a Year or Key Stage when information from a number of units of work, in a number of contexts, may give you a clear picture of the level at which the child is working. The essential function of the Level Descriptions is to help you to make summative assessments. Level Descriptions detail the development of capability. Two key principles of capability are 'designing' and 'making', the two Attainment Targets. The Level Descriptions refer to the development of knowledge and understanding in general, and not to specific facts. They describe the uses of knowledge that children have obtained. For each Attainment Target, you will need to assess which Level Descriptor describes best the Level at which the child is working.

Record keeping is an essential feature of assessment. This does not simply mean recording the experiences and work that the children have covered. You need to record what the children have learnt and also by how much their competence has increased. By doing this you will be giving an indication of whether or not any additional activities are necessary to reinforce concepts and skills. Discussion with colleagues about judgments of children's work will help you to come to consistent interpretations of the Levels within the Level Descriptions.

Enquiry Task

Identify a design and make assignment that is linked to a topic you are interested in. Investigate the knowledge and skills that will be necessary for the children to perform this assignment. Check through the Programmes of Study for your Key Stage so as to plan focused practical tasks and investigate, disassemble and evaluate activities that will allow children to design and make in a meaningful way.

Below we describe two assignments that we taught in school.

Designing and Making a Sandwich — An Example of a Key Stage 1 Assignment

Within the half term topic 'The Teddy Bear's Picnic', many design and technology activities took place. The children:

- designed and made invitations;
- selected, from a display of party hats, and then made one hat for their teddy and one for themselves, and then told a friend what they would need;

- made a picnic box for themselves and their teddy;
- made a chair for their teddy;
- made a list of party games or made up some games and were prepared to explain how to play them;
- prepared cakes and biscuits, discussed storage, and then designed and made sandwiches.

Some sandwiches were brought into the classroom and the children discussed what a sandwich was and listed what each sandwich contained. The children drew their favourite sandwiches. The history of sandwiches was discussed. (These are investigate, disassemble and evaluate activities, IDEAs.)

Linked with work in science — for example, discussion about healthy sandwich fillings — the children tasted and selected their preference from four types of bread and four fillings. Younger children might look at a smaller selection of breads and fillings. Discussion about healthy fillings took place before final choices were made. The bread and fillings were brought in by small groups of children. Linked with work in mathematics, information was gathered and displayed by means of a block graph. Linked with work in English, the children were told stories about picnics and making sandwiches (for example, *The Lighthouse Keeper's Lunch*, Ronda Armitage (1994); *This is the Bear and the Picnic Lunch*, Sarah Hayes (1988)).

The children then brainstormed how to make a sandwich. From this class brainstorm, a plan was written on a flipchart to sequence the order of activities. The need for hygienic working conditions was discussed, as was the type of utensils needed to complete the task. The children were then asked to consider how they all could be involved in the sandwich making. This led to the children working in two production lines; for example, butterers, fillers, cutters and arrangers. This work links with early ideas about economic and industrial understanding.

The children drew on their own experiences as well as their designing skills. They clarified their ideas through discussion to make suggestions how to proceed. Their making skills included selecting materials, tools and techniques. They were involved in assembling, joining and combining materials and components. The children made suggestions about how to proceed and applied simple finishing techniques. The knowledge and understanding gained by the children, through focused practical tasks, was mainly linked to health and safety. They learnt how to spread, cut and grate.

Designing and Making a House — An Example of a Key Stage 2 Assignment

The children involved in this assignment were in Years 5 and 6 and were studying a topic on 'Homes'. The children had to design and make a house, or part of a house, that was to be built from a frame structure, and which had electrical circuits in it somewhere. The children had constructed simple circuits with switches in Years 3 or 4. The use of a switch and the need for a complete circuit with no gaps were reinforced through focused practical tasks where children looked at varying the flow of current in the circuit; for example, dimmer switches and parallel circuits. The children were shown how to construct different types of switches — for example, tilt, pressure, rotating — which they might use in their houses. Clearly, within these focused practical tasks the link with science is a very close one. The children were shown how to draw circuit diagrams and to make card mock-ups to aid their design work. As part of their 'investigate, disassemble and evaluate activities' (IDEAs), the children carried out a survey to identify all the different things in their homes that used electricity. They examined manufactured switches and conducted a survey to find out the variety of switches that were used at home. The safety aspects of electrical work had to be constantly reinforced throughout the project.

The second focus was the framework for the house. In the past, the children had made a wooden rectangular frame which had been strengthened with triangular corner pieces made out of card. This time, the children had to manufacture a 3-D frame so the need for accuracy was more important. Again, safe use of tools was emphasized. The children worked in groups to design their house. They examined the materials that their teacher had available and then, on paper, drew annotated sketches of their first ideas. These sketches were transformed into card mock-ups so the children could see how their circuits could be fitted in. The children needed to turn the lights on and off, and they had to design switches to do this. Some children made burglar alarms from pressure switches under carpets and also switches that operated when a door opened. Some children wanted a fire-effect, so they made flames from tissue paper; lamps were put behind this to show when the fire was burning.

Issues Affecting the Development of Capability

Teachers' Knowledge and Skills

The main aim of design and technology teaching is to increase children's capability. If you are to increase children's understanding then you must understand the subject yourself. Effective assessment of children's design and technology capability depends, to a great extent, upon your level of understanding of capability.

Three main forms of knowledge will increase your effectiveness as a teacher. The first form is your own design and technology knowledge. Development of your own capability should include an understanding that goes beyond the primary school level and into the wider world of technology. It should include knowledge of technical vocabulary; for example, what are cams and cranks, and how do they operate? When you feel content with your own understanding and skills you are likely to become more effective in your teaching, and be more relaxed (and therefore adventurous), allowing children greater freedom to explore more complex ideas.

The second form of knowledge is pedagogical content knowledge (Shulman, 1986). This will include: knowledge of the best ways to organize children's learning; what construction kits will best illustrate particular concepts, for instance, gearing up and down; what relevant help to give children in their constructions; and the examples and illustrations to use that will aid children's understanding of technological concepts and vocabulary.

The third form of knowledge is curricular knowledge. You need to understand the Design and Technology National Curriculum, the content of the Programmes of Study and the Level Descriptions. This knowledge can be enhanced by reference to *Key Stage 1 and 2: Design and Technology The New Requirements* (SCAA, 1995), and to published schemes (see bibliography for examples).

Enquiry Task

The Programme of Study for Key Stage 2 states that: 'pupils should be taught:
how simple mechanisms can be used to produce different types of movement.'
Meeting this requirement could involve pupils in using pulleys, gears, levers, cams and cranks.

- Find out what the terms pulley, gears and cams mean.
- Plan focused practical tasks, and investigate, disassemble and evaluate activities to develop children's understanding of these terms.
- What design and make assignments might use this knowledge?

The Classroom Environment

Your classroom needs to be organized to maximize children's experience of technology, and to allow and encourage the children to select materials, resources and tools for themselves. If the classroom environment can meet children's needs then they may be more likely to be able to solve problems which are concerned with the needs of others. You may wish to create space for children to work, with access to resources and tools. Some assignments may take weeks to complete and, therefore, storage arrangements for unfinished work may need to be organized. Displaying work will show that you value what the children have produced, so you may want to plan this space. In this way you may stimulate divergent thinking, creativity and inventiveness, all of which are essential parts of design and technology capability.

Enquiry Task

When you are beginning to plan out your next unit of work for design and technology the following task should aid you to teach it more effectively.

- Review your classroom environment. In what ways does it provide inspiration and encouragement for design and technology?
- How might the classroom environment be improved to allow freer access to tools and resources?
- How could displays be developed that celebrate children's achievements?
- Are there 'hands on' displays, linked to units of work, that can be prepared?

Your choice of tasks and contexts should be carefully selected so that it does not reinforce stereotypes. Children's capability and range of interests need to be extended beyond conventional horizons. Ethical, moral and National Curriculum 'law' considerations should be examined when design and technology units of work are planned. All children should be given opportunities to use all the materials and components encompassed by design and technology. It is 'good' for children to see male and female adults working together on food, textiles, electricity, and mechanical and construction activities. If your school does not have both male and female teachers, you may wish to consider how to provide children with other appropriate role models. Children's awareness needs to be raised so as to acknowledge the roles of female designers or engineers and male cooks or fashion workers. Children of both sexes need to know and understand that they all need practical skills as well as the ability to record and communicate. You may consider it your duty to ensure that children see that technology can lead to worthwhile careers, and that it can raise understanding of the world and of human issues.

Remember, you are preparing children to live in a multicultural society, and one way that you can do this is to draw attention to and value artefacts from other cultures; how they are made, how they have evolved, and how we acknowledge through, for example, investigate, disassemble and evaluate activities (IDEAs), the contribution they make to people's lives. It is easy for children to think that a society without advanced technology is primitive. Lower levels of technology may still incorporate a balance of needs and available resources, and will, almost certainly, be appropriate for that particular community. You might use case studies to enhance your teaching of a particular topic; for example, a study of 'Homes' may look at mud huts and emphasize the energy efficient nature of their design. The annotated reading list at the end of this chapter provides details of valuable sources of ideas and information.

For a variety of reasons, many children may lack confidence and may be easily put off working on design and technology activities. The tasks that you plan should have differentiation built in. Some tasks may need modifications so as to meet the needs of specific children: other tasks may need no modification since differentiation is by outcome. The more capable children should have higher expectations put upon them; for example, be asked to make more careful measurements, record results more precisely and annotate sketches more accurately. This may be planned so each child knows what is expected of her/him, and she/he is able to use her/his knowledge and understanding to achieve success.

Every child needs to be made very aware of what each activity demands and what your aims are. Some children will require step-by-step guidance or a simple sheet that will lead them through the activity. *Time* is another way that you may like to differentiate; for example, you may wish to assist less able children more than other groups. Focused practical tasks help to build confidence by carefully adding to children's skills and knowledge. Small group work builds up self-confidence and prevents a less confident child becoming an onlooker. You may wish to try to counteract interference and the dominance of some children as both are likely to lower the self-esteem of some others. The use of praise and encouragement, being aware of what is happening in each group, and quiet intervention, when needed, are skills that you may need to acquire. Asking the children what they have done, what they have learnt and whether they need more experience in an aspect of their skills or knowledge, may help in your planning of differentiated activities and will, in addition, involve the children more in evaluating their own needs and their work.

Enquiry Task

- How might you use construction kits to develop children's ideas about mechanisms and control?
- What aspects of design and technology capability are developed by this activity?
- Observe children working to see if everyone in a group is included in the activity. What steps will you take to ensure that all children are involved?

References

ANNING, A. (1994) 'Dilemmas and opportunities of a new curriculum: Design and technology with young children', *International Journal of Technology and Design Education*, **4**, pp. 155–77.

APU (1989) *Science at Age 13*, London, HMSO.

ARMITAGE, R. (1989) *The Lighthouse Keeper's Lunch*, London, Oliver Boyd.

DATA (1995) *Guidance Materials for Design and Technology, Key Stages 1 and 2*, Wellesbourne, DATA.

HAYES, S. (1988) *This is the Bear and the Picnic Lunch*, London, Wallen.

DE BONO, E. (1978) *Teaching Thinking*, Harmondsworth, Penguin Books.

DFE (1995) *Key Stages 1 and 2 of the National Curriculum*, London, HMSO.

KIMBELL, R. (1994) 'Progression in learning and the assessment of children's attainment in technology', *International Journal of Technology and Design Education*, **4**, pp. 65–83.

NAAIDT (The National Association of Advisors and Inspectors in Design and Technology) (1992) *Make it Safe*, Eastleigh, NAAIDT Publications.

NCC (1990) *Technology in the National Curriculum*, London, HMSO.

NCC (1993) *Technology Programmes of Study and Attainment Targets: Recommendations of the National Curriculum Council*, York, NCC.

SCAA (1995) *Key Stages 1 and 2: Design and Technology the New Requirements*, London, HMSO.

SCAA (1996) *Exemplification of Standards in Design and Technology: Key Stage 3*, London, HMSO.

SHULMAN, L. (1986) 'Those who understand: Knowledge growth in teaching', *Educational Research Review*, **57**, 1, pp. 4–14.

Annotated List of Suggested Reading and Resources

BAGSHAW, H. (1992) *STEP: Design and Technology 5–16*, Cambridge, Cambridge University Press.

(This contains teachers' resource files for Key Stages 1 and 2, a story book pack and flip book for Key Stage 1, and information books for Key Stage 2. There is a particularly useful DATA file for Key Stage 2 that contains photocopiable sheets covering all aspects of D & T.)

BUDGETT-MEAKIN, C. (1992) *Make the Future Work*, London, Longman.

(This is an important book in which contributors, by examining values and appropriate technology, provide a range of views and thus set technology within a world-wide perspective.)

DATA (1995) *Guidance Materials for Design and Technology, Key Stages 1 and 2*, Wellesbourne, DATA.

(This pack contains a guide book with details on developing design and technology in your school. It contains 30 units of work encompassing a comprehensive range of activities for children.)

DATA (1996) *Technical Vocabulary for KS 1 & 2 — Design and Technology*, Wellesbourne, DATA.

(This contains words and definitions of the terms used in design and technology.)

GIBSON, C., HARDING, J., HUTCHING, J., MAPSTONE, J. and PENGELLY, B. (1991) *Rainbow Technology*, Cheltenham, Stanley Thornes Ltd.

(A useful resource for developing design and technology in primary schools. It consists of workcards with challenges and ideas, a teachers' guide with comprehensive notes to each card, 36 context cards and a techniques book which provides a bank of photocopiable materials that will help to develop working skills.)

MACAULEY, D. (1988) *The Way Things Work*, London, Dorling Kindersley Ltd.

(This is a clear and easy introduction to machines and how they work.)

SCAA (1995) *Key Stage 1 and 2: Design and Technology the New Requirements*, London, HMSO.

(This give a clear, concise interpretation of the National Curriculum. It explains what terms mean, shows progression between Key Stages and illustrates this with examples of children's work and ideas for activities.)

12 Information Technology

Chris Higgins

Introduction

Information technology (IT) has a place throughout the primary school as a cross-curricular tool for both children and teachers, and as such you will find that it appears in many different places in the National Curriculum document (DFE, 1995). The first task in this chapter is to consider how IT is represented in the formal National Curriculum and to consider the philosophy behind its inclusion.

The National Curriculum sets out the essential knowledge and skills of IT capability for children, and as this definition of the legal curriculum must stand unchanged for a reasonable length of time, it is phrased in terms of the processes involved and is independent of current software and curriculum practice. This means that the teacher has to have the expertise and experience to put the flesh of classroom activities onto the skeleton of the legal framework, and so some ideas for using IT in practice are offered: in language, using a word processor; in mathematics and geography, using a spreadsheet; and in any context, using a multimedia authoring package. Some strategies for gathering more information about ideas and resources are discussed, followed by an introduction to the Internet as a source of information.

Next, the issues that the use of IT might raise for you in teaching and learning are considered. You might well ask yourself how you can tell if a particular activity is worthwhile and what is actually going on when the children are using some IT in their work. Some approaches are introduced for you to consider using as you attempt to evaluate the complexity of IT activities in the classroom. Then some of the implications IT use might have for your general planning and assessment are considered, followed by a discussion of the need for a whole school approach to planning the IT curriculum to ensure that each child is exposed to the full range of IT activities, at the right stage for them, and that there is a progression in their activities over time.

Finally, what might constitute an IT capability for teachers is considered, which would enable today's teachers to deliver to their children all that is required in the IT realm. As the recent evidence, both from the national research project on the impact of IT on children's learning (Watson, 1993) and from the latest review of OFSTED inspections (OFSTED, 1995), shows that the quality, and indeed quantity, of current IT use in schools is still very patchy, there is still some way to go.

The Philosophy

There are two aspects to the use of information technology in the primary school for the teacher: first, the development of each child's personal IT capability and skills; and second, the possibilities for IT to enhance children's learning in all areas of the curriculum. The National Curriculum describes what is meant by IT capability as follows:

> Information technology capability is characterised by an ability to use effectively IT tools and information sources to analyse, process and present information, and to model, measure and control external events.
> This involves:
>
> - using information sources and IT tools to solve problems;
> - using IT tools and information sources, such as computer systems and software packages, to support learning in a variety of contexts;
> - understanding the implications of IT for working life and society. (DFE, 1995, p. 67)

The philosophy inherent in the National Curriculum is that the development of a child's IT capability and skills should take place generally in context in other areas of the curriculum, and not in specific IT time or sessions. For example, rather than talking about databases in the abstract, you could wait until you were collecting some information together in class, perhaps as part of a science activity. Then, as one of the ways the children might work with this information, you could explain about databases in context and get the children to enter the information into one. They could then investigate the data, and so develop and practise their database skills as well as answer the questions they had started with.

The two different aspects of IT use in the primary school are emphasized by the fact that IT appears in two distinctly different ways in the National Curriculum. It is treated as a subject in its own right, with an Attainment Target and associated Programmes of Study; but it also appears in the detail of the Programmes of Study for other curriculum areas. Indeed, with the exception of PE, all other curriculum subjects have the following statement in their Programmes of Study: 'Pupils should be given opportunities, where appropriate, to develop and apply their information technology capability in their study of . . .'

You can start to make sense of what is required in the classroom for IT by first concentrating on the part of the National Curriculum that talks about IT as a subject (DFE, 1995, pp. 67–71). The Programmes of Study at each Key Stage (KS) start with overarching statements, which provide a focus for the activities at that stage and help you to get a feeling for the progression between the stages. They state:

> KS1 Pupils should be taught to use IT equipment and software confidently and purposefully to communicate and handle information and to support their problem solving, recording and expressive work.

> KS2 Pupils should be taught to extend the range of IT tools that they use for communication, investigation and control; become discerning in their use of IT; to select information, sources and media for their suitability for purpose; and assess the value of IT in their working practices (DFE, 1995, pp. 68–9)

The substance of the Programme of Study is then set out in more general terms in just three sections: what opportunities should be given to pupils; what should be taught about communicating and handling information; and what should be taught about controlling and modelling. Thus in Key Stage 1, pupils are essentially gaining experience of a variety of IT applications in a range of contexts; whilst in Key Stage 2, they are essentially extending their experience of using IT, and becoming more sophisticated in their choice of IT to use. IT capability is seen to be more than just the skills of IT use, it combines the ability to use IT effectively with an understanding of its purpose.

The next step in becoming familiar with the position of IT is to see how it is used in other curriculum areas.

Enquiry Task

Analyse the National Curriculum document (DFE, 1995) to discover where IT is mentioned in other curriculum areas.

- Highlight the explicit references to IT use in other subjects.
- Decide which of these references would fall within the work in your class.
- Draw up a diagram of the whole year scheme of work for your class, showing where the IT activities would occur and in which part of the curriculum they would be.
- Decide what part of the IT capability they also address, if any.

You can now start to see what parts of the IT capability will be covered by the activities suggested by these explicit references in other curriculum areas, and what areas you will still need to work on.

IT Use in Practice

Having got a feel for what the documentation says about IT requirements, let us look at some examples of what you can do in practice. First, let us consider writing activities in English (see also Chapter 3). Word processing is one of the most common IT applications used in school, and the ability to use a word processor is obviously one element of IT capability. However, to use a word processor only for copying previously handwritten text wastes the potential of a powerful tool.

As you may have found from the previous enquiry task, there are explicit references to IT use in the English curriculum for writing:

Pupils should have opportunities to: plan and review their writing, assembling and developing their ideas on paper and on screen (KS1); plan, draft and improve their work on paper and on screen (KS2). (DFE, 1995, p. 9 and p. 15)

The relationship between the use of a word processor and the teaching of writing skills is very complex. At Key Stage 2 it is suggested that pupils should think of the writing process as having five stages:

To develop their writing, pupils should be taught to:

- plan — note and develop initial ideas;
- draft — develop ideas from the plan into structured written text;
- revise — alter and improve the draft;
- proofread — check the draft for spelling and punctuation errors, omissions or repetitions;
- present — prepare a neat, correct and clear final text. (DFE, 1995, p. 15)

You might consider whether any of the stages could be enhanced by the use of IT. For example, for some children the planning stage is best carried out with pen and paper using a diagrammatic format, with an initial brainstorm of phrases or single words being joined by circles, boxes and arrows to indicate intended links. However, at the revision stage it may be a benefit to be working with text in a computer. The cut-and-paste facilities make it easier to make amendments and alterations to the text and obtain a new draft than it would be if the children had to write out the whole text each time by hand. The use of a spellchecker at the proofreading stage has interesting implications for the children. It draws their attention to spelling mistakes and offers corrections, and therefore can be a powerful teaching aid. It also reinforces the need for careful proofreading, as a spellchecker cannot check for meaning, and an unintended word may be passed by the spellchecker with unforeseen results. Using a word processor during the writing process will therefore give a different character to the various stages. You can see that it will fulfil some of the requirements of the IT capability development, but it can also enhance the language work.

There are other language activities that you can organize with a word processor that implicitly practise and develop word processing skills, but which are worthwhile in their own right. For example, you could give the children a piece of writing on the screen with the punctuation removed and then ask them to put it back so that the text makes sense. You might get a pair of children, or a group, to write something collaboratively. You could present a poem on screen with the lines mixed up and ask the children to use the cut-and-paste facilities to put them into the correct order. You can use this re-sequencing activity with many other texts as well for different purposes, for example a recipe, an experimental procedure, the dialogue in a play, a sequence of logical deductions, and so on. Again you will be enhancing other areas of the curriculum while carrying out in a meaningful way the requirements of developing the children's IT capability with a word processor.

Another rich source of IT activities that can enhance a number of curriculum areas is the use of spreadsheets. Obviously, spreadsheets can be used in mathematics as a vehicle for introducing and practising the use of algebraic concepts; for working with variables; and for investigating patterns and relationships. Spreadsheets can also be used in a number of curriculum areas for presenting and manipulating data. One innovative use of the presentational power of more powerful spreadsheets comes when working with maps in geography. Contour data can be taken from 25 points in a 5-by-5 grid on a map, and entered into an array of cells on the spreadsheet. If a 3-dimensional surface chart is now drawn of this data, a fair perspective view of the area represented on the map will be obtained. This can then be rotated at will and viewed from various elevations, providing a powerful tool to make links between the topography of the map and the reality of the countryside it represents.

An IT activity that incorporates many of the stated elements of IT capability is the use of a multimedia authoring package. Multimedia is the term used to describe multiple forms of information (such as text, graphics, sound, animation and video material) which are available at the same time from a single computer. A multimedia authoring package enables you to create links between the computer screen and the various computer-based multimedia resources, and so allows the user non-sequential access to text, pictures, sound and so on. This allows an interrelation between the resources, so that topics can be explored in multiple ways and the concepts involved can be used in different ways in different situations. For example, a map could be displayed on the screen which had links to pictures and text about the places on the map. Children could use such a package to present information on a topic for many parts of the curriculum. First they would have all the traditional information-gathering parts of the activity to carry out. Then they would have to prepare their resources in the form of text, drawings, photographs, sound and so on, and input them to the computer. Finally, they would have the task of organizing and presenting the material by means of the links, together with explanatory text or captions. The production of such a presentation would show understanding of the topic in question, and demonstrate the children's IT capability.

These examples give you a flavour of the kind of IT activities that you can incorporate into your classroom. But where can you get more ideas? Obviously there are many books and articles on the subject, and some are mentioned in the list of further reading at the end of the chapter. One particular organization that provides much useful material is the National Council for Educational Technology (NCET) which has put together a range of useful documents about IT use.

One of the most recent innovations that you can take advantage of is itself an application of IT, and that is the Internet. This worldwide network of information providers, with its interconnected databases, libraries, archives and so on, is a valuable source of information for the teacher about IT resources and activities.

Enquiry Task

Interrogate the Internet databases for teaching ideas and resources.

The Internet is an example of a multimedia package, consisting of linked 'pages' of information in the form of text, graphics, sound, video, etc. Each page has a unique

---

address which enables you to go straight to it, or you may go from one page to another by selecting a link such as a highlighted word in the text. The Internet is like a vast library: it doesn't have a catalogue but it does have the capacity to allow you to search electronically for what you seek.

- Choose a topic on which to search for information.
- There are a number of different ways to start your exploration:

    - you could start by looking at some of the general educational pages such as those maintained by NCET, BT (CampusWorld) or Research Machines (Pathways);
    - you could look at the pages of some of the subject associations such as the Association of Teachers of Mathematics;
    - you could employ what is termed a 'search engine' such as Alta Vista, to search for topics by means of keywords.

- As you read through the pages you will find items you can print out, and details of resources you can send off for. You might also make a note of the addresses of other pages of interest, and so develop your own personal list of sites from which you will be able to obtain news, ideas and resources.

For more details on using the Internet see *Highways for Learning* (NCET, 1995b).

Teaching and Learning Issues

One outcome of reflecting on the effects of using IT on the teaching and learning process might be a desire to evaluate activities in the classroom to see how they progress and what is happening that is worthwhile. The ideas that the social context of the learning process has an important role to play, originally proposed by the Russian psychologist Lev Vygotsky and developed in the writings of Jerome Bruner (Vygotsky, 1978; Bruner, 1986), lead to a theory of teaching and learning in which the effects of a child's peers and the choice of teaching process employed have to be considered in any evaluation. Viewing IT use in this context, if you want to collect evidence about an IT activity you must try to capture as much data as possible about all facets of the activity. The implication of this is that observational techniques will be required to record all the interactions between children, IT materials and teacher.

Enquiry Task

Collect evidence about an IT activity in the classroom and analyse what is going on.

- Gather as much data as you can about what takes place. You could:

    - videotape the activity;
    - tape record the activity;
    - (either yourself or a colleague) watch the activity and take notes or complete observation schedules;

- interview the children;
- record a navigation trace of how the program was used (this is a facility some programs have, that notes the order in which parts of the program are used);
- collect printouts giving information on the state of the program;
- take copies of screen displays.

- You can then carry out a detailed study of what happened during the activity. Use this to evaluate the nature and quality of the educational processes that took place.
- Introduce a form of discourse analysis:
  - create a transcript of what was said;
  - break what was said down into small units;
  - relate to these units the interactions that took place, the participants' views of why they did whatever they did, and the screen displays and outputs as representations of the state of the program.

- Analyse what was successful and what was worthwhile, both in terms of the development of IT capability and in the terms of the enhancement of the learning process.
- Consider how you might use the results of your analysis to guide your future use of IT.

Another issue raised by the use of IT in teaching and learning is that, as a cross-curricular activity occurring at so many points of the curriculum and at so many different times, you require an effective means of recording and assessing what each child has achieved.

As IT resources are bound to be scarce, it will not be possible for all your children to carry out a given activity at the same time. For instance, it may not be possible for them all to carry out an extended piece of writing using the word processor as fully as previously described, during the same period of time. However, with effective record keeping you can ensure that each child can go through this process at least once each year, say, during their work on various topics.

Similarly, your record keeping could enable you to ensure progression for each child by revisiting specific IT activities at intervals, with new work reflecting the children's increasing expertise. These ideas of providing progression themselves have an inevitable impact on the need for both short- and medium-term planning of opportunities for IT activity to occur in context.

Implications for Assessment and Planning

The evaluation of IT activities to discover how they may enhance the teaching and learning process for a class has been discussed in the previous section. Here, the more specific task of how to assess your children's individual IT capability is considered. Assessment may focus on a particular element of IT capability, or it may be that more holistic assessment is needed to decide a child's level of attainment at the end of a Key Stage. The Level Descriptions for each Key Stage describe the types and range of performance that pupils working at a particular level should characteristically demonstrate. The purpose of assessment in this area is no different to that in any other subject: it is to establish each child's progress in order to determine what is needed for them next.

As IT is a tool to support and enhance learning, its use may be part of an activity in some other context, and so the assessment of IT capability will probably be wrapped up with the assessment of the other activity. For example, you could assess how successful a child was in communicating ideas in text by looking at their use of a word processor. However, you should be considering the child's use of the word processor in the fullest sense of our previous discussion, not just measuring their ability to use a particular package (important though that would be), but also assessing how they approached the different stages of the writing process.

As part of your record keeping you will need to consider what evidence you might collect on which to base your assessments. Obviously, you can have examples of whatever the product of the IT activity is, such as printouts of text, pictures and so on. You might collect two or three printouts showing different stages in the development of the finished article. You could photograph screen displays or other finished work. You could also get the children to keep a written log of the progress of their work if it developed over a period of time, such as in the exploration of an adventure game.

You may want to assess the children's understanding of what they are doing as well as their ability to use IT. For this you could use any of the data gathering techniques mentioned in the previous enquiry task. For example, you might want to tape record the children's discussion as they are carrying out an activity, as one of the outcomes frequently reported when a small group of children carry out an IT activity is the focused discussion that takes place. Having observed the activity and made some notes, you may need to spend a few minutes talking to the children individually about what they have done. You could ask them to explain to you what they did and why. If they can describe their use of IT and suggest alternative ways of doing things then they are demonstrating a high level of IT capability. You might get the children to make some written comments on what they have been doing.

The assessment of a child's IT capability cannot be completed on a single occasion. A variety of situations will be needed to give opportunities for the various forms of IT activity. Also, to allow progression, children should be revisiting activities so that they can move on to more challenging uses of IT as their capability develops. This leads us to the whole question of planning IT activities.

The first enquiry task of the chapter asked you to draw up a map of your class's complete scheme of work, showing where the IT activities would take place which were generated from explicit references to IT use in other curriculum areas. You can now use this map as a framework to help you to plan where to place other IT activities you wish the children to engage in, to develop their IT capability or to enhance other parts of the curriculum. This gives you a chance to see the IT curriculum that the children will follow. You now really need to place your map into an overall map for the whole school.

Enquiry Task

Create a whole school IT curriculum map.

- The first step is to gather the information. Essentially you need to create an equivalent map to the one you have created for each of the classes in the school. You can do this in a number of ways:
    - ask your colleagues to fill in a questionnaire providing you with the information you require;
    - obtain the same information by means of structured interviews;
    - work with your colleagues in a staff meeting to create the maps.
- You can now amalgamate the individual class maps to create an overall IT map for the school, and then you can see the IT curriculum your school is offering.
- From this you can:
    - check that you are providing all the required opportunities for the children to develop their IT capability;
    - see where you are enhancing teaching and learning;
    - ensure that you are providing progression across the whole school, thus avoiding duplication.

IT Capability for Teachers

To use IT in the classroom, both for teaching and learning, and to help children to develop their own skills, you will need to have what might be termed a teacher's IT capability. IT capability for a teacher would include some pure IT skills, but more importantly it would include other educational skills which you might need to use IT effectively.

NCET worked with a group of teachers, advisors and teacher educators to come to a consensus of what might be considered as *IT capability for teachers*. They considered it to have seven elements:

- positive attitudes to IT;
- understanding of the educational potential of IT;
- ability to use IT effectively in the curriculum;
- ability to manage IT use in the classroom;
- ability to evaluate IT use;
- ability to ensure differentiation and progression;
- technical capability.

The group then expanded on each of these elements to give a full characterization of IT capability for teachers. This characterization could be considered a counsel of perfection, in the sense that it represents an ideal situation which is not realistic or feasible, but it can give a useful indication of where your own IT strengths and weaknesses lie.

Enquiry Task

Audit your personal IT capability by rating yourself for each of the seven elements on a 1–5 scale.

Capability in each element could be characterized in more detail as follows (adapted from NCET, 1995c):

Positive attitudes to IT
- use a range of IT resources with skill and confidence;
- tackle new applications with confidence;
- recognize the potential of new technologies in education.

Understanding of the educational potential of IT
- reflect on and adapt your teaching in the light of your knowledge, understanding and experience of IT.

Ability to use IT effectively in the curriculum
- plan schemes of work which integrate IT use within the context of the National Curriculum;
- plan, deliver and support learning activities involving the selection and use of IT at appropriate levels for all pupils;
- use and support the use of a range of IT resources and applications;
- encourage pupils, through their use of IT, to ask questions, solve problems, and work collaboratively.

Ability to manage IT use in the classroom
- effectively integrate IT into lessons, taking account of the availability and proposed use of IT resources;
- provide differentiated activities for pupils using IT;
- monitor and evaluate pupils' progress in using IT;
- provide opportunities for all pupils to make demonstrable progress in their use of IT.

Ability to evaluate IT use
- evaluate the usefulness and appropriateness of a range of IT resources for pupils of all ages and abilities, in differing curriculum contexts and with different teaching styles;
- evaluate the contribution IT has made to your pupils' learning;
- appraise your own use of IT for personal and professional purposes.

Ability to ensure differentiation and progression
- plan, implement, evaluate and review schemes of work for individual pupils incorporating IT use;
- effectively assess, record and report on your pupils' achievement in IT as well as in other subjects;
- use this process as the basis for cyclic planning to ensure pupil progress in developing IT capability;
- use IT as a personal and professional tool to support differentiation.

Technical capability
- use and manage a range of IT resources for information access, development and presentation of materials, communication and management;
- reflect on, evaluate and develop your own IT skills;
- seek out information and opportunities for updating your IT skills.

Having audited your personal IT capability, you could now decide on a personal development plan to work on any area of weakness. For example, if you wanted to improve your ability to use IT effectively in the curriculum, you could decide to concentrate on planning schemes of work that integrated IT use into other curriculum areas. One possible source of inspiration, as we have already mentioned, might be NCET documents, in particular *Approaches to IT Capability Key Stages 1 and 2* (NCET, 1995a). Another very useful source would be *Microscope*, which is the journal of Micros and Primary Education (MAPE), the national association for primary teachers interested in this area. This regular journal also produces occasional special editions on particular topics, and 'IT Starts Here!' (MAPE, 1994) could be a good starting point.

On the other hand, perhaps you feel that you would like to work on improving your ability to ensure differentiation and progression. This might be an opportunity to work with colleagues on agreeing a simple common system for recording IT achievement, which could assist you all in planning differentiated progression.

Whatever you decide to do, a planned approach which makes explicit the tasks you are intending to undertake and the goals you are hoping to achieve will assist you in developing your own IT capability.

References

BRUNER, J.S. (1986) *Actual Minds, Possible Worlds*, Cambridge, Massachusetts, Harvard University Press.

DEPARTMENT FOR EDUCATION (DFE) (1995) *Key Stages 1 and 2 of the National Curriculum England*, London, HMSO.

MICROS AND PRIMARY EDUCATION (MAPE) (1994) *Microscope Special: IT Starts Here!* Kettering, MAPE/Castlefield.

NATIONAL COUNCIL FOR EDUCATIONAL TECHNOLOGY (NCET) (1995a) *Approaches to IT Capability: Key Stages 1 and 2*, Coventry, NCET.

NATIONAL COUNCIL FOR EDUCATIONAL TECHNOLOGY (NCET) (1995b) *Highways for Learning: An Introduction to the Internet for Schools and Colleges*, Coventry, NCET.

NATIONAL COUNCIL FOR EDUCATIONAL TECHNOLOGY (NCET) (1995c) *Training Today's Teachers in IT*, Coventry, NCET.

OFFICE FOR STANDARDS IN EDUCATION (OFSTED) (1995) *Information Technology: A Review of Inspection Findings 1993/94*, London, HMSO.

VYGOTSKY, L.S. (1978) *Mind in Society: The Development of Higher Psychological Processes*, Cambridge, Massachusetts, Harvard University Press.

WATSON, D. (ed.) (1993) *The Impact Summary*, London, King's College.

Annotated List of Suggested Reading

LOVELESS, A. (1995) *The Role of IT: Practical Issues for the Primary Teacher*, London, Cassell.
(A useful book discussing the purpose of IT in the curriculum and its role in teaching and learning.)

NATIONAL COUNCIL FOR EDUCATIONAL TECHNOLOGY (1994) *Information Technology Works*, Coventry, NCET.
(A handy summary of the research evidence on the value of IT for teaching and learning.)

NATIONAL COUNCIL FOR EDUCATIONAL TECHNOLOGY/NATIONAL ASSOCIATION OF ADVIS- ERS FOR COMPUTERS IN EDUCATION (1994) *Reviewing IT*, Coventry, NCET.
(A pack to help schools assess their IT provision, with particular reference to preparing for a school inspection.)

SCRIMSHAW, P. (ed.) (1993) *Language, Classrooms and Computers*, London, Routledge.
(A useful collection of articles about IT in the context of learning theories, using language activities as examples.)

SEWELL, D. (1990) *New Tools for New Minds*, Brighton, Harvester Wheatsheaf.
(A very readable account of the cognitive perspective on the use of computers with young children, written by a psychologist.)

STRAKER, A. (1990) *Children Using Computers*, Oxford, Blackwell.
(A useful practical discussion of using IT in the classroom. Things have moved on though, since this was written, so some of the comments are dated.)

UNDERWOOD, J. (ed.) (1994) *Computer Based Learning: Potential into Practice*, London, David Fulton.
(A discussion of the extent to which theoretical ideas about IT use have been able to be put into practice.)

Section 3

The Whole Curriculum

13   Religious Education

Gwyneth Little

Introduction

If you began your initial teacher training in the late 1990s, the likelihood is that you will have been in primary school when the 1988 Education Reform Act was passed. In the early 1990s, the impact of the then new National Curriculum on teachers was such that working to fulfil requirements in subjects had to be prioritized; very often Religious Education was at the bottom of the list, not being part of the National Curriculum (see Chapter 1 for more details). National Curriculum subjects had guidelines, curriculum folders, inservice training, curriculum advisers, teacher assessments, and some even had SATs (Standard Assessment Tasks); RE had locally Agreed Syllabuses: all these subjects needed urgent and significant changes in response to new requirements.

Enquiry Task

- What was your experience of Religious Education in the primary school you attended?
- At the time, were you aware of any changes being made in the teaching of RE?
- How would you describe your teacher's attitude to RE?
- What effect do you think your previous experience is likely to have on the way you approach the teaching of RE with your class?

Surveys have shown that in general the RE experienced by student teachers in their own education was:

- largely Christian and Bible based until they reached GCSE level;
- limited in activity to stories and drawings;
- only interesting if delivered by an enthusiastic teacher;
- unlikely to be relevant to those who had no personal or family faith commitment.

If the above description matches your experience of RE, no wonder you may feel lacking in confidence at the prospect of teaching this subject for the next forty years! However, teachers are at the same time keen and professional people with open minds and an eagerness to provide all round quality education for their pupils. Most teachers express the personal opinion that RE, if taught properly, adds an opportunity and a dimension to a child's whole education which is not only interesting but immensely valuable in terms of personal and social development. Without RE, the curriculum offered is likely to lack any real opportunity for children to reflect on a range of human experiences. It is a fact that most people in the world express some form of attachment to a particular faith, or at least to some awareness of a spiritual dimension to (human) existence. This may not always be obvious, or frequently discussed, but surveys have shown this to be the case. The ways in which these attachments and beliefs are responded to and expressed provide the outward evidence of an inner experience. This evidence provides some of the material for study in RE.

In this chapter, I shall look at the aims of RE and how these can be the foundation of your planning and practice for effective RE with your class. But first, what are the legal requirements?

The Legal Requirements

You may have found the legal requirements listed in various publications, but to ensure that you have them to hand here is a summary for you to reflect on and ask questions about.

- RE is included in the Basic Curriculum for all registered pupils aged 5–18 in maintained schools, though children may be excused at the request of a parent; teachers also have the right of withdrawal.
- Any syllabus produced by an LEA must 'reflect the fact that the religious traditions in Great Britain are, in the main, Christian, whilst taking account of the teaching and practices of the other principal world religions represented in Great Britain'.

Subsequent to the introduction of the National Curriculum, the Department for Education provided guidance (DFE, 1994) suggesting that:

- any Agreed Syllabus should ensure that it contributed to a broad and balanced curriculum for pupils and had sufficient depth to challenge their thinking.
- 36 hours a year should be devoted to RE at Key Stage 1 and 45 hours a year at Key Stages 2 and 3.
- Agreed Syllabuses should specify at what ages or stages particular subject matter should be taught. It is recognized that all religions will not be taught in equal depth or at each Key Stage. The balance between Christianity and other religions should take account of both the local and national situations, and should also take account of the local population and the wishes of parents.

- an Agreed Syllabus should extend beyond factual information about religions so as to include the wider areas of spirituality and morality, and the way in which people's values and behaviour are affected by religions.
- RE must not seek to convert pupils, nor urge a particular religion or religious belief on pupils.

A Brief Rationale

Pupils are made aware of the presence of religion in the world almost every day through the media as well as local life, and often realize the tensions which exist within, and between, religions. Questions of morality and ethics are frequently discussed and responded to with religious and philosophical debate. Even younger primary school children have the capacity to discuss ideas, news items and issues associated with 'religions'.

Enquiry Task

- Find out which religious issues are currently being discussed by children.
- What ideas and opinions do the children have about these issues?
- How skilful are the children in being able to see more than one point of view?
- What influence does your awareness of these views have on how you might approach the teaching of RE?

Many people have supported the teaching of RE in the anticipation that learning about other faiths will increase tolerance of diversity and respect for individuals and groups different from one's own. This is an admirable aim and an outcome we would work for in RE, but two things need to be set beside this aim. Firstly, religions do not have a good track record when it comes to understanding and appreciating each other, and children are very aware of this. Secondly, such attitudes, whilst being particularly pertinent to RE, should be part of the whole curriculum and ethos of the school. However, knowledge and understanding of the beliefs and practices of other faiths significantly removes the sort of ignorance which contributes to prejudice, and which leads inevitably to racism.

The Aims of RE

Most Agreed Syllabuses contain a statement outlining the aims of RE — check this by looking at the syllabus of a school that you know. Although worded differently, syllabuses tend to express commonly held ideas about what their aims are. Several recent syllabuses base their aims on those set out in the model syllabuses published by the School Curriculum and Assessment Authority (SCAA, 1994).

Let us then consider the main aims of RE and see how these can be effectively demonstrated and fulfilled in the primary classroom.

Knowledge and Understanding

Religious Education aims to help pupils to acquire and develop knowledge and understanding of Christianity and other principal religions represented in Great Britain. (SCAA, 1994, p. 4)

Almost without exception, the above aim is the first one in the list of aims of all Agreed Syllabuses. Clearly, it is based on the recognition that accurate information and a realization of why things are as they are, is the foundation of learning in RE. Since the 1988 Education Reform Act, RE has taken on a wider and more exciting prospect than ever before. The recognition of Britain as a diverse society of many faiths and cultures, and an increasingly global perspective throughout the curriculum, have contributed to a flowering of awareness of the need to be well informed about the beliefs and practices of major world religions.

We have noted already the requirement that a syllabus should reflect the fact that the religious traditions in Great Britain are, in the main, Christian but that it must also include teaching about other principal religions represented there.

- What might this statement mean in the school context?
- How much is 'in the main', and how many (and which) religions do you choose?
- What religious beliefs and practices are most appropriately introduced in each Key Stage?
- To what extent must you recognize the faith commitments of the children in your school?
- How can you teach children about a world faith of which you have only very limited, or no, personal knowledge?
- If you have a firm personal faith, how can you teach about other faiths without compromising that, and still retain the integrity of the teaching of the other faiths?

How can we 'understand' other faiths and, more importantly perhaps, what implied messages are there in the requirement to develop pupils' knowledge, understanding and awareness of Christianity as the 'predominant' religion in Great Britain? (DFE, 1994).

It is easy to see how this apparently straightforward requirement to acquire knowledge and understanding can become a practical and ideological minefield. Whilst recognizing the problematic nature of the aim stated at the beginning of this section, I nevertheless believe that it offers children and their teachers together an area of exploration which can lead to creative, active, positive and delightful learning experiences in RE.

Gwyneth Little

Christianity

In a secular society, and one which some people would say is becoming increasingly so, the aim to help pupils to acquire knowledge and understanding of Christianity might appear inappropriate. Yet understanding the importance of the Christian heritage of Britain, and its influence on individuals and society in general, can be a jumping off point for children in their learning. Children are surrounded by the evidence of Christianity; in local religious buildings; in their daily act of collective worship in school (a requirement of the 1944 Education Act), which should be of a broadly Christian nature; and, for many, by an active involvement in a living, worshipping community. The influence of Christian belief and teaching on society cannot be underestimated. In addition, Christianity is supported by the most obvious and readily available resources.

Although you are likely to recognize the need for children to encounter different denominations within Christianity, you may fail to recognize that Christianity is a world-wide religion, with many different forms of expression. By the year 2000, it is predicted that the centre of strength in Christianity will no longer lie in Europe, but in Africa. Therefore, through your teaching you will need to inform your children of the symbols, stories, art and music through which Christians of a variety of cultures express their worship and beliefs. Such diversity should be celebrated, and may well be the first step in children's awareness of the rich variety of expression in all religions, world wide.

As with any religion, the actual content of the Christian material to be taught will be set out in the local Agreed Syllabus. Whether or not you are a Christian, it might be helpful to reflect on what you consider to be the essential elements of Christianity which pupils should have encountered before they leave primary school.

Enquiry Task

- Make a list of what you would consider to be the ten most significant elements of Christianity which pupils should have encountered before they leave primary school.
- Compare these with the areas of Christianity required to be taught by your local Agreed Syllabus. What similarities and differences do you notice?
- Discuss with a group of colleagues which areas you would feel comfortable teaching and which you may find difficult. Try to establish reasons for this. Prioritize the list and then compare your priorities with those of others in your group. How closely do they agree? What reasons can be given for any differences?

Alan Brown (1994, p. 10) suggests the following content should be covered in the primary school:

i)   A basic knowledge of the events in the life of Jesus and an understanding of the importance for Christians of his life, death and resurrection.

ii) A knowledge of some of the Bible stories from both Old and New Testaments with the opportunity to explore them at the level appropriate to the pupils.

iii) Some knowledge of the major Christian festivals and the meaning of the events celebrated by Christians (including both the Christmas and Easter cycle of festivals).

iv) A knowledge of some of the different rites of passage as they occur within the different traditions of Christianity.

v) Knowledge of some important Christians of contemporary times and in history, and an understanding of how their faith was important to them and to others.

vi) A knowledge of some selected events in Christian history (an obvious place to link with other areas of the curriculum).

vii) An understanding and awareness of how the creative arts have helped Christians to express their faith.

viii) A knowledge of some important Christian prayers, and how and when they are used.

ix) An understanding and awareness of how important the Eucharist is for most Christians — noting some differences between groups.

x) An exploration of how a person's Christian faith may help that person to arrive at certain ethical decisions and provide a framework for behaviour.

xi) A knowledge and awareness of the diversity of Christian belief and practice throughout the world.

Christianity contains paradoxes which may ultimately be inexplicable; the humanity and divinity of Jesus, for example, or extraordinarily difficult concepts such as original sin, as well as some areas like the crucifixion, regarded as too bloodthirsty for young pupils. Yet children have a great capacity to deal with difficult and controversial issues at a level appropriate to their ability and experience, and can, often, because of their freshness of approach, provide teachers with a new insight.

To teach the story of Christianity demands that we don't only concentrate on the 'gentle Jesus meek and mild', but enable children to reflect on the pain, suffering, anger and humanity of Jesus, the reforming revolutionary. Careful planning for introducing complex concepts in progressive stages will ensure that pupils' understanding deepens throughout their school years. By revisiting concepts such as 'salvation' in different ways and at different stages, understanding can be achieved by breaking down these concepts into underlying ideas. So, *doing wrong* and *saying sorry, forgiveness, action to alleviate another's pain*, and *loving relationships* can all contribute to children's understanding of the Christian concept of salvation. Asking children to share their own experiences, enlightening stories, real-life action, news, poetry and modern songs can all be vehicles for getting the discussion going which will creatively explain and expand the meaning of such concepts.

Other Religions

The most recent statistics regarding religious affiliations in Great Britain show that 6.7 million adults in the UK are members of Christian Trinitarian Churches, a drop of almost 25 per cent since 1970: only the Orthodox Churches and 'other' Free Churches show an increase in numbers. Membership of other religions more than doubled in the same period (1970–1992), but still remains small in comparison with Christianity. In 1992 (HMSO, 1995) these were:

- 0.52M Muslims;
- 0.27M Sikhs;
- 0.14M Hindus;
- 0.11M Jews;
- 0.08M 'Others'.

Although numbers can demonstrate almost anything, there are, nevertheless, interesting implications here for the RE teacher.

- Christianity is decreasing, other faiths are increasing.
- Certain denominations of Christianity, in particular charismatic and evangelical denominations, are increasing, and more of the population is holding onto religious affiliation.

These are all factors to be taken into consideration if you are to make the teaching of RE relevant to, and topical for, children.

Obviously, the balance of religions taught in any one school will need to reflect the ethnic diversity of that school. Where there are significant numbers of Hindu, Muslim, Sikh, Buddhist or Jewish children, there needs to be a programme of teaching which acknowledges and values the faiths of these pupils. Equally though, and what is often forgotten, is the necessity to teach a variety of faiths in schools where no cultural diversity exists. This is necessary to acknowledge that there are different religions that pupils will encounter at some point in their lives; an introduction to the main practices and beliefs of some of these will enable pupils to meet believers with confidence and respect. Learning about and reflecting on religious beliefs enables anyone to recognize that ultimate truth lies beyond human understanding, but that this quest is one of the dimensions which make humans unique within creation. Offering the opportunity to learn, reflect and internalize ideas and concepts is crucial to children's personal, spiritual, moral, and social development.

Beliefs and practices differ, and different religions attach major importance to different aspects of their faith. Children need to face up to, and realize, the importance of these differences, whilst recognizing the common human experiences and ethical responses which influence the people who have a commitment to a religion.

Religious pluralism has always been a fact in the history of mankind. With rapid means of travel and increasing cultural exchange between different nations and also with communities of Hindus, Buddhists and Muslims living together with Christians in several countries of the West, religious pluralism is no longer an academic point to be discussed, but a fact of experience to be recognised. (Stanley Samartha, source unknown)

Enquiry Task

- Find out which faith communities are represented within a 20 mile radius of where you live.
- How large is each community?
- Do they have a local place of worship?
- Make contact with someone from a religious community, or visit their place of worship. Discuss his/her attitude to RE and its role in primary school education.
- Compare points made in the discussion with your own views. How might this comparison influence your teaching of RE?

I asked earlier how schools choose which religion to teach. The model syllabus (SCAA, 1994) recommends that Christianity should be studied at all Key Stages, one other religion at Key Stage 1, and two others at Key Stages 2 and 3. Some local Agreed Syllabuses differ in their recommendations. All recognize the need for careful planning to avoid confusion in the minds of children. All also recognize the need to take account of the faiths followed by the children in any particular school.

Preparation and Planning

To become confident in the teaching of unfamiliar material you can employ several strategies. Courses on particular faiths are available at local and national RE centres (details of programmes are available from addresses provided at the end of the chapter). Distance learning courses enable you to study at home and at your own speed. Such courses are available from, amongst others, Westminster College in Oxford and The Open University. Providing yourself with a good GCSE textbook is also helpful since it can give concise and accurate information, sufficient to enable you to provide appropriate material for your children. Examples of suitable titles are given at the end of the chapter, together with books covering methods, approaches and activities.

Planning to teach about a world faith can be stimulated in a variety of ways. Visits and visitors provide a good way for children to experience the reality of religion and can also enhance your own knowledge and appreciation of the subject. For example, you may find it helpful to contact local clergy if you are not too sure of how to teach about church colours and vestments, or the service of Baptism. Many clergy are willing to be involved, to welcome children to the local church or chapel, to talk to them appropriately, to demonstrate ritual, and to allow exploration.

Members of many faith communities are very pleased to answer queries, to visit schools, and to conduct children on a visit to their place of worship or local shops selling the artifacts of that faith. Such encounters need approaching with sensitivity and a very clear idea of the educational outcome expected. Asking around your locality about availability and suitability can often produce good results. Sometimes, initiating the contact yourself can produce fascinating results. Names and addresses of communities willing to engage in this way with schools are frequently published in Agreed Syllabus documents, or held by the local RE self-help group or advisor. Such experiences will repay the initial effort made to establish the links in terms of children's interest and involvement, as well as the breaking down of assumptions and prejudices that are all too often held.

Stories from religious traditions not only fascinate pupils but develop understanding of important beliefs. They also provide opportunity for creative responses through drama, art, writing and movement. Artefacts are one of the most interesting and thought-provoking introductions to a world faith. The visual stimulus is essentially mysterious and with a life of its own, but shaped by key events and experiences. This sense of mystery arouses children's curiosity, allowing the teacher to encourage development of close observational and questioning skills. Ambiguously, artefacts are also 'real', created objects: they can give children a sense of the reality from which they (the artefacts) came and of the experience encountered within that reality. They have the ability to bring children into real contact with the faith of people. Because they are special objects, there is a need to look at the intentions of the creator, and the meanings they have for people, in order to discover the reasons why they are special and valued. Artefacts are symbols, silent teachers, pointing children to the story and meaning enshrined in the object. The concrete brings the unknowable closer to the material world. Importantly, an artefact has the potential to reveal its own truth, to speak for itself. Children often recognize that, and make their own responses to the object.

Displays of pictures, photographs and objects promote questions. Good videos for RE are being produced all the time. Watch out for schools broadcast programmes such as the BBC 'Believe it or not' series: many are excellent for introducing or reinforcing a topic in RE.

Enquiry Task

- Read through a local Agreed Syllabus. Choose a year group, a religion and a Programme of Study which interests you.
- How would you introduce one of the topics suggested in the Programme; for example, 'Places of Worship' or a festival?
- What would you expect the children to know and understand at the end of this topic?
- How might you find out what the children did know and understand? What activities would you provide that would allow you to assess this knowledge and understanding?

Assessment

A major factor in planning for any subject relates to how learning is to be assessed. Assessment opportunities allow you to determine the levels of knowledge, understanding and skills attained by the children so that subsequent planning is well informed and enables the children to progress. This is as true in RE as in other areas. Taking note of End of Key Stage Attainment Targets in an Agreed Syllabus will give you ideas as to appropriate tasks to set children for assessment purposes. Assessment of knowledge can be achieved through written work, such as 'reports from the scene' on pilgrimage or sequencing a cut up story of the life of Muhammad. Levels of understanding can also be assessed through such written work, as well as in teacher-led discussion; for example, are the children able to explain why Muhammad is important to Muslims?

It is important to note that, because RE encourages more sensitive and personal reflections and ideas, there are aspects which are inappropriate, if not impossible, to assess. You cannot make judgments about a child's beliefs, for example; you can only assess their language skills in expressing these beliefs. Clearly, in allowing children to respond personally to experiences and activities, any response made is individual, and, therefore, valid. You cannot say that one child's response is 'right' and another's 'wrong'. So you need to be clear in your planning about what knowledge and understanding you want children to acquire, and how you will assess that. At the same time, you need to plan for opportunities for children to be creative, express ideas, and respond freely to experiences.

Developing an Understanding of the Influence of Religions on Individuals, Societies and Cultures

The second aim in most syllabuses is about recognizing that religion is not abstract philosophy, only to be thought about, but that its beliefs are dynamic in the lives of followers. For many, religion affects how the individual behaves in every part of everyday life; in the food they eat, the way they dress, the rituals they perform, the activities they engage in.

Religion will be also influential in shaping relationships within the family, between friends and within society more generally, the rituals with which the milestones of life's journey are marked, the observation of seasons and festivals, and the interaction with the faith community in worship and learning. In the wider scenario, religion determines people's responses to issues of national and cultural identity, to people of other faiths, to the needy and deprived, to economic and political structures, and to ecology and the environment. How can you begin to show children the significance and enormity of this influence? Needless to say, a gradual approach to all these is essential — again, wise and thoughtful planning is needed.

Begin slowly. At Key Stage 1, children's conception of a wider society is limited. They do understand individuals, however, and we need to start with their experiences. How many Key Stage 1 classes use the topic 'All About Me' as a cross-curricular theme? It may be that for some children the religious affiliation of their family is very obvious and important. You could explore some of the following type of questions and issues:

- Why is Ahmed away today? Because his family is celebrating the festival of Eid.
- Look at the beautiful photographs of Gillian when she was a bridesmaid at her Auntie's Christian wedding.
- Why doesn't Reuben ever have ham sandwiches in his lunchbox? Because Jews have special food rules they wish to obey.

If you are fortunate, many such examples will present themselves, providing you are an observant and interested teacher. Sensitive discussion, delight and pleasure in learning about the interesting things other children do, and practical activities, such as inviting a visitor into school to show children objects and books which are special to them, will greatly contribute to children's awareness of the influence of religion on the individual and family.

Stories of children who belong to practising religious families are now being produced and are very helpful; for example:

- *Sam's Passover* (Hannigan, 1985)
- *Bridges to Religion* (Jackson, 1994)
- *Gift to the Child* (Grimmitt, Grove, Hull and Spencer, 1991)

Simple activities suitable for Key Stage 1 children can develop understanding of the influence of religion on people and cultures. These could be making diva lights for the Hindu festival of Divali, or, for Easter, hot cross buns made out of clay. Simple cooking, such as burfi, an Indian sweet, or sampling matzos eaten by Jews at Passover, gives children a taste of religion — literally.

At Key Stage 2, children can grasp a much wider picture of the influence of religion. Within the family, rites of passage, such as birth ceremonies, may be common. Visits to the local church can include looking at what people in the wider community do; for example, visit the elderly, run drop in centres, visit Lourdes; as well as recognition of global issues.

Looking at the lives of the eminent followers of a faith, as well as ordinary people doing what they see as appropriate, can give children the opportunity to reflect on what motivates these people's actions.

At Key Stage 2, there is the opportunity to study aspects of various cultures, such as music, art and story, and to consider the extent to which the religious beliefs of a society have been expressed in and through them.

Developing the Ability to Make Reasoned and Informed Judgments

The third general aim focuses on skill development. If approached with openness, the teaching about world faiths can start your children on one of the most absorbing journeys of discovery they will ever make. It is important, however, that they develop the skills that will allow them to be critically aware of the sensitivities and paradoxes involved.

What skills will enable the children to fulfil the aim of developing the ability to make reasoned and informed judgments? Some suggestions include:

- *observing* an Arti ceremony at a Hindu temple;
- *listening* to the Hallelujah chorus;
- *reflecting* on religious stories about the origins of the universe;
- *critical* analysis of issues in medical ethics;
- *empathy* with religious people undertaking a pilgrimage.

Religious beliefs stem from that which is most deeply human, and perhaps the most important skill in this context is empathy. Can we help children to lay aside their preconceived notions and assumptions, and understand how an experience is for other people? What is it like to walk in another's shoes? In an exercise called *Walk My Walk* (Hammond, Hay, Moxon, Netto, Raban, Straugher and Williams, 1990), children are invited to watch closely a friend walk in her/his normal style. They then try to walk alongside their friend in the same way. Children greatly enjoy trying this out! The discussion afterwards can focus on what that felt like. How difficult was it? What did the children need to think about? What were they really trying to do? Can they understand their friend any better now? This discussion presents an active metaphor to the children of the difficulties, delights and achievements to be experienced in meeting people of different faiths. Therefore, in planning schemes of work you should provide opportunities for active learning which involve pupils in developing empathy and other skills. Role play, drama, discussion, debate, interviews and visits are all strategies that may be employed in the learning process.

In exploring and examining their own beliefs, values and experiences, children have the opportunity to develop further their personal and moral stance, and their world view. These may differ, but children — if they are encouraged to give reasons for their beliefs and actions, as well as listening to those of others — will effectively acquire understanding and respect for other people.

To Provide Opportunities for Pupils' Spiritual, Moral, Social and Cultural Development

For many teachers this is the most vital yet sensitive aim of RE. You may consider ways of enhancing children's moral and social development by encouraging an understanding of right and wrong, and the effect of personal behaviour on society. You may welcome the opportunity to study a variety of cultures in geography, art and music, as well as in RE. But what about *spiritual development*? What does this term mean? How can we identify it? How can we encourage its development? It may seem to be a slippery area. I will work with the OFSTED definition of the scope of Spiritual Development that is contained in the supplement to the Handbook for Inspection.

> Spiritual development relates to that aspect of inner life through which pupils acquire insights into their personal existence which are of enduring worth. It is characterised by reflection, the attribution of meaning to experience, valuing a non-material dimension to life and intimations of an enduring reality. 'Spiritual' is not synonymous with 'religious'; all areas of the curriculum may contribute to pupils' spiritual development. (OFSTED, 1993, p. 8)

The spiritual dimension includes self-awareness and self-knowledge, but it is also concerned with relationships with others, and with those experiences which relate to our place in the universe, feelings of awe and wonder, and a need to question our origins, purpose and destiny. Imagination and creativity play an important role in developing the spiritual dimension. No matter how 'spiritual' is defined, it seems that RE has a unique and particular role to play. However, it is worth stressing that in the OFSTED statement . . . 'all areas of the curriculum may contribute to pupils' spiritual development'.

Religious Education is centrally concerned with questions of fundamental importance to human beings.

> Why am I here? Why does anything exist?
> Is there a God? What is truth?
> Why is there suffering? Who loves me?
> Do I matter?

Raising an awareness of such fundamental questions of life, and of how religious teachings can relate to them, is the first step towards understanding the spiritual development I have been considering. Children are naturally inquisitive and need little prompting to ask questions. However, by their nature, the above are major philosophical and religious questions. You will need to consider how you might help children to formulate, and then respond to, fundamental questions of the type outlined above.

There are many stimulus ideas which you can use to identify the spiritual and moral aspects of life. All of the following provide suitable starting points:

- pictures, for example, of sunsets;
- news items;
- family events, such as birth;
- leaves, flowers, stones and other natural objects;
- photographs showing pollution of the natural world.

Possibly, *story* is the most important stimulus and aid to developing awareness. It has been said that story is a net for catching 'truth'. Invariably, stories arise out of human experiences, such as relationships, journeys, conflict, and loss. Herein lies the 'truth' of such a story. In engaging with the story, the child engages in a process of discovery — about themselves and others. In doing so, religious concepts, such as transformation, forgiveness, the nature of reality, can be discovered and understood. Take, for example, the story *The Velveteen Rabbit* (Williams, 1995), or *The Rainbow Fish* (Pfister, 1992). In the first story, the Rabbit asks, 'When do you become real?' and the answer seems to be, 'When you have been loved into existence.' The Velveteen Rabbit is a story about relationships, and the meaning and purpose of life; it expresses human concerns, doubts and questions. *The Rainbow Fish* refuses to give away his shining scales, and so becomes lonely and miserable, but by sharing his good fortune he eventually finds friendship and joy. These and many other tales offer opportunities for reflection, which in turn can create awareness of questions and issues, and allow children to explore their individual responses to them. There is a dynamic of communication between story and child which creates opportunities for growth, and perhaps spiritual and moral development.

If treated with imagination, the great traditional stories of religions have the same potential and opportunities for interaction. In addition, these stories offer children a wider perspective on issues, and so increase the opportunity for social and cultural development. Such stories need to be told within the context of their importance to that religious community, but children will find common human themes embedded within them all.

Guided by the sensitive teacher, offering time for reflection develops the pupils' ability to apply spiritual and moral ideas to everyday life. Sensitive questions about how children may care for one another, the responsibility to share, and even the grief felt in the loss of someone or something much loved by others can be freely and sympathetically discussed in relation to children's own experience. The skill of understanding the feelings and beliefs of others can be developed, and positive attitudes encouraged.

Enquiry Task
- Collect and read some stories used in the primary classroom.
- List the central ideas and concepts in each. To what extent are these ideas and concepts 'religious'?
- What open-ended questions would you use with children to extend their opportunities for personal reflection and response?
- Try them out. How will you evaluate the children's understanding of these ideas and concepts?

RE should help pupils to learn to be aware of, and to take seriously, their own inner experience and their potential to be aware. Hence learning to respect the inner experience of other people. (Hammond et al., 1990)

References

BROWN, A. (1994) *Religious Education*, London, The National Society.

DFE (1994) *Circular Number 1/94, Religious Education and Collective Worship*, London, DFE.

GRIMMITT, M., GROVE, J., HULL, J. and SPENCER, L. (1991) *A Gift to the Child*, Hemel Hempstead, Simon & Schuster.

HAMMOND, J., HAY, D., MOXON, J., NETTO, B., RABAN, K., STRAUGHER, G. and WILLIAMS, C. (1990) *New Methods in RE Teaching*, Harlow, Oliver & Boyd.

HANNIGAN, L. (1985) *Sam's Passover*, London, A & C Black.

HMSO (1995) *Social Trends*, London, HMSO.

JACKSON, R. (1994) *Bridges to Religion*, Oxford, Heinemann.

OFSTED (1993) *Handbook for the Inspection of Schools*, London, HMSO.

PFISTER, M. (1992) *The Rainbow Fish*, London, North-South Books.

SCAA (1994) *Model Syllabuses for Religious Education*, London, SCAA.

WILLIAMS, M. (1995) *The Velveteen Rabbit*, London, Puffin.

Annotated List of Suggested Reading

BROWN, A. (undated) *Religions: A Study Course for GCSE*, London, Longman.

(The six major world religions are concisely described under ten section headings; for example, Celebrating and Belonging. An admirable handbook for teachers needing a basic introduction to a specific religion.)

BROWN, E. (1996) *Religious Education for All*, London, David Fulton.

(The book sets out to explore a differentiated approach to teaching Religious Education. Imaginative use of resources and sensory experiences provide an exciting approach to the subject.)

BASTIDE, D. (ed.) (1991) *Good Practice in Primary RE*, London, Falmer Press.

(Practitioners in the field of RE offer practical advice on ways of developing understanding in the subject.)

COLE, W. and EVANS-LOWNDES, J. (1991) *Religious Education in the Primary Curriculum*, Norwich, RMEP.

(An excellent introduction to teaching RE, with discussion of how to plan what approaches are appropriate.)

WATSON, B. (1993) *The Effective Teaching of Religious Education*, London, Longman.

(A book which deals with some of the complex and controversial issues arising in the teaching of RE. Theory and practice are tightly integrated to provide a challenge to those who want to look in depth at the issues.)

Journals

RE Today, CEM, Royal Buildings, Victoria Street, Derby, DE1 1GW.

British Journal of Religious Education, CEM, Royal Buildings, Victoria Street, Derby, DE1 1GW.

Religious Education Centres

National RE Centre, West London Institute of Higher Education, Lancaster House, Borough Road, Isleworth, Middx., TW7 5DU.

The National Society's RE Centre, 23 Kensington Square, London, W8 5HN.

The Regional RE Centre (Midlands), Westhill College, Weoley Park Road, Selly Oak, Birmingham, B29 6LL.

The RE Centre, Westminster College, Oxford, OX2 9AT.

The Welsh National Centre for RE, School of Education, University College of North Wales, Deiniol Road, Bangor, Gwynedd, LL57 2UW.

York RE Centre, University College of Ripon and York, St John, Lord Mayor's Walk, York, YO3 7EX.

14 Drama

Suzi Clipson-Boyles

Introduction

This chapter begins by defining primary drama and explaining the extent to which teachers are required by the National Curriculum to teach drama. The value of drama as a pedagogical approach is explored through an examination of the different processes it can offer to children's learning. It then goes on to describe the different ways in which this drama can be delivered, including teaching drama through English, through other subject areas, as part of an Arts curriculum, and through cross-curricular themes. Guidance is given on drama teaching, planning and assessment, and whole school issues are also considered.

What is Primary Drama?

Drama in the primary school encompasses a broad range of activities which are employed for different purposes. At one end of the spectrum, there are performance-based activities such as assemblies and school plays which enable children to participate in and experience a specific form of communication to an audience. This theatre-orientated type of drama is also developed through visits from outside companies and trips to professional performances where children can experience and respond to an alternative form of communicating ideas and story.

At the other end of the scale there is what has traditionally been called 'educational drama' which involves children in the active creation and exploration of situations based on fact or fiction which are purely for the benefit of the participants — in other words, which are not for an audience. Such drama is not training children to be actors, but is enabling them to learn in a way which is active, experiential and memorable. As such, it is regarded by many teachers as a learning method rather than a subject area because it can be employed to deliver many aspects of the curriculum very effectively.

Along this continuum, there are many variations of these two extremes. For instance, a class may explore the human dimensions of a biblical story through improvisation in order to gain a deeper insight into the meaning, but they also present their ideas to the rest of the class or even develop the work further into an assembly performance. The latter would serve a very different purpose to the first example in terms of the pupils' experiences.

Different schools adopt different approaches to drama. Some schools feel that there is no longer time for performance drama and the inevitable rehearsal time this takes; others create such performances with the children, making it a useful and relevant part of their work. Some schools have a firm commitment to educational drama as an effective teaching method, seeing it as an additional means of delivering some parts of the curriculum, including English, and others see drama as a subject in its own right, sometimes employing it as a tool for delivering personal and social education. However, it is important for you to acknowledge that drama now has an explicit place within the National Curriculum in addition to offering a pedagogical approach to certain aspects of primary education, and as such it should have a recognized place in all primary school curricula.

Drama and the National Curriculum

The National Curriculum has undergone many changes before reaching its present form and drama has appeared in various places during those developments. In addition to the requirements within English, the original Non-Statutory Guidance for history, geography and science all referred to drama as a useful mode of learning, giving examples of how it might be used within those subject areas.

Today's National Curriculum is heavily content based, and subject areas appear to be much more independent of each other. (Those who are new to the profession may be interested to note that many teachers still find the original Non-Statutory Guidance a very useful source of reference to good practice, particularly the provision of constructive examples of integration between the subject areas.) As a result, drama does not appear in any curriculum area other than English. Indeed, the references to drama in English now have a much higher profile in response to considerable feedback from teachers during the consultation process leading to the most recent changes (see DFE, 1995).

Drama is discretely embedded in the Programmes of Study at Key Stages 1 and 2, where there are explicit requirements for a variety of drama activities within the Programme of Study for Speaking and Listening. These include opportunities for pupils to respond to drama they have watched, in addition to active participation in different drama activities. Drama is also implicit in the Reading Programme of Study; here, the wide range of texts requires consideration, response, discussion, acting out, performance and so on — all skills which can be usefully developed through drama.

> If children are to develop sophisticated and creative responses to texts they need opportunities to explore these processes through practical, interactive activities. Drama can allow this to happen. (Clipson-Boyles, 1996, p. 85)

It is thus apparent that drama is not only a clear requirement of the National Curriculum, but also has a core place within primary education. As such, it is creating renewed interest in the vast potential it can offer to language, humanities, and cross-curricular work, in addition to the Arts curriculum. This upsurge of interest in the value of drama is resulting in a 'new wave' of drama taking place in primary schools. Many teachers and other educationalists are welcoming the growth of this 'new wave drama', and the inclusion and quality of drama is now under close scrutiny by OFSTED during inspections of primary schools and teacher training institutions.

New Wave Drama

Drama in primary schools enjoyed recognized educational status from the late 1960s into the early 1980s. However, as educational foci moved from pedagogy to curriculum matters during the late 1980s, teachers became increasingly occupied with content. This trend was reinforced from 1989 as the National Curriculum requirement documents started to appear. Understandably, teachers prioritized content delivery above all else and the consequential return to more formal teaching methods meant that drama virtually disappeared from many schools. HMI (1990) noted this demise with concern:

> Only a minority of primary schools have a well-developed policy and guideline for their work in drama. Consequently drama rarely receives consistent attention either as a means of enriching work in other subjects or as an activity in its own right. (p. 7)

Nevertheless, the evidence of good practice cited in the above mentioned HMI report supported the belief that drama was an important part of primary education as it 'often contributes powerfully to good standards' (p. 7).

However, six years on, the tide is turning once again, and drama is beginning to return to an increasing number of primary schools. As teachers feel more familiar and confident with the National Curriculum they are able to return to pedagogical issues. For while it is vitally important that there are clear goals for children's developing curriculum knowledge and skills, it is equally important that teachers understand the most effective ways in which that knowledge and those skills can be acquired. In other words, it is as important for teachers to understand **how** children learn as it is to know **what** children need to learn. Drama represents ways of learning which are known to be effective and appropriate within primary education.

Enquiry Task

Imagine that, as part of a topic on 'Food' with Year 2 pupils, you have set up a café rôle play corner.

List six ways in which you think the children's learning and understanding in the following four areas might be enhanced by playing there:

---

i)   oracy;
ii)   reading;
iii) writing;
iv)   science.

Alongside each item on your list, note down how you might promote such learning by the way you structure the activity; for example, providing ice and jugs of warm water during the play.

Try to arrange a visit to a classroom with a role play corner. Observe the children at play, making notes on one of the four aspects listed above.

Introduce an additional stimulus resource and continue to make observation notes. What changes do you notice?

Another contributing factor to 'new wave drama' is the recognition of pupils' entitlement to a high quality Arts curriculum. In addition to the benefits which drama has to offer language work and humanities subjects, drama also has an important part to play in the primary arts.

> While drama is recognised in the National Curriculum as an invaluable teaching method, it is first and foremost an art form in its own right. (Arts Council of Great Britain, 1993, p. i)

Whilst the 'first and foremost' might be more relevant to secondary education where drama is taught discretely by specialist teachers, it is appropriate for primary teachers to recognize that drama is **also** an art form in its own right. Drama which is performed for an audience — for example, in assemblies, plays and concerts — is much more aligned to theatre studies than the experiential and exploratory educational drama which may not actually be performed at all.

The Processes of Drama

The true nature of educational drama lies in the exploration and communication of ideas, issues, subject content, themes, stories and feelings through participatory action and imagination. This is very different from the notion of 'acting', although presenting drama can sometimes, but certainly not always, be an appropriate part of the work. Drama in the primary school is about offering pupils opportunities to develop understanding from within through active experience. It also provides strong and meaningful contexts for evaluation and reflection.

When engaged in drama, children become involved in educational processes which can make a valuable contribution to their learning. These processes encompass knowledge, skills and concepts, some of which relate directly to specific aspects of curriculum and some of which are transferable.

Drama can provide many different contexts for language. Not only do the pupils talk in rôle for a variety of purposes, they also engage in a considerable amount of talk during the planning and sharing of ideas. Communication is an important function of drama, and there are many excellent ways in which an integrated language approach can be achieved through drama. A topic on television, for example, might include planning, writing and reading news scripts, with interviews and features.

Children can be helped in their thinking by concrete experiences. Experiential active learning experiences offered by drama give children opportunities to explore, challenge, question, control and change. For instance, it is very common for children who are struggling with writing to create wonderful stories in drama — a skill they can rarely develop when bound by the limitations of their literary ability. Good teachers can often utilize this extension of their imaginative thinking by using drama as a stimulus for writing. In drama, pupils are required to discuss their thoughts, and sometimes change their thinking. They also have to organize their ideas in order to communicate them to a larger audience.

Drama enables pupils to see issues from a variety of perspectives, and sometimes puts them into situations where they have to represent a view which is not necessarily their own. For example, a whole class improvisation of a planning meeting about the building of a new motorway across farming land would enable the pupils to prepare arguments and 'represent' different groups (government, local villagers, farmers, builders, environmentalists, etc.). Not only would they experience their own participation, they would also be immersed in the debate as they hear other views and engage in heated argument! Reflection takes place on different levels. Sometimes pupils may reflect on the issues or problems with which they are working, sometimes they may reflect on the responses of others, and perhaps the biggest challenge for a teacher is to help them reflect upon their own learning. Evaluation is also a valuable part of drama, and this is arguably at its most powerful when children are giving feedback to each other and then acting upon that in order to make further changes.

Creative skills can flourish and grow within a sound, developmental drama curriculum. Pupils are given full permission to use their imagination — a skill which should be natural to children in their play, but which increasingly seems usurped by the visual impact of television and video. Children are often brimming with creative ideas and yet the school environment may be unable to provide space for growth. Drama provides that space and enables children to develop and shape their ideas into forms that will communicate to others. Likewise, children's organizational skills can be helped enormously by drama as they move through the processes of brain-storming ideas, shaping ideas into an order, representing information symbolically, arranging furniture, and finding props, for example.

The development of social skills can be assisted greatly by drama in two ways. Firstly, the discipline of working in groups with shared tasks, planning and targets can help children to learn to cooperate and communicate. It is more often than not the case that children enjoy drama so much that they soon overcome their reluctance to work with particular individuals. Secondly, the subject matter of social skills can actually be introduced into the drama for exploration in itself; for example, bullying, loneliness, consideration and so on. This provides opportunities for empathy, looking from other perspectives, discussion and questions. The cloak of disguise drama provides means that children can explore the social skills of others in a way that is safe because it is distanced from reality, and can therefore be discussed objectively once the drama experience is over.

It is appropriate to mention at this point the importance of 'de-rôling' the children at the end of a drama session. Apart from the fact that other teachers and pupils might be disturbed by marauding Vikings hurtling back to their classroom, the drama needs to be put into its proper perspective, particularly if you have been dealing with difficult emotional issues. A 5-minute calming down discussion about the drama out-of-rôle, and preparation for the next (non-drama) activity before moving back to the classroom are ways of disconnecting from the experience so that it does not cause confusion, distraction or distress.

Enquiry Task

Plan a drama activity which is helping to explore areas of your current geography teaching. After the activity ask for four volunteers to discuss the session with you during a time when you are not teaching the whole class. Plan carefully beforehand what you want to find out. For instance, what was their response to this way of working? How much did they learn? What did they like or not like about the lesson?

Try to record on tape the discussions if possible, and afterwards, when playing the tape back, note down the main points of interest. You may like to consider the following questions as you reflect on the findings:

- How did the children's learning measure against my planned outcomes for the activity?
- How do the children perceive drama as a means of learning?
- What differences were there in the children's responses?
- How effective was my role in the activity?
- What advantages/disadvantages were there in this way of working on this particular occasion?
- What can I learn from that for the future?

The Multi-faceted Nature of Drama

There are many different ways that drama can happen in primary classrooms. Sometimes, it might be a whole class activity in the hall for half an hour. On other occasions it might be working in pairs in the classroom for 10 minutes. The following framework comprises a list of variables which are possible when planning drama activities. The framework is by no means definitive. The aim is to demonstrate that there is no such thing as the stereotypical drama lesson. Instead there is a rich range of choices and opportunities for you to use for different purposes.

In addition to these variables, there are also many different modes of working. Figure 14.2 lists the main modes which are commonly used in primary school drama.

Figure 14.1: Framework of working variables for drama

Category	Variable	Example
Purpose	stimulus for other work	air-raid simulation in shelters — followed by diary writing
	discrete work	nativity play for Christmas
	follow-up to other work	assembly presentation of topic work
Context	specific oracy work	pretend interviews in police station (question/answer)
	vehicle for reading	searching newspaper for story to dramatize
	vehicle for writing	writing astronaut's checklist for Moon journey
	integrated language work	improvise, plan, write plays — exchange and read scripts
	specific curriculum area	Viking funeral rituals
	exploration of cross-curricular themes	gender roles in the workplace
	drama as an art form	reworking Shakespeare's plays
	integrated arts work	responses to a visit to Imperial War Museum
Content	revisiting prior knowledge	re-enacting a poem or story chapter
	extending prior knowledge	shaping of historical facts into a context
	exploring/researching new knowledge	geography problem-solving
	imaginative development	story-making
Organization	pair work	job interviews
	pairs plus observer (trios)	parent/child improvised argument — discuss with observer
	groups	six pupils developing a storyline
	whole class	Pied Piper simulation
Location	classroom — at tables	improvised 'meeting'
	— tables cleared	creating tableau pictures
	— in carpet area	turn-taking mimes of foods
	hall	exploring another planet
	playground	stylized 'bully' sequences
	theatres	stimulus or follow-up
	places of interest (during school visits)	Victorian school room (e.g., Black Country Museum)
Teacher role	directing	creating a performance for assembly
	instructing	setting a group task
	questioning	preparation or follow-up
	listening	to children's ideas
	observing	to check the need for intervention
	participating in role	Mayor of Hamelin leading the decision making about the rats
	participating out of role	questioning a character in the 'hot seat' (see 'MODES')
	providing stimuli	'Three Bears' artefacts in home corner
Time	short focused 'one off'	miming and guessing occupations before topic work
	whole session 'one off'	exploration of a fairy story
	developmental series	aspects of the way of life in Ancient Greece
	large project	performance about World War II based on children's work

Figure 14.2: Modes most commonly used in primary school drama

Mode

Guided imagery   where the children listen to commentary and instruction from the teacher to explore an imaginary situation.
Example: imagining that they are only six centimetres tall and exploring a kitchen.

Mime   where the children explore and present stories or situations through movement and facial expression.
Example: miming emotions for children to guess as a preliminary to discussion on feelings.

Tableaux   where the children make statue pictures (sometimes called 'freeze frames').
Example: in groups of six making tableaux to represent the seasons.

Tableaux sequence   where tableaux are linked into a series to tell a story — sometimes linked by movement, narration, music, poetry, etc.
Example: evacuees leaving home, arriving in the country, living in the country, returning home.

Role play   pretending to be another character, real or imaginary.
Example: in rôle play corner set up as a hairdresser's salon.

Spontaneous improvisation   developing a situation whilst in role without any prior planning, and without an anticipated ending.
Example: characters meeting on a train journey.

Reconstructed improvisation   revisiting an improvisation in order to shape it into story form by using, changing and developing the original spontaneous ideas.
Example: using the characters which emerged on the train journey to weave into a story.

Interviews   where the children work in pairs, either both in role or with just the interviewee in role.
Example: reporter interviewing Red Riding Hood for her story.

Hot seating   where the whole class or a group of children ask a 'character' (played by a pupil, teacher or even an outside visitor) questions.
Example: group of four children researches Tudor food. They then present themselves as Tudor cooks for questioning by the rest of the class.

Simulated experience   where the teacher plans and creates an 'experience' for the children to explore. The teacher is usually also in role.
Example: preparing and loading a ship ready for a voyage with Francis Drake.

Story shaping   where the children create a story together but present it 'live' rather than writing it down. (Follow-up work might include writing at a later stage.)
Example: an adventure which takes place through a time tunnel.

Script reading   where children read scripts (either their own, their peers', or published texts) in groups. Interpreting and playing out stage directions provides an excellent reading-for-meaning exercise.

Script writing   where the children follow up their activities with planning, shaping and writing.

Staging   where the children are included in every stage of the process involved in presenting to an audience — those stages might include planning, script writing, musical composition, costume/scenery making, box office, programme writing, etc.
Example: reworking of *Oliver Twist* by Charles Dickens.

The choice of drama mode needs to be well informed by a good understanding of drama methodology, and there are many good books available on this subject, some of which are listed at the end of this chapter to help you get started.

The following example demonstrates how the framework described in Figures 14.1 and 14.2 might be used.

Purpose	stimulus for other work
Context	integrated language work
Content	making a complaint/responding to a complaint
Organization	pairs
Location	classroom
Teacher's role	instructing and observing
Time	10 minutes
Mode	spontaneous improvisation

In the above example, the main teaching focus is on writing letters of complaint (Year 6). A preparatory discussion with the whole class is needed, in this case about holidays and what can go wrong. The children then sit facing each other in pairs and imagine that one is a travel agent and the other an angry customer who has just returned from a disastrous holiday. The children are encouraged to ask/ answer as many questions as possible, and are told that you are going to observe their speaking and listening skills as they work. (A countdown at the start of the activity helps to build up the suspense and focus the commencement of the improvisation! Likewise, a cooking timer helps to set the challenge that they must not come out of role until the bell rings!) After the drama, you would give appropriate input on letter writing skills; the children are required to put their experiences onto paper in the form of a letter of complaint to the travel company.

Enquiry Task

Using the drama variables framework, as in the previous example, plan an activity which might be appropriate for your history plans for next term. Remember that you can 'pick and mix' the variables as much as you like to suit your children's needs!

Design an observation sheet to use during the lesson. You will need to consider who you are observing, how this observation will happen, and what evidence you will need to see in order to make an objective assessment. Reflect on how your assessments of particular children compare with other data you have collected about them in other ways.

The Importance of Clear Learning Objectives

The enjoyable and lively character of drama sometimes belies its potential for significant and relevant learning. Teachers who are already engaged in delivering a full-to-brimming curriculum may feel that they simply do not have the time to give up to a subject which is just for fun! In reality, drama should not be seen as neither an activity without substance nor as an added extra. Rather, it should be regarded as an invaluable way of learning.

However, if time allocated to drama activities is to be fruitful, it is vital that those activities are carefully planned with clear learning objectives in mind. At any one time the objectives might relate to:

- English — e.g., giving reasons for opinions and actions
- Other subject areas — e.g., use of geographical vocabulary
- Drama skills — e.g., speaking clearly for an audience

It is also highly likely that there will often be overlap between any two or all of these three areas at any given time.

Drama and English

English is an important subject in its own right, but it also serves the whole curriculum. The centrality of English in primary education is not just about academic achievement but is also about the fundamental place of language and language development in the lives of human beings. Language is pivotal to our lives, as communication takes place continuously during our waking hours. The effectiveness of that communication depends on the experiences through which we learn. It is the responsibility of teachers to provide quality language experiences which make sense to children and which move them along a progressive developmental pathway towards ever-increasing competence.

Language is a complex set of communication modes which overlap and interweave; for instance, reading can only take place because of what someone has written. Reports can include accounts of what has been spoken; written work is often the subject of discussion. In recognition of this, good primary English teaching is characterized by an integrated approach where oracy, reading and writing are linked together in ways which enrich and inform each other.

The National Curriculum requirements for English repeatedly use the word 'range'. For instance, it is used to refer to *purposes, audiences, texts* and *opportunities*. Drama can help you provide an interesting and stimulating range of experiences through which children can develop the required skills of oracy, reading and writing. Children tend to work at their best when the task in hand has a meaningful purpose. Resource stimuli, (e.g., actual report forms on clipboards for police interviews), can also make a tremendous difference to children's motivation and the quality of their output as they add to the direct experience on which the work can build. If you want children to write well it is important to give them something meaningful to write about! For example, infants would far rather write a letter to the 'monster' they have just befriended on the moon than a practice letter in an exercise book. Drama can offer both these resources to language activities — meaningful

Figure 14.3: Language activities served by drama

Drama	Oracy	Reading	Writing
Travel agent rôle play corner	Customer service	Checking brochures	Form filling
Space mission	Use of scientific language Giving instructions	Research before/ after Checking reports	Astronaut's report form Checklist of equipment
World War II evacuees	Describing home Explaining new rules	Examples of letters Old recipes	Letters Diary
Police interviews (house burglary)	Formal speech Questioning	Newspaper reports Security catalogues	Statements Security leaflets
Hamlet (story exploration)	Shakespearian language Describing feelings	Text portions Annotated versions	Ghost story Eye witness account
Three Little Pigs (tell in own words)	Re-telling Responding	Text portions Letters from wolf	List of furniture to buy Letters to the wolf

purpose and concrete stimulus experience. Figure 14.3 illustrates the points which have been made so far with some examples of how language activities might be served by drama. There are many more examples which could be included under each heading. The chart simply illustrates points made earlier to help you start thinking about the potential language situations that drama can offer. Thoughtful and creative planning can result in interesting and meaningful activities for pupils which keep them on task and promote learning.

Enquiry Task

Talk to teachers you meet about the use of drama as a stimulus for language work.

- What techniques work best?
- How often do they use drama?
- How do the pupils respond?
- Why do some teachers prefer not to teach drama?

Try to gauge the levels of awareness about how much drama can offer to language work. Extrapolate examples of good practice for your own information and development. Identify any doubts about drama and what you believe to be the root causes of these doubts. Consider how teacher's views on drama are affected by their own value systems. Reflect on your own value system in relation to the employment of drama both as an Arts subject and as a teaching method across the curriculum.

Curriculum-based Drama

Drama can be used to provide contexts for language skills development through other curriculum areas, but it can also be used to help children to develop subject specific skills, concepts and knowledge. Ken Byron (1993) describes how a class of 5–7-year-olds learned about rocks and underground exploration during a one-week project using a drama approach. The work involved, amongst other things, discussion, rôle play and improvisation, researching using books and samples of rocks, recording, problem solving, and reporting. It is not hard to see that those children are likely to have a far better understanding of the rôle of a geologist than if they had just been told. It is also more likely that they would remember for much longer because of the experiences they had undergone.

History, geography, science, technology and RE all encompass bodies of knowledge which children need to understand and remember. But it is not enough for children to merely hear the facts — for you to impart chunks of knowledge in a similar way to distributing pencils and paper! You need to assist and support the children in developing an understanding of those facts, so that they may integrate them into their conceptual frameworks. Drama can help you to provide appropriate learning experiences which will assist your pupils in acquiring and practising skills, building concepts, and integrating and remembering knowledge.

The value of drama here lies in its potential to set facts, skills and concepts into situations where they are meaningful. Where children cannot only make sense of them but also apply and use them. However, if this is to be done effectively, the skills, concepts and knowledge need to be clearly identified when the drama is being planned. The following examples are designed to demonstrate how this might be applied.

Example 1: Geography at Key Stage 1

Key knowledge Purpose of maps/physical features of countryside
Key concepts Differences between town and country
Key skills Making maps/using symbols/discussing locations
Drama activity Visiting the 'site' of the 'Three Little Pigs' story. Re-enacting, with the introduction of physical features (e.g., hill, river, wood, field). Planning locations in the hall (or playground). Making maps in pairs for the 'Story Tourists' Information Centre'.

Example 2: History at Key Stage 2

Key knowledge Law and punishment in Tudor times
Key concepts Capital and corporal punishment/reasons for change
Key skills Describing events/change/research and communicate knowledge
Drama activity After initial research and discussion about crime and punishment, the teacher would lead a guided imagery through a Tudor town — describing streets, buildings, smells, characters, etc. Assign characters and bring the streets alive. Create a story about the theft of bread and the placing of the culprit in the stocks. Work this into a repeatable sequence, building in new responses each time. Discuss pros and cons of abusing people in the stocks. A second lesson could require the pupils to work in groups of eight on a story where the punishment is hanging. They would construct a story sequence based on their research, this time without

the leadership of the teacher. A further development might include a debate on hanging.

As teachers, we must always remember that our perceptions of the subjects we teach are different from those of our pupils. We have a wealth of experience behind us! We cannot rely on transmitting that experience purely by telling — we need to create situations in which children can experience for themselves, and in doing so their learning will be enjoyable, meaningful and effective.

Exploring Cross-curricular Themes through Drama

Cross-curricular themes such as gender issues, equal opportunities, bullying, and economic and industrial understanding need real contexts if they are to be truly understood by children. Helen Vick (1990) describes how she used drama with 9- and 10-year-olds to challenge their assumptions about gender roles. Using improvisation techniques where the children followed an instruction card to play out a family situation, they then discussed how the roles were distributed. The improvisation then ran again with the roles reversed.

If children are going to discuss and consider challenging issues, they need to be given something to talk about. Drama helps to simulate situations through which children can empathize. But perhaps more importantly, it also enables a 'distancing' effect. For instance, whilst children might find it difficult to openly discuss a bullying incident during the lunch hour, they are more likely to find it easier to discuss an incident created by the drama where they can be more objective.

Whilst not wanting to undermine the importance of considering cross-curricular themes within primary education, teachers may be helped through their concerns over shortage of time by remembering that such themes can provide excellent material for language work.

Dramatic Form

Drama has a significant part to play in the primary arts curriculum although it has never been given a discrete place as an arts subject during the development of the National Curriculum.

> The practice of the arts, in whatever form, involves the creation of objects or events that express and represent ideas and perceptions. The arts emerge from the fundamental human capacity for making sense of experience by representing it in symbolic form. (NCC, 1989, p. 5)

Drama can help children to express their ideas through an alternative form. The main difference between discussing drama as an arts subject and regarding it as a teaching method is in the emphasis on skills. The *raison d'être* of drama as an art form is to create something in order to communicate it to others. If this is to happen effectively, children need to learn the skills of such communication and develop an awareness of the power and effect of different forms of presentation. Form, likewise, is an area where specific knowledge is going to influence the style of communication. Media studies can help enormously here, particularly analysis, discussion and appraisal of television and film.

Responses to, and appreciation of, the work of others is also a major component of drama. This should include opportunities to reflect on the work of peers and also live theatre performances both in and out of school.

The place of performances in schools has notably declined since the pressure of delivering government requirements has meant that some teachers are now regarding school plays as 'luxury items' which time can ill-afford. One positive consequence of this is that many school performances are now much more closely integrated with the children's other work. The best practice allows children to be involved in every stage of the production from start to finish. Such involvement might include such processes as:

- planning;
- improvising;
- script writing;
- rehearsing and learning;
- costume and scenery design;
- costume and scenery making;
- box office maths;
- backstage organization;
- sound effects production;
- musical composition and accompaniment;
- programme writing and illustrating.

Enquiry Task

Design a questionnaire for parents to find out their views on assembly presentations, school plays and concerts. Areas of interest to consider might include:

- how much parents value these as an audience;
- how parents perceive themselves to be of value to their children's learning;
- how the children talk about such activities at home;
- what memories parents have of their own school days.

Reflect upon how parental views and understanding compares with your own. Consider whether you need to provide parents with further information about the place of drama in the primary curriculum. How might you go about communicating this?

Assessment and Reflection

When regarding drama totally as an arts subject it has been suggested (Arts Council of Great Britain, 1993) that it is assessed in a similar two-part framework as music (performing/composing and listening/appraising) and art (investigating/making and knowledge/understanding). Readman and Lamont (1994) recommend a three part assessment framework requiring the ability to:

- create drama;
- engage in drama;
- reflect on drama.

Each of these 'abilities' can be broken down into skill components. These might include:

- planning in a group;
- listening to the ideas of others;
- researching for a purpose;
- organizing ideas into a shape;
- sustained concentration and involvement;
- sharing of individual responses;
- ability to empathize;
- application of imagination;
- communication of ideas through movement;
- communication of ideas through speaking;
- retrospective discussion of feelings and experiences;
- suggestions for continued development of the drama;
- reflection on own part in the drama;
- critical analysis of form.

To ensure that progression is taking place and that staff are building on previous learning, it can be a worthwhile exercise for whole school teams to decide upon a developmental scheme of skills applicable throughout the primary years. If children are provided with a drama curriculum which is underpinned by such a developmental framework, they are more likely to develop a confident approach which might also benefit their work right across the curriculum. This 'confidence' is not merely about performing but, perhaps more importantly, can be applied to their ideas and their ability to discuss, reflect upon and further develop their own work.

It is important to assess children's drama skills if we wish them to achieve maximum benefit from a drama curriculum. Again, this works best where schools have a whole-school policy and it is up to teachers, guided by relevant professional information, to decide what is most useful and relevant to their particular situation.

It is also possible to assess children in other areas of the curriculum during a drama activity; for example, speaking and listening in English, or the use of geographical language during a 'journey'. It is up to the individual teacher to decide what is to be assessed and why. The appropriate use of geographical vocabulary could be observed during a drama session, where it is not appropriate to assess the use of such words in writing because the children concerned do not yet have the writing skills to record them. Drama can give those pupils the opportunity to demonstrate that they understand and can apply those words correctly or incorrectly, as the case may be.

When children are highly involved in creating their own drama it can be relatively easy for you to stand back, observe and assess. (Of course, when you are in role with the children this is not feasible!) Likewise when the children are watching each other, you can be watching them! However, if assessment is to be useful, it is important to be clear about what is being assessed. Self-assessment and peer assessment are also elements of learning and reflection which are complementary to the drama mode. Indeed if it is only ever the role of the teacher to comment on the activity then the emphasis on 'performance' is arguably reinforced by the notion that the *raison d'être* of the drama is to be 'watched'. Although this is inevitably a facet of all assessment, the opportunities offered by drama for children to reflect on their own experiences, learning, feelings, opinions and input are very valuable indeed. Likewise, drama enables children to give feedback to each other, and to engage in useful discussion of a reflective nature.

Summary

Thus, drama has been presented to you here with all the rich opportunities it has to offer. Not only can it be an exciting inclusion in its own right, it also provides a pedagogical approach to many aspects of the primary curriculum, and, as such, it can actually support and enhance children's learning. It should not be seen as yet another requirement to be squeezed into an already crowded curriculum, but rather as a valuable tool for you to employ as part of your regular practice.

References

ARTS COUNCIL OF GREAT BRITAIN (1993) *Drama in Schools*, London, ACGB.

BYRON, K. (1993) 'Caving Expedition', *Projects for Science and Technology with Drama, Questions*, London, Watts.

CLIPSON-BOYLES, S. (1996) 'Teaching reading through drama', in REID, D. and BENTLEY, D. *Reading On! Developing Reading at Key Stage 2*, Leamington Spa, Scholastic.

DFE (1995) *Key Stages 1 and 2 of the National Curriculum England*, London, HMSO.

HMI (1990) *The Teaching and Learning of Drama*, London, HMSO.

NCC (1989) *The Arts 5–16: Practice and Innovation*, Harlow, Oliver & Boyd.

READMAN, G. and LAMONT, G. (1994) Drama: *A Handbook for Primary Teachers*, London, BBC.

VICK, H. (1990) 'The use of drama in an anti-sexist classroom', in TUTCHELL, E. (ed.) *Dolls and Dungarees*, Milton Keynes, Open University Press.

Suzi Clipson-Boyles

Annotated List of Suggested Reading

HEALD, C. (1993) *Role Play and Drama*, Leamington Spa, Scholastic.
(A useful resource book for early years teachers, giving ideas on a range of types of activity including how to promote play in role play corners, drama through fairy tales, rhymes and puppets, and recreating places of interest.)

KAY, M. and COTTERILL, A. (1989) *Learning Through Action*, Wisbech, Learning Development Aids.
(An inspiring book which offers guidance on the management of experiential drama to help children's learning, particularly in geography and history. The book includes detailed lesson plans with tight frameworks for teachers' support.)

NATIONAL ASSOCIATION FOR TEACHERS OF ENGLISH (1993) *Move Back the Desks*, Sheffield, NATE.
(A useful practical A4 size book of drama ideas for the 9–14 age range. It is divided into two parts: techniques and case studies.)

RANKIN, I. (1995) *Drama 5–14*, London, Hodder & Stoughton.
(A practical approach to classroom drama with detailed lesson plans for a range of topics at each Key Stage. The teacher's role and children's activity are carefully explained along with details of National Curriculum Levels, learning outcomes, resources and assessment guidelines.)

RAWLINS, G. and RICH, J. (1992) *Look, Listen and Trust: A Framework for Learning Through Drama*, Walton-on-Thames, Nelson.
(A skills-based resource book which addresses the issue of progression as well as offering many suggestions for practical activity.)

READMAN, G. and LAMONT, G. (1994) *Drama: A Handbook for Primary Teachers*, London, BBC.
(An excellent resource book for drama with children from pre-school through to Key Stage 3. The book provides a framework for planning and assessment along with useful Key Stage statements. A sound methodological base, with some inspiring practical ideas.)

SOMERS, J. (1994) *Drama in the Curriculum*, London, Cassell.
(A useful book which covers drama methodology, including the role of the teacher, underpinned by a sound theoretical base. The practical examples are designed to support teachers' own planning.)

TAMBLING, P. (1990) *Performing Arts in the Primary School*, Oxford, Basil Blackwell Ltd.
(This book is specifically about drama within the arts curriculum and it provides teachers with useful guidance on working towards creative quality and performing skills which are relevant and educationally appropriate.)

WOOLLAND, B. (1993) *The Teaching of Drama in the Primary School*, Harlow, Longman.
(A readable balance of theory and practice, this book offers excellent details on using drama to deliver the National Curriculum and also includes performance elements and ideas for working with very young children at Key Stage 1.)

15   Dance

Carol Beth

> Dance makes a distinctive contribution to the education of all pupils. It uses the
> most basic of human expression, movement. Through its use of non-verbal com-
> munication pupils are able to participate in a way which differs from any other
> area of learning. It provides aesthetic and cultural education, opportunities for
> personal expression, and it also introduces the students to a wealth of traditional,
> social, and theatrical forms. In a broad and balanced curriculum this important area
> of human experience should not be neglected. (CDET/NATFHE/NDTA/SCODE,
> 1989 p. 1)

This chapter deals with the place of dance within the curriculum, both past and
present, together with its processes, planning and progression.

Dance within the Curriculum

It may surprise you to see dance referred to as an Arts subject, rather than as part
of PE. Indeed, its relatively recent place (since the late 1950s) in the general
curriculum did come about through the development of PE. From the 1960s onwards, specialist PE courses evolved for the training of teachers, and during the
development of these courses, the importance of the need for educational dance
was recognized.

This recognition coincided with the greater availability and appreciation of the
pioneering work of Rudolph Laban (1869–1958) on the analysis of movement and
dance, and their notation. The application of his teachings in the field of movement
was taken up enthusiastically by many PE and dance teachers.

During the 1970s and early 1980s, dance developed as a subject that was
recognized in its own right. Performing arts courses proliferated and enabled growing numbers of students to study dance as their first degree subject. This consolidation of dance in the higher education training establishments was mirrored in the
wider educational and public world.

Dance became a creative force and, when taught in primary schools, became
known as creative dance. It attracted funding from government, local authorities
and arts boards, and arts institutions, such as the Gulbenkian Foundation. Schools
identified teaching posts for dance, inservice programmes and workshops focused
on dance, and collaborations took place between educational dance companies and

schools. There were cross-curricular Arts projects with local authority dance animators and mainstream dance companies. At national level, dance in the arts was finally acknowledged by the government with the appointment of a National Dance Officer.

Dance and the National Curriculum

Dance has not had an easy time since the introduction of the National Curriculum. The order in which subjects were introduced meant there was a time lag of three years between the Core subjects of science, English and maths being put in place and the establishment of the curriculum for the other subjects. There were several major refinements to preceding Orders for Foundation subjects which reduced content, time allocation, and assessment. Dance was reduced to one aspect of PE. In addition, PE was the last subject Order to be published. This not only affected the status of PE but led to a decline in the opportunities for dance to flourish in its own right. The constraints placed on PE meant there was a corresponding squeeze on the time and space for dance.

We are now in the 'Post Dearing' stage of delivering the National Curriculum: dance has remained one of the three Areas of Activity in PE at Key Stage 1 and one of the six Areas of Activity at Key Stage 2. With this simplification of activities at Key Stage 1, there should be sufficient time for the development of a rich movement vocabulary and well-grounded kinesthetic awareness in the children. Movement vocabulary is the range of movements, actions and gestures that each individual draws upon in everyday life and which dance catches, frames and expands into expressive and repeatable phrases. Kinesthetic awareness may be described as the 'seventh sense'. It is the ability of the nerve endings on the skin and in the muscles and joints, to feed the brain with information about where in space the limbs and body are at any given moment. Dances tap into this awareness and use it to inform their understanding of what is happening to their body while dancing.

Dance has its own core language and terminology to enable the observer (whether audience, teacher, other dancers) to put into precise terms what they are feeling about what they are seeing. This is no different to any of the Arts subjects. Each has its base of particular knowledge, skills, philosophy, and values.

When you start planning your dance curriculum you may find the terminology difficult. You may question the value of these new terms on the ground that dance is about 'doing'. Foster (1976) points out that, 'dance is another language, a language that springs and comes entirely out of another place than the literary one.' Rudolph Laban created a notational form of recording dance composition as well as the qualities of the actions, precisely because dance needed its own form of recording. However, we also need to share the seeing and feeling experience, and this is particularly important for the teacher. You may want to talk with your children about their dances and to check, confirm and help them to refine their movement ideas.

As with poetry and music composition, you might begin by setting the children to spontaneously move and dance. When you have observed them, you may feel that in order to complement the visual, you need to understand and share a common dance language, both verbal and written, with colleagues and the children. You can talk to the children and they to you about what they are doing, feeling, seeing, and sharing. To give a sense of purpose to the children, you can guide the discussion by shading in the detail of 'what' they did, 'where', 'how' and 'with whom': I discuss these four ideas in some detail below. There are additional ways to help your children develop and deepen their dance skills and understanding: again, I will discuss some of these ways later on in the chapter.

Dance at Key Stage 1

At Key Stage 1, dance includes movement patterns and existing dance traditions as well as creative educational dance. The creative perspective can be used to energize the movement pattern work and to enhance any selected traditional dance. This can be achieved by identifying the key qualities from creative dance: for example, body awareness; sensitivity of footwork; focused spatial awareness; expression in gesture, and confidence in using and selecting rhythmic phrases. These qualities are part of dance skills.

The emphasis in the Order for PE has moved from evaluation to participation. This shift has the potential to detract from the quality of the children's learning. You (and your children) will need to find a balance between freedom to experience and learn the basic actions of dance (such as, travelling, jumping, turning, gesture and stillness), and giving attention to the quality of the children's movement performance and the quality of the choices that they make as to what movements to include, where to move, how to move and with whom to move.

Enquiry Task — Video Analysis of Children's and Teachers' Experience

With the knowledge and permission of your children and their parents, set up a project to video movement in the playground.

Decide which play area gives you most potential for observing a mixture of quiet movement and a wide variety of games and activities. Suitable activities may include standing, wandering, sitting and watching, and actions and small gestures. Actions that you might see include running, sliding, hopping, jiggling on the spot, skipping, turning around, or jumping in different ways. Gestures might include the hands and arms moving about near or far from the head and upper body. You might like to make your own list both before and while the video work is ongoing.

Select an area of the playground which is used by all or most children at some time. Avoid any area which might have become a no-go zone for some children (for example, because of footballers).

Decide whether you want a random sample or a selected group. In either case keep the number of children that you hope to observe to a manageable number, probably

---

no more than six. Note what you base your choice on, and at the end of the observation period, who was left out.

Designate an area of the playground and video movement in that area. Set up the camera in an unobtrusive place (maybe even inside and shooting through a window). Set up the camera each playtime (preferably on a swivellable tripod) a few days before you put in a video tape. Stand with the camera for those few days so that the children become used to you. Use this time to watch with one eye (like a camera) and tune in to the space and to what unfolds within it. Use your eye like a camera to zoom in on a movement or gesture and then pan out and take in the whole of your designated space. Be flexible about changing the area of playground if it proves unsuitable to your needs. Accept that any movement or part of a movement begins and ends at the boundary you have designated, even if that means finishing with a bodiless leg, or a foot.

- Watch and video movement within the designated space for not more than 10 minutes each time.
- Video over a week or a day a week for a month.

Each time you place yourself in the position of observer/video recorder in this activity, try to open yourself to seeing movement as though for the first time.

Analyse your tapes. Develop a vocabulary (or a set of symbols) to help you with this analysis.

In the enquiry task above, you were asked to give particular attention to children's spontaneous and natural free movement. When you are teaching them dance, this observation may inform how you seek to develop your children's dance skills. The attention you brought to your observations can be transferred to the way you teach dance to your children. Two of the characteristics of this attention are the intensity of focus and involvement (the extent it enables you to empathize). There are others which you might like to identify as you proceed.

Video recordings and notes of children's movement serve as a record for future reference, for example, in assessing the movement characteristics of children. They may also provide evidence of how images and words together can enhance the teacher's enquiry into movement material for dance.

Dance at Key Stage 2

At Key Stage 2, the PE Programme of Study includes six Areas of Activity, but dance is still prioritized as an element to be taught in all years of this Key Stage. The primary school curriculum has always contained an element of folk and country dance (dances of different times and places, as well as traditional dances of the British Isles) and this is now included in the National Curriculum.

The curriculum for dance emphasizes body control and aesthetic awareness through responses to different stimuli. You may find the children deal with body control in the natural ebb and flow of their playground movement. From an early age, some children have a facility for coordination and seem fluid when they move, whether running, jumping or stopping. Other children have a natural grace which catches the eye and makes us want to watch. An appreciation in watching these individuals, the analysis of form, of the body in movement, is aesthetic awareness in action. This way of 'seeing' develops knowledge about movement dance. It can help you develop an understanding of body control and aesthetic awareness needed for creating dance.

Enquiry Task — Reflective Diary of a Teacher's Feelings

Buy or make a notebook or folder in which you can include different sized drawings and sketches, photographs and newspaper pictures, as well as your notes. Find a shape and colour which is pleasing and makes the diary personal and aesthetic.

List ways to record information about movement, for example:

- handwritten, or word processed paragraphs, cut and pasted in.
- a block of writing with key points bordered in colour.
- different fonts for different information.
- an article with key points identifying by highlighting.

Allow yourself a space and a time for creative reflection, and your own creative experiences. In the foreword to Gough (1994), there is a description of dance being intimately connected with feeling, with one's emotional life, and, as with other Arts forms, the demands of dance to openness, commitment, and honesty. This will be as true for the teacher as for the children.

Remember times when you danced. In your notebook, jot down words or sentences to describe those memories. Add sketches or line drawings or colour shapes if you wish.

- Do the memories fall into categories? (Some examples of categories are included at the end of the chapter.) Allow time to reflect on this question.
- Can you order them?
- Were some of the emotions involved in the memories negative as well as positive?
- List them.

Close your eyes and remember some aspect of the dance in your body. See if you can dance it now even if it's simply a twirl, or a turn or a sway. Repeat it until you can connect it with an emotional response. Take some quiet time to write about what you experienced in the dancing. If you were unable to rediscover a dance, did you find yourself making one in the 'here and now'?

- What were your feelings?
- Did they get expressed in the way you found yourself moving?
- Could they have?

The enquiry task above is not about using emotions to stimulate dance but about discovering that dance can have an emotional content. Dance can help children access an emotional feeling or imaginative memory. Any of us may jump for joy, cringe with shame, feel wrung out like a rag, flee from threat, freeze with terror, turn cock-a-lorie with the coming of Spring. People are often captured by rhythms and atmosphere. It might be a marching band, or a busker in the Underground, or the swaying and jumping to the roar on the football terraces. All around it is possible to see and to read the movement responses of the human body. You may find it useful to note them in your reflective diary and to think about how they might be used within the dance curriculum. As your confidence and observational abilities grow, these notes may provide you with more ideas for dance and a means to continue clarifying what dance is about.

Another way to build up an 'ideas bank' and set of data for analysis is to scan the daily press and the educational papers for illustrations which have actions or moods captured in photographs. These may include images of sport, dance, street action — anything which carries the feel and look of authentic involvement. As you analyse, compare and contrast what you are seeing, you may develop the ability to identify and feel the actions and moods in your body, and recognize those of others.

Processes

Below, I look at ways to deepen and develop the children's and teachers' dance skills.

In order to support and enable us to understand mathematics, music or art, we learn about number tables or basic music notation or the principles of colour. These are part of the 'language' of each subject. As mentioned earlier, there is also a fundamental method of movement analysis (given to us by Laban) that will give your dance material a secure framework from which to launch into creativity.

The aims of dance are very important, if you are to continue to develop an understanding of what the lesson needs, and why. They are not about finding a series of simple movement descriptions which get repeated and perhaps tell a story. Nor are they necessarily about fitting in with Core or cross-curricular themes of the National Curriculum. The aims of dance are capable of embracing the needs of the individual child and the class as a whole. If you are to develop as a teacher of dance, you may need to develop your own answers to questions such as:

- How do you find a point for lively interaction between the teacher and the children?
- What interests you?
- What are the interests of the children?
- How can they be channelled into dance work?

Creative dance lessons may be based upon a central structure encompassing four questions:

- *What* movements do we do?
- *Where* do we move?
- *How* do we move?
- *With* whom do we move?

Below, I discuss each of these questions briefly. Any good dance book which uses Laban's analysis will contain more detail and explanation.

What concerns the body actions, the detailed physical aspects of any dance movement: the jumping, rolling, running, stepping, and so on indicated in Key Stage 1. Knowing the detail of this will transform your movement observation skills. It includes the range of actions of which the body is capable, all the body parts and the whole body's ability to be involved, as well as the shapes that the body can achieve. This 'what' develops and moulds the child's natural and instinctive movement — the movement you may have already begun to observe and note in the first enquiry task.

Your role as the teacher includes finding ways to help the children question the validity of their movement answers, to see what is needed to take this action further, to make that more delicate, or perhaps to think about what was learnt when several dance ideas were linked together to make a little composition. Assessment provides an important way to help, through the process of reviewing and refining. Repetition of dance ideas may be encouraged, to incorporate the identified refinements.

Where concerns space, which is part of the fabric of dance. As a teacher of dance, part of your role is to enable the children to see and to use space knowingly and knowledgably: to deal with the space which is near to them and far away; to use directions, levels and pathways both on the ground and in the air; and to develop patterns.

How concerns the expression and the artistry of the body moving: 'how' is the aspect that takes a movement into the realm of dance. It is to do with *intention* and this idea of intention is what affects the quality of the movement. For example, if a child is learning a dribbling skill in football, the *intention* will influence the quality of the movement and the body while dribbling the ball. If that same child was attentive to the energy and the flow of their body while travelling through space, exploring, for example, the movement idea of sudden and percussive actions, the *intention* would be quite different: that in itself would change the affective quality of the movement. Of course, it would also change what the viewer or observer saw and felt. *How* is also to do with dynamics, of how movement becomes dance, through notions of weight and time — see below for more detail.

Whom concerns making connections; for example, between body parts. A starting point for the children might be giving attention to playing with hand patterns. This would bring into focus one way of making movement relationships; for example, hand relating to fingers, hand synchronizing with the other hand. For older children *whom* might include working in pairs and in groups, or it could involve solo work where the relating is concerned with something other than another human; for instance, a focusing on the unfolding of thematic music, a prop, or a specific quality. For younger children (5- to 6-year-olds) dancing alone, with someone else, or simply sharing the space with others (including the teacher) is sufficient.

The concepts involved in the relationship aspect of dance include harmony, unison (dancing together at the same time and in the same pattern), canon (moving off one after another or in groups), contrasting (where dancers use contrasting movements), opposition (where there is a dramatic tension between dancers), and leading and following. The environment and props and objects are also included in the possibilities for the 'with whom' of dance.

Dynamics is about the energy and the flow of movement. It involves opposites, so it is not just about fast and strong and getting there: it is also concerned with slow and gentle, and hesitating. As dancers, and as observers, we also need to feel these qualities of energy and opposites in our bodies: feel it with our kinesthetic sense which informs our body awareness. It is when we can connect with this feeling that the kinesthetic process can retain the sensations. It can become a movement memory and a wonderful resource accessible to all of us, made up of movements we have performed and our observation of others. You can give yourself a powerful teaching tool by harnessing your feeling, attention, and aesthetic awareness, and provide you with a storehouse and databank of movement memory, enabling recognition and comprehension of the movement qualities and characteristics of others.

As the children learn to build their movement vocabulary, they can also be helped to cultivate a matching movement memory. They will need these skills to be able to rehearse and reshow their dance ideas and dance compositions with accuracy and precision. Below is a list of adjectives and verbs that encapsulate the expression of dynamics. You may find it helpful and fun to use your reflective diary to record observations and photographs which illustrate for you a movement connection.

- smooth and irregular;
- sustained and sudden;
- regular and irregular;
- bursting and flowing;
- contained and explosive;
- fluent and erratic;
- continuous and percussive;
- slow and fast;
- controlled and unstoppable.

These words conjure up movement. Each one has qualities the body can experience.

Weight is a vital component of dynamics: it does not mean fat. Weight is a means to give quality to the management of the body and develop an awareness of gravity when managing oneself and/or others; for example, when supporting someone in a coordinated, safe and fluent manner. Playing with and discovering new ways to manage gravity and weight gives the body and movement its tension and elasticity. It clarifies the transitions during movement. Weight is a key aspect when working on the PE Key Stage 2 aspect of body control. Qualities that are involved in 'weight' include:

- heavy and light;
- strong and gentle;
- firm and delicate;
- powerful and fine.

The list above is about differentiation. You may find it useful to discuss with a friend which one of these pairs you think you have a natural movement preference for, and then perhaps explore through simple activities what you see as the differences in the qualities. You might also look out for sessions in school or at home where these qualities are in evidence; for example, threading a needle (fine and delicate), or examining and playing with a collection of feathers (gentle and light). You might look for pictures which capture the attention and concentration of physically using these qualities.

Progression

Progression involves moving forward in terms of material, concepts and knowledge: gradually building up children's awareness, sensitivity and understanding of the dance curriculum. The elements of dance are encountered repeatedly as you and the class return to them in a developmental continuum.

Between the ages of 5 and 9 years, children will mature physically, intellectually and emotionally. The movement ideas that they encounter need to develop in an appropriate way. The children need a curriculum that develops coordination, strength, stamina, an ease of movement, and a physical confidence in developing movement ideas. You need to take each of these aspects of development into account when developing the dance curriculum for your class. The Programmes of Study for PE should help you to plan a curriculum that is progressive. The questions you ask yourself should be directed at monitoring this progression.

Progression requires sensitivity to the 'readiness' of children. It is easy to follow a plan or to suggest specific actions which are directed into a dance, but you will need also to utilize your growing understanding of the readiness of each class and the members within it to take the ideas that you give them and to use them in a meaningful way. You may need to look for real development and quality in movement, rather than praising children merely for finishing a dance or because they worked with energy and enthusiasm. Progression occurs through guided questioning by the teacher, and eventually by the children themselves. It is essential that you tease out the deeper implication of the *what*, *where*, *why* and *with whom*, to enable the children to come to an understanding of the significance and potency of dance activity. The following enquiry task is allied to a simple dance activity that may illustrate some of the ideas developed above.

Enquiry Task — Catching the Bird

The idea is based on thinking about birds. It might arise from a news article about threatened species or birds trapped by pollution or fishing lines.

- Watch a video or film or visit a bird park to watch birds in the wild.
- Find illustrations and photographs of wild birds in the air and on the ground.
- Develop some questions for/by the children that will encourage observation and the expression of opinions: for example;

What sort of birds do you see?

How are the birds' bodies structured?

How are birds sometimes caught?

How might the birds respond to being trapped?

What might loss of freedom feel like?

What might loss of freedom look like (its form and qualities)?

- Discuss movement content that could be used for action; for instance, stalking, stillness, lifting, tipping, looking, reaching, snatching, struggling, holding, enclosing, trapping, and losing freedom.
- Analyse the quality and feeling connotations in these actions and their movement potential; for example, at Key Stage 2, travelling and stopping, balance and off balance, lifting and lowering body parts, weight aspects of strong and light, sudden movements.

Ask yourself:

- What might you do with the learning and movement ideas that have emerged from this analysis?
- How might you excite and lead the children into exploring the movement potential of the ideas?
- What might be significant moments in this piece of work; for instance, the moment of realization that freedom is lost?
- How might you explore this significant moment in dance?
- How might you help the children express feelings of loss, for example?
- How might you guide the children to refine their ideas?

In the enquiry task above, it may be better to explore the significant moments of the dance through association, rather than the specific situation. Thus, rather than the children copying 'being a bird', they might investigate the feelings and qualities of the moment when freedom is lost. You might ask them how they could express loss, and then help them to explore and refine their movement into a symbolic form so that the movement represents the loss, rather than the bird.

During Key Stage 1, much of the experience in this dance might be concerned with personal space and relating to the teacher, while the body aspects could involve the arms and hands in expressing and exploring loss. During Key Stage 2, the whole body and body parts might be investigated, including complex aspects of time and weight, as well as children relating to each other in duets or trios. A much greater area of space might be utilized for special pathways to be explored.

Progression in dance calls for involvement in the art of dance. This may be achieved through visits to see dance companies or by inviting dance-in-education companies into the school.

Concluding Remarks

Valuing the subject and the children's work, while demanding quality from them is a complex matter that requires time for reviewing, reflecting, and renewing the connection between curiosity, joy, quality and attention to the process which is dance.

The material in this chapter is basic to the National Curriculum for Dance. Although the description within the PE Order is brief, the concepts, skills, knowledge, and learning involved is as deep, and can be as difficult, as for any other subject. The basic essentials have been identified. Your continuing journey of reflection and questioning can be greatly supported by referring to the recommended texts.

References

CDET/NATFHE/NDTA/SCODE (1989) Plenary Paper, *Dance in the School Curriculum Conference*, Bedford, October.

FOSTER, R. (1976) *Knowing in My Bones*, London, Black.

GOUGH, M. (1994) *In Touch with Dance*, London, Whitethorn Books.

Annotated List of Suggested Reading

DES (1972) *Movement: Physical Education in the Primary Years*, London, HMSO.
(The definitive all-round text of the 1970s, which lifted movement into the whole curriculum and identified key issues such as gender, equal opportunities and differentiation. It contains wonderful, joyous photographs.)

DFE/WELSH OFFICE (1992) *Physical Education for Ages 5 to 16*, London, HMSO.
(This has detailed information on dance and assessment.)

GOUGH, M. (1994) *In Touch with Dance*, London, Whitethorn Books.
(This book is highly recommended, particularly for Key Stages 2 and 3. It contains comprehensive illustrations and categories of dance materials, and is rich on resources and stimuli.)

FOSTER, R. (1976) *Knowing in My Bones*, London, Black.
(This book is out of print, but is available in most education libraries. It has a magical entry on the fabric of the creative process and a guide to understanding aesthetics.)

LOWDEN, M. (1989) *Dancing to Learn*, London, Falmer Press.
(This is essential reading for teachers of dance. You can dip into it for lesson ideas or revisit it for in-depth information. Each reading reveals key knowledge and brings fresh understanding.)

SHREEVES, R. (1982) *Children Dancing: A Practical Approach to Dance in the Primary School*, London, Ward Lock Educational.
(A lively and accessible book that incorporates the basic theory with many practical ideas.)

16   Special Educational Needs

Gary Thomas

Introduction

It is one of the guiding principles behind the National Curriculum that all children should study the same curriculum. This includes children with special needs. The same principle applies to all children in special schools: all children should receive the same curriculum.

The application of the National Curriculum to all children is welcome. For many years there was much discussion about whether children with special needs should receive the same curricular experiences as other children. Some commentators thought that these children needed a completely different curriculum — one concentrating on basic skills — while others suggested that the content should be the same, but that it should be made easier to digest; it should be diluted.

A moment's thought will reveal how sterile is such a debate. 'Children with special needs' is a huge catch-all category which comprises those with learning difficulties, those with sensory disabilities, those with physical disabilities, and those with emotional problems. These children's needs will differ enormously. Some will require a carefully managed and adapted curriculum in which it is certain that they will not continually be faced with failure, while others will be able to engage in experiences which differ little from those of the majority of the class, perhaps only needing additional equipment which will help them to see or hear. To talk of a curriculum for children with special needs is therefore quite inappropriate.

It is also inappropriate to think in terms of a specific group of children having special needs. The Warnock Report (DES, 1978) made it clear that many children, around one in five at any one time, would have special needs. These may not necessarily be the same children from day to day or from year to year. Some children will have problems with one subject, or one aspect of the curriculum; other children may have difficulties due to an emotional upheaval, a medical crisis or a personality clash with a teacher. In fact there are myriad reasons why a child might experience problems with the curriculum.

In other words, the current opinion is that there is not a specific group of children who have special needs. It is the job of the teacher to identify each child's needs and to attempt to meet them. Some children's needs will be more pressing or more difficult to meet than others and it is these children on whom I shall be concentrating in this chapter. It should then be clear that if the group of children with special needs is not a static group but rather a fluid group comprising different children at different times, it is doubly important to think of these children all receiving the same curriculum. Indeed, it is one of the central tenets of today's practice that all children are *entitled* to the same curriculum. This *entitlement* underpins the comprehensive principles of today's education and it is also one of the underpinning notions behind *inclusion* — namely, the idea that all children should be fully and comprehensively included in the complete activity of the school. No children will be excluded because of their special needs.

If this is the case — if all children receive the same curriculum, and if this is such an important principle — you may reasonably ask how it is possible to meet all children's needs within the same curriculum. It would be wrong to pretend that it is in any way easy to do this, but there are some important strategies, techniques and principles to remember in doing this and some of these will be considered here:

- First, there is *differentiation* — namely the tailoring of a specific curricular issue or area to the precise needs of a child or group of children.
- Second, it is important to consider what *assessment* means in the context of special educational needs. Much of the mumbo-jumbo that characterized special needs assessment of the past has now been thrown out and this frees us to think far more constructively about what is needed from assessment and how it can contribute to teaching. Good special needs assessment and teaching is simply good practice for all children. There are no special methods or procedures which have been shown to be of especial value to children who have special needs.
- Third, it is important to consider how classroom organization can help in the delivery of the curriculum for all children. In particular, it is important to consider how additional people can be employed in the classroom and the judicious use of group work and peer tutoring, such that expertise in the classroom is used effectively.

Each of these shall be considered, addressing the National Curriculum where appropriate. It should be remembered, though, that special educational needs is not a specific area of the National Curriculum and children may experience difficulty in each or all of the subject areas. Where necessary, though, examples of adaptations to teaching shall be given, which may enable children who are experiencing problems to have access to the National Curriculum.

Enquiry Task

Much of the thrust of this chapter will be that there is no special set of procedures or methods which are appropriate for children designated 'special' and that good teaching in the National Curriculum is good for *all* children. One of the assumptions behind this is that 'learning difficulty' is something of a misnomer and that everyone's learning needs are very similar.

To examine this last idea . . . think about a piece of learning which you as an adult may have had to do recently. It might have been learning to drive, to use a word processor, to hang wallpaper. Was it a rewarding experience? Use the following checklist (adapted from Thomas, 1996) to think about the learning you undertook:

- Was it a happy experience? What made it so?
- Was it an unhappy experience? What made it so?
- Was it rewarding? Why?
- Was it unrewarding? Why?
- Was it frustrating? What made it so?
- Did you feel stupid? What contributed to that feeling?
- What helped you to learn?
- What hindered your learning?

The following may have been included in your answers:

- I learned by watching someone
- The person teaching me was warm and supportive
- The person teaching me was sarcastic
- I do not learn well if others are watching me

You will have many other observations and answers here. Consider on the basis of these what you *need* in order to learn. What do we therefore mean by *learning needs?*

Differentiation

Differentiation is a difficult-sounding word which in fact means something very simple. It means the adaptation and modification of the curriculum for the purpose of making that curriculum meaningful to and accessible by all children. In other words, ways of teaching the curriculum are changed so that children can engage with it. Simply presenting work in a flat, undifferentiated way would mean that many children would not understand what was being presented and would become bored and alienated.

And we should not feel diffident about such adaptation — it should be remembered that the new National Curriculum Orders allow Programmes of Study to be modified such that the curriculum is 'wholly relevant and meaningful' to children.

So, it's official. It is perfectly legitimate to adapt the curriculum in order to make it meaningful to most children. Note, though, that differentiation does not imply that a different curriculum is presented. There is no assumption that children will need a different curriculum content if they have special needs. Nor is there any assumption that the aims of the curriculum will change because children have special needs. The central assumption is that methods and strategies must change to accommodate children's particular circumstances and needs. For instance, in discussing children's spoken language, Lewis (1996) identifies in the eight (plus two extension) stages in the National Curriculum a number of references to such language. These include:

- listening responsively;
- taking account of the listener;
- conveying the intended message;
- providing appropriate levels of detail;
- recognizing the need for adjustment to audience;
- showing awareness of standard English;
- providing variety of expression;
- using increasingly sophisticated vocabulary;
- structuring talk appropriately;
- responding to discussion.

Lewis goes on to give some advice on ways in which these criteria can be met through certain teaching methods and strategies (see below). Note that there is nothing very special about these strategies and methods. They simply represent good, imaginative teaching, and this sums up the modern approach to meeting special educational needs. There are no magic formulae or extra-special devices which have to be used with children who experience difficulties. There is no need to assume that the teaching styles or strategies that are appropriate for children with special needs are accessible only to those who have had long training or experience. The main requirement is for creativity and imagination to make the curriculum come alive for all children — and if such creativity and imagination are used, then all children will benefit, not simply those with lower achievement. The following suggestions are adaptations of some of the strategies Lewis (1996) suggests in the context of spoken language:

- Use audio recordings relevant to a particular activity or display; for instance, if there has been topic work on birds, a table or classroom area could include sound or video recordings of a local naturalist talking, extracts from TV or radio programmes, or children talking about their own work on birds.
- Exchange messages with other schools — locally, nationally or internationally — using audio, video or e-mail. This will provide a rich source of data for discussing and analysing differences in expression, dialect, pronunciation and register.
- Set up phone links with other classes using real telephone lines, mobile phones, string-and-can phones or computer networking.
- Set up a recording studio area in which children can record, for example, news bulletins, debates, quizzes, jokes, messages and reviews of books, TV programmes or music. Encourage children whose first language may not be English to use their own language, with or without translations.
- Find ways of stimulating spoken language in all curricular areas — don't assume that it is just the preserve of 'English'. For instance, discussing mathematical problems, hypothesizing and reporting findings in science, collecting oral history accounts, using scripted or unscripted role playing in history.

- Use home–school audio-tapes or video-tapes instead of written diaries.
- Make a guide to the school on a video- or audio-tape.
- Encourage children to think about and use varying tone, timing and non-verbal cues.

To reiterate, there is nothing 'special' about Lewis's ideas here. They are simply imaginative ways of developing spoken language and listening skills which will help to involve and include all children. Those children who appear to be slower at academically oriented tasks may be slower for a variety of reasons, and it is only through creative thought about the presentation of curricular experiences that they will be helped to become engaged.

Cox (1996), a headteacher, gives some similar examples of excellent activities in design and technology which accommodate, stimulate and include all children. He reminds us that although some pupils may have limited practical skills they should not be fed token design projects. He goes on to describe the development of a number of primary school topics in his own school which met the National Curriculum Order specifying the need to integrate design and construction skills. He gives details of one of these topics, on 'Wheels', and specifies some of the ways in which children could be helped, namely by:

- making sure that many and varied hand tools were provided;
- supplying wood cut into centimetre sections;
- showing children clearly how to make a corner joint;
- obtaining appropriate books on wheels from the local schools' library service;
- encouraging parents to be involved in the project;
- ensuring that there was adequate time and adult assistance available.

Here again, as with the example from English, there is nothing revolutionary, remarkable or specialized needed to help children with special needs. All that is needed is a modification of good practice. (It should be remembered, of course, that some children may need special help or supervision when working with certain kinds of equipment or tools.)

Given that the emphasis in the above examples has been on the imaginative use of presentation (or 'delivery' as it is sometimes called) it is worth pausing for a moment to consider the content of the curriculum as an aspect of differentiation. Talking of content presents a knotty problem, since I stated at the outset that one of the tenets of today's thinking is that children — whatever their ability or disability — should receive the same content. Moore (1996) comes up with some useful ideas concerning this problem. Writing in the context of History in the National Curriculum, she develops the idea of *a minimum entitlement* for pupils who learn more slowly. She suggests that this entitlement should ensure that pupils can acquire essential skills and understanding of the subject whilst not being hampered by too much historical content.

History is, of course, an appropriate subject area for such a distinction between understanding and content to be drawn, since it is in this subject that there has been so much discussion about whether children need to learn specific pieces of information, such as dates, or whether it is better to equip them with the conceptual skills needed to think about, interpret and understand history. The new National Curriculum gives the opportunity to put the emphasis more firmly on understanding than before, while still retaining a skeleton of factual knowledge, and armed with this knowledge Moore makes a convincing case for suggesting minimum entitlements within the National Curriculum. She suggests that teachers should be able to select content from earlier or later Key Stages and decide for themselves what the minimum entitlement should be for particular pupils or groups of pupils. She goes on to suggest that pupils' minimum entitlement will be assured if teachers examine the focus statement to be found at the beginning of each history study unit and select those materials from the list of historical content which will give pupils an adequate understanding of the focus statement. An example she gives is that at Key Stage 3 (relevant for primary/middle school pupils) all pupils must be taught about some of the major features of Britain's medieval past, including the development of the medieval monarchy and the ways of life of the peoples of the British Isles. She suggests that teachers will still be meeting the requirements of the focus statement if children with learning difficulties are given a minimum entitlement. For example, with the aspect of the focus statement concerning major features of Britain's medieval past the content could be the Battle of Hastings in 1066. For that concerning development of the medieval monarchy, Moore suggests that William the Conqueror and the Domesday Book, together with castles and castle building, are appropriate content. Moore's ideas are imaginative and helpful and a thorough read of them is recommended, whether or not you have any special interest in or responsibility for history.

From these snapshot examples of the imaginative adaptation and presentation of the curriculum it should be clear that differentiation is simply about the creative and intelligent use of methods and materials in order to make a subject meaningful and interesting for all children. Any teacher can do it. Unfortunately, one of the legacies of the special education tradition is the idea that there is a whole raft of special assessments, procedures and methods which are only understood and administered by appropriately trained experts. This is now agreed to be not the case. There is a great deal of evidence which shows that the special assessments and procedures which have been developed over the years by special educators are no more effective in helping children learn than are the 'naive' assessments and programmes devised by ordinary class teachers working only on their instinctive, professional response to a child's difficulties. This is perhaps an appropriate time to pause and think about assessment in the National Curriculum with children with special needs in mind.

Assessment

There has been much mumbo-jumbo in special education assessment. For too long, professionals who have been concerned with children experiencing difficulties have relied on supposedly 'objective' tests of children's weaknesses, and following such assessments a 'programme' of help would be provided which would 'remedy' the child's deficits.

There were two problems with this approach. First, it placed all the problems *within* the child, whereas often the cause of a child's difficulties would comprise a composite of factors, many possibly originating in the school. Second, and more important, there is no evidence that the approach works. Detailed follow-ups and evaluations of such methodology show that it is all an elaborate waste of time (Thomas, 1995).

However, the fact that this reliance on special tests and special programmes has been shown to be without value should not be seen as a problem, but rather as an opportunity. Indeed, the idea that there is not a specific set of special assessments which are applicable to, and appropriate for, a certain set of children is quite in keeping with the philosophy that I have just explained now governs our thinking about the curriculum generally. In other words, there is not a specific diet — of assessment *or* curriculum — appropriate for children with special needs. Having said this, it must be reiterated that this does not mean that special attention should not be given to those who appear to be having difficulty. Indeed, there are now specific guidelines laid down in the *Code of Practice*, which is produced by the Department for Education (DFE, 1994), specifically to regularize and improve assessment practice. (An outline of the Code of Practice *stages* is given on p. 240)

If, then, assessment does not depend on the tests on which it once relied, what now characterizes assessment for children with special needs? In answering this question it is perhaps worth outlining in general terms what sort of things teachers should be looking out for and considering while doing National Curriculum assessments at Key Stages 1 and 2. The principle here is the same: all children (unless extraordinary procedures are followed to exempt children from assessment) undertake the assessment procedures. It is important to stress, though, that the specific assessments associated with the National Curriculum will not give the teacher enough detailed information on which to base a plan of work. Specific plans of work concerning differentiation or classroom organization will depend on your own knowledge of the child, what he or she likes, finds interesting or experiences difficulty with. The answer (and this answer is backed up with decades of research) is that *you the teacher* are in the best position to know what the child needs. You — who see the child's work every day, who talk to the child and know his or her style of learning, and fears or weaknesses — are in the best position to plan out the child's work. It is important to have confidence in your ability to make your own assessments of the child's problem and not to blame yourself or admit defeat if the child seems to be learning very slowly. Some children *will* learn slowly — for whatever reason. Remember that some adults pass their driving test on the first attempt while others take six or seven attempts — the latter group do not need specially devised tests and procedures; they may need extra help and extra practice and this is what is usually provided.

This is not to say that there are not forms of assessment which are not valuable. In the area of literacy, for example, miscue analysis (Goodman, 1981) and an informal reading inventory combine to provide an excellent means of assessing any child's current ability and reading strategies, but it is especially useful with children who are struggling with reading. Basically, the combined method comprises taking a sample of text (say, 100 words) and presenting it to the child. You count the errors the child makes in the sample of text and produce a percentage figure for the child's success. Thus, if the child makes 15 errors in the 100 words, they have achieved an 85 per cent success rate, which would be low. For a child to be at the correct instructional level he or she would have to be at 90 per cent or above. This element would thus tell you on what sort of text to teach a child. Miscue analysis then involves looking at the kind of error (or miscue) children make. Do they, for example, tend to make errors on the basis of an over-use and misuse of phonics? Or do they make errors by too much guessing on the basis of the picture or the meaning in the text so far?

Analysing errors in this way is a powerful tool in gaining access to the child's preferred strategies in reading and it suggests avenues on which to proceed if a child does seem to have got into bad habits (for example, the over-use of contextual cues).

Enquiry Task

Take a small group of children from your class and undertake informal reading inventories comprising a simple miscue analysis, as outlined above.

- What do the group's results tell you about the level of the children's work?
- Are they roughly at the right level? Or are they tending to be reading material which is consistently too easy or too hard?
- What sort of miscues are the children making?
- Are there any consistencies among the children's miscues, and does this indicate anything to you about the way they have learned to date?
- If there are such consistencies, how will you go about encouraging more effective strategies among the children?

Miscue analysis is just one example of an assessment method, and there are, of course, different kinds and methods of assessment in each of the National Curriculum subjects. The point of giving this example is to show that it is a form of assessment which is useful for all children, not simply those who are assumed to have learning difficulties. There are two keys to this kind of assessment: first, finding out where the child is now, and working from there — there is no point working on something far too hard or far too easy; second, the intelligent analysis of a child's learning, saying to yourself, 'What is the child thinking here; how is s/he going wrong?' This is not very complicated and can be adapted for use in any of the National Curriculum subjects.

Having said all of this, it is important to remember that the Code of Practice does specify procedures which should be followed at the class and school level which are set in place in order to ensure that children do not slip through the net. It is worth specifying these as there will certainly be children in your class who are at one or other *stage* in the Code of Practice assessment procedures.

> *Stage 1*: Children who are at stage 1 (and there are likely to be several in every class) remain the primary responsibility of the classroom teacher, who will gather information about the child, ensure appropriate differentiation of the child's work and develop classroom management strategies (perhaps through the use of a learning support assistant) which increase individualized help for the child. Parents should be kept informed of the child's difficulties and the strategies being employed to help him or her.
>
> *Stage 2*: At stage 2 (and at stage 3) the teacher will, with the special needs coordinator (SENCO) for the school, develop an individual education plan (IEP) which will give details of 'curricular and non-curricular need, individual teaching requirements and the arrangements for monitoring and review' (DFE, 1994).
>
> *Stage 3*: Stage 3 involves the consultation with outside professionals and specialists (such as a visiting peripatetic advisory teacher) who may be able to offer additional information about the child, or may be able to suggest further developments in the strategy for helping the child and refinements of, or adaptations to, the IEP.
>
> *Stages 4 and 5*: These essentially involve outside specialists who will consider the need for an assessment with a view to the issuing of a formal statement of special educational needs for a child.

Placement of the child at one stage (up to stage 3) or another is a matter for the school, and in particular the SENCO in consultation with the class teacher and head. Progression from one stage to the next represents a recognition of more serious concern about the child's difficulty, so while there may be several children at stage 1 in each class in a primary school, only one child in 50 to one in 100 will proceed to stage 5. Cowne (1996) gives helpful advice on how to record concern at stage 1 (for which class teachers will have most direct responsibility), and she also gives useful guidance on the structuring of an IEP and the steps which should be gone through in writing and developing it.

The full title of the Code of Practice is *The Code of Practice on the Identification and Assessment of Special Educational Needs* and it is a key document in organizing not only identification and assessment, but also the monitoring and review of children's needs. It is an easily read and well-constructed document which has been well-received by the teaching profession. There should be a copy in every school and it is important that you read it for a full explanation not only of these specific procedures but also as an explanation of current thinking on assessment, especially assessment in the context of the National Curriculum.

Enquiry Task

Under the Code of Practice, each school must have a policy for special educational needs. Ask to see a school's policy and note its contents. Note in particular the use of the Code's notion of *stages* in the policy, and how the school interprets this. Arrange to meet the school SENCO to discuss how the placement of children at different stages works in practice. You might like to find out:

- how many children are at each stage;
- how the school communicates with parents when a child is put at stage 1.

You might also like to consider what the policy says about integration of children with special needs, and to find out from the SENCO what arrangements the school has put in place to realize any policy ambitions.

Organization

One of the corollaries of this individualistic way of looking at special needs in the curriculum is that a great deal of effort has to be invested in tailoring the curriculum to the needs of individuals and providing a good deal of individual help. Though this is bound to be difficult, it is not as difficult as it once would have been since one of the positive consequences of the move to integrating children with special needs into ordinary schools is the increasing provision of learning support assistants (LSAs) in classrooms.

These assistants go under different names in different local authorities (general assistant, teaching assistant, learning support assistant) but their duties are similar in each. They may be employed to give help specifically to a child with a statement of special educational needs, perhaps for 10 hours per week. Or they may be employed out of the school's special needs budget to provide general assistance to teachers. There are now far more of these assistants than there were only ten years ago.

It is important, though, that the work of assistants is organized well since the finding of much research (see Thomas, 1992) is that the mere provision of help does not necessarily and automatically free-up the teacher for more (or improved) contact time with children. Indeed, some research (e.g., DeVault, Harnischfeger and Wiley, 1977) has indicated that having an assistant in the class seems to result in the teacher spending *less* time with children, and more time on routine administrative and procedural matters. Organization is also important since the great majority of LSAs are untrained and many are unsure about how to work in the classroom.

Enquiry Task

One possible way of organizing the work of LSAs alongside the class teacher lies in the technique known as *room management*, where specific roles are allotted to each adult in the class. This has been shown to work in primary classrooms (e.g., Thomas, 1985) and with the advent of IEPs offers a useful way of making individualization

---

more of a real possibility, and more meaningful when it does occur. Essentially, it involves the following:

- One person (teacher or LSA) takes on the role of an **individual helper**, concentrating on the work of individual children, working intensively with them for short, specified periods of time. A programme of children to be worked with is established before the lesson. The individual helper would thus be responsible for managing the teaching element specified in the IEP.
- One person (again, teacher or LSA) takes on the role of **activity manager**, working with the rest of the children, and concentrating on their work in groups. This is at a less intensive level, and the activity manager will also take on responsibility for managing the routine and control of the class, dealing with interruptions and other matters.

Now draw up a lesson plan (in any subject) and adapt it so that you deliver the curriculum using two members of staff, one of whom is an LSA. Specify likely tasks for five groups of children in a class, and likely work for individuals using the following table, adapted from Cowne (1996).

	Group 1	Group 2	Group 3	Group 4	Group 5
Task; Resources; Intended learning outcomes					
Role of activity manager					
Role of individual helper					

During the session keep notes of learning outcomes that seem to be being achieved (or not) by individual children. After the session, with your assistant analyse and note what various children learned. Compare these notes with those taken during and after a session organized in a different (perhaps your usual) way.

Room management provides a good way of addressing the organizational demands of individualization and differentiation. Cowne (1996) gives a good account of how it might be used in a classroom and gives a useful planning sheet for specifying the work of individuals and groups.

References

COWNE, E. (1996) *The SENCO Handbook: Working Within a Whole-school Approach*, London, David Fulton.

COX, D. (1996) 'Design and technology at Foxyards Primary School', in WIDLAKE, P. (ed.) *The Good Practice Guide to Special Educational Needs*, Birmingham, Questions Publishing Co.

DEVAULT, M.L., HARNISCHFEGER, A. and WILEY, D.E. (1977) *Curricula, Personnel*

Resources and Grouping Strategies, St. Ann, Mo., ML-GROUP for Policy Studies in Education, Central Midwestern Regional Lab.

DES (1978) *Special Educational Needs (The Warnock Report)*, London, HMSO.

DFE (1994) *The Code of Practice on the Identification and Assessment of Special Educational Needs*, London, HMSO.

GOODMAN, K.S. (1981) *Miscue Analysis: Applications to Reading Instruction*, Urbana, Illinois, National Council of Teachers of English.

LEWIS, A. (1996) 'Developing spoken language — making school experience meaningful', in WIDLAKE, P. (ed.) *The Good Practice Guide to Special Educational Needs*, Birmingham, Questions Publishing Co.

MOORE, A. (1996) 'Making National Curriculum history more accessible', in WIDLAKE, P. (ed.) *The Good Practice Guide to Special Educational Needs*, Birmingham, Questions Publishing Co.

THOMAS, G. (1985) 'Room management in mainstream education', *Educational Research*, **27**, 3, pp. 186–93.

THOMAS, G. (1992) *Effective Classroom Teamwork*, London, Routledge.

THOMAS, G. (1995) 'Special needs at risk?' *Support for Learning*, **10**, 3, pp. 104–12.

THOMAS, G. (1996) 'The needs of teachers of children with special needs', in SMITH, C. and VARMA, V. *A Handbook for Teacher Development*, Aldershot, Arena.

Annotated List of Further Reading and Resources

ACE Centre, Ormerod Sch, Waynflete Rd, Headington, Oxford, OX3 8DD.
(The ACE Centre does much innovative work on developing IT for those with special needs, particularly for those with serious physical or learning disabilities.)

DFE (1994) *The Code of Practice on the Identification and Assessment of Special Educational Needs*, London, HMSO.
(The Code of Practice is an essential read.)

LEWIS, A. (1995) *Primary Special Needs and the National Curriculum (2nd edn)*, London, Routledge.
(This is a comprehensive, thorough and up-to-date text and is full of practical ideas.)

LOCKE, A. and BEECH, M. (1991) *Teaching Talking*, Slough, NFER Nelson.
(A carefully structured guide through language difficulty with many good ideas.)

Maths Links: available from NASEN Publications, 4–5 Amber Business Village, Amber Close, Tamworth B77 4RP.

Maths Steps: LDA, Duke St, Wisbech, Cambridge, PE13 2AE
(Ideas for maths and those struggling with it.)

National Music and Disability Information Service, Foxhole, Dartington, Totnes, Devon, TQ9 6EB

ORT Trust (1995) *Enhancing Design and Technology in Special Education*, London, ORT Trust.
(Ideas for design and technology. Available from Malcolm Jacobs, ORT Trust, 99 Belmont Ave, Cockfosters, Herts, EN4 9JS.)

Questions — Exploring Science and Technology KS1–KS3
(This is a magazine on science and technology produced by the Questions Publishing Company, 27 Frederick St, Hockley, Birmingham, B1 3HH.)

WIDLAKE, P. (ed.) *The Good Practice Guide to Special Educational Needs*, Birmingham, Questions Publishing Co.
(A treasure chest of practical ideas on special education and the National Curriculum. Good chapters on individual subjects as well as information on assessment and IEPs.)

Notes on Contributors

Kate Ashcroft is Professor and Dean of the Faculty of Education at the University of the West of England. Formerly Head of the School of Education at Westminster College, Oxford and Principal Lecturer at Oxford Polytechnic, she has extensive primary teaching experience as a class teacher, Deputy Head and Advisory Teacher. She has a distinguished research and publication record in the area of educational management. She is co-editor and chapter author of an earlier book, *The Primary Teacher's Guide to the New National Curriculum*, also published by Falmer Press.

Carol Beth is Senior Lecturer in Arts Education at Oxford Brookes University. Previously, she was Inspector for Arts in Merton Local Education Authority. For many years, she taught dance within initial teacher education and in professional development programmes for teachers. At present, she is undertaking research into, and working with, clients in dance/movement therapy.

Jackie Chapman is Lecturer in Art and Education at Westminster College, Oxford. She is an experienced teacher in both primary and middle schools where she was coordinator for art. She spent seven years as an educational consultant in Development Education and published extensively in that field.

Suzi Clipson-Boyles is Senior Lecturer at the School of Education, Oxford Brookes University, where she coordinates the primary English team. She has a broad experience of teaching across the full primary age range and her drama work with primary pupils has been featured on radio and television. She has produced a number of publications in the field of language and literacy, including drama.

David Coates is Senior Lecturer in Science and Design and Technology in Primary Education at Westminster College, Oxford. Previously, he worked as the Design and Technology Coordinator in a primary school. He has a range of publications in the areas of Science, Design and Technology, and mentoring in primary schools in the UK and abroad. He is a chapter author of an earlier book, *The Primary Teacher's Guide to the New National Curriculum*, also published by Falmer Press.

Jennifer Gray is Lecturer in Physical Education at Westminster College, Oxford. She has extensive experience of school teaching and of educational consultancy. She has published a number of books and articles on teaching swimming and diving, and is a chapter author of an earlier book, *The Primary Teacher's Guide to the New National Curriculum*, also published by Falmer Press.

John Halocha is Lecturer in Primary Humanities in the School of Education, University of Durham. Previously, he was Principal Lecturer in Geography Education and Teaching Studies at Westminster College, Oxford. He has taught in primary and middle schools and was Deputy Head of two schools. He is a chapter author of an earlier book, *The Primary Teacher's Guide to the New National Curriculum*, also published by Falmer Press.

Jean Harding divides her time between lecturing in Design and Technology within initial primary teacher education at Westminster College, Oxford, and leading Design and Technology workshops for primary school teachers. She has been a class teacher, a Head of Infants within a primary school and an Advisory Teacher for Design and Technology.

Chris Higgins is Senior Lecturer in Information Technology and Head of Mathematics at Westminster College, Oxford. He is a member of the Editorial Board of *Information Technology for Teacher Education* and has taught extensively within primary and secondary teacher education courses on information technology in the classroom. He is a chapter author of an earlier book, *The Primary Teacher's Guide to the New National Curriculum*, also published by Falmer Press.

Ann Jordan is a Senior Lecturer in Primary Education at Worcester College of Higher Education where she teaches on a range of initial teacher education, Humanities, and Pedagogy and Management courses. She previously taught in a variety of schools, most recently as a Deputy Head in a large primary school.

Margaret Jones is Senior Lecturer in Mathematics Education at Westminster College, Oxford. She has previous experience as a secondary and primary teacher, as a Head of Mathematics Department and as an Advisory Teacher in Mathematics. She has extensive experience of the development of curriculum materials in Mathematics and is a chapter author of an earlier book, *The Primary Teacher's Guide to the New National Curriculum*, also published by Falmer Press.

Gwyneth Little is Lecturer in Religious Education at Westminster College, Oxford. Formerly, she was Advisory Teacher in Religious Education in Leicestershire and Head of Religious Education within a secondary school: she is a regular contributor to the journal *Religious Education Today*, and is a chapter author of an earlier book, *The Primary Teacher's Guide to the New National Curriculum*, also published by Falmer Press.

Cliff Marshall is Principal Lecturer in Primary Education and Science, and is BEd Course Leader at Westminster College, Oxford. He has previous experience as a primary school teacher and as a Deputy Head. He has published a number of papers in journals and at conferences on Primary Science, and is a chapter author of an earlier book, *The Primary Teacher's Guide to the New National Curriculum*, also published by Falmer Press.

Helena Mitchell is Principal Lecturer in Language and Literacy and PGCE (Primary) Course Leader at Westminster College, Oxford. She has experience of early years education at class teacher and Deputy Head levels. She has published in the area of Language and Literacy and has recently completed her PhD research which focused on early years reading. She is a chapter author of an earlier book, *The Primary Teacher's Guide to the New National Curriculum*, also published by Falmer Press.

Jenny Monk is Senior Lecturer in Language Education and Teaching Studies at Westminster College, Oxford. Previously, she worked in primary schools as a class teacher, Deputy Head, and Language Advisory Teacher. She has contributed to a number of books on Language and Learning, and is a chapter author of an earlier book, *The Primary Teacher's Guide to the New National Curriculum*, also published by Falmer Press.

David Palacio is Head of Research in the School of Education and Science Subject Leader at Westminster College, Oxford. He has taught in primary and secondary schools, and has wide experience of working with teachers in the United Kingdom and abroad. He has published extensively in the areas of Science Education and Assessment, and is co-editor and chapter author of an earlier book, *The Primary Teacher's Guide to the New National Curriculum*, also published by Falmer Press.

Maureen Roberts was Senior Lecturer in Teaching Studies and Primary Geography at Westminster College, Oxford. She has studied Interdisciplinary Studies in the USA and Comparative Education in the UK. She has experience as a Geography Curriculum Support Teacher within UK and USA inner city primary and nursery schools and is currently working as a Registered Inspector for the nursery voucher scheme. She is a chapter author of an earlier book, *The Primary Teacher's Guide to the New National Curriculum*, also published by Falmer Press.

Paul Taylor is Senior Lecturer in History and Humanities Education at Westminster College, Oxford. He has taught in a range of schools and has published a number of articles in books and journals about History and Humanities Education. He is a chapter author of an earlier book, *The Primary Teacher's Guide to the New National Curriculum*, also published by Falmer Press.

Gary Thomas is Professor and Reader in Education at the University of the West of England, Bristol. Before moving into teacher education he was a primary school teacher and an educational psychologist. He has an interest in, and commitment to, inclusive education and has directed a Barnardo's-funded project on inclusion.

Patricia Thompson is Head of Performing Arts at Coventry University. Formerly, Head of Pedagogy and Principal Lecturer in Music and Music Education at Westminster College, Oxford, she has a range of experience as a class teacher and Head of Music Department and has an international profile in the world of Music

Education. She is a chapter author of an earlier book, *The Primary Teacher's Guide to the New National Curriculum*, also published by Falmer Press.

Mike Threlfall has been a class teacher, Deputy Head and Head Teacher of three primary schools. Since leaving headship in 1994, he works independently mainly in the fields of education management, environmental education and special educational needs: he also works as a part-time tutor on professional development courses and as a lecturer on teacher training programmes.

Index